CITY OF SACRIFICE

City of Sacrifice

The Aztec Empire
and the Role of Violence in Civilization

DAVÍD CARRASCO

Beacon Press

BOSTON

Beacon Press
25 Beacon Street
Boston, Massachusetts 02108-2892
www.beacon.org

Beacon Press books
are published under the auspices of
the Unitarian Universalist Association of Congregations.

05 04 03 02   8 7 6 5 4 3

This book is printed on acid-free paper that meets the uncoated paper
ANSI/NISO specifications for permanence as revised in 1992.

Text design by Elizabeth Elsas
Composition by Wilsted & Taylor Publishing Services

Library of Congress Cataloging-in-Publication Data
Carrasco, Davíd.
    City of sacrifice : the Aztec empire and the role of violence
in civilization / Davíd Carrasco.
        p.   cm.
    Includes bibliographical references and index.
    ISBN 0-8070-4642-6 (cloth)
    ISBN 0-8070-4643-4 (pbk.)
    1. Indians of Mexico—Rites and ceremonies. 2. Aztecs—Rites and
ceremonies. 3. Human sacrifice—Mexico. 4. Human sacrifice—Central
America. I. Title.
    F1219.3.R38 C28 1999
    299'.78452—dc21   99-23752

THIS BOOK IS DEDICATED TO
LUGENE ANN WHITLEY

CONTENTS

Introduction

Performing the City of Sacrifice

> Thus, they had captured five hundred men of Chalco. These were
> sent to Tenochtitlan and on the day after their arrival, by order of
> Tlacaelel and the king, they were immediately sacrificed to the god
> Huitzilopochtli. In this way the vow that had been sworn was fulfilled,
> and the temple was reddened with the blood of five hundred men.
> A fire sacrifice was ordained; this was the most terrible and horrendous
> sacrifice that can be imagined . . . A great bonfire was built in a large
> brazier placed on the floor of the temple. This was called "the divine
> hearth." Into this great mass of flames men were thrown alive. Before
> they expired, their hearts were torn out of their bodies and offered to
> the god.
>
> Fray Diego Durán, *The History of the Indies of New Spain*

Jonathan Z. Smith said to me when he heard I was writing this book
on sacred violence and the city, "Everyone really thinks religion is a
marginal social force until you run into a human sacrifice and the
matter is opened up again." This book intends to open up the matter
of religion by focusing on two of the most vital expressions in human
culture, the sacred city and ritual violence. I chose this combination
because my encounters with sacred cities in Mesoamerica eventually
forced me to confront the practice of ritual human sacrifice in the social world. Aztec settlements in particular were organized around ceremonial complexes, which served as theaters for many kinds of performances, including the ritual slaughter of humans and animals. Our
understanding of the history of Mesoamerican religions becomes extraordinarily rich and problematic when we are confronted with prodigious acts of violence, most of which were carried out in the monumental ceremonial centers of cities and in relation to a particularly

complex, hierarchical ordering of social life that has been identified as urban. When we try to face up to the accounts of human sacrifice, our assumptions about human nature, social order, and the human imagination are shaken, and the issues of what religion is, does, and means are opened, like cuts in our scholarly position, and the discourse is lit up. These lights from sacred cities and violent acts, which are full of religious meanings, challenge our blind spots.

I remember the day my academic deadpan about cities and sacrifice cracked into a tight grimace. I had just looked down into the offering cache at the Great Aztec Temple in Mexico City where the skeletal remains of forty-two children lay as a messy remnant of a fifteenth-century, precious offering to the rain gods. The Mexican archaeologist Eduardo Matos Moctezuma was giving me a tour of the site, which was under intense excavation, and said, pointing, "Here is something beautiful and profound in its terror." Peering down into the ritual receptacle where children's skulls and infants' bones lay strewn and tangled in what looked like a chaotic, even wild, arrangement, I could see greenstone beads near several mouths, flakes of blue pigment that had been sprinkled on the bodies, necklaces of greenstone, and several disks with appliquéd turquoise mosaics and turtle shell. I knew from my study of Aztec cosmology that this spot might be one of the entrances to Tlaloc's paradise, the rain god's aquatic afterlife. I felt a visceral response that relocated my attention from ideas to feelings, from my head to my stomach and heart, for I was a father of a young child and I wondered what possible creative hermeneutic turn I could spin onto this scene. When I stood up and gazed around the site with its giant grinning serpent heads, stone warriors leaning against stairways, stone skulls strewn around the site, and the monumental disk sculpture of a dismembered warrior goddess, it was evident that violence against humans was a profound human necessity and practice for the Aztecs in their capital city.

The topic of ritual killing has been difficult to gain insight into. This has been especially so when ethno-historical descriptions present us with the density of Aztec violence in the various forms of human slaughter. I used to rationalize difficult questions about who was sacrificed by saying that "The majority of the victims were enemy warriors," as though that "distancing" response settled the matter. Numerically this is true, but a perusal of the eighteen yearly ceremonies carried out in and around the sacred city of Tenochtitlan shows that women and children were also sacrificed in over a third of them. Faced with the ritually choreographed, publicly performed human sacrifices that transported enemy warriors for miles over difficult terrain into the capital; dismembered male and female bodies and hung skulls on monumental racks; painted the shrines, celebrants, and faces of gods with animal and human blood; slashed open the throats of infants; beheaded young women; and dressed teenagers in flayed human skins, I am stimulated to see that religious violence is a major motivating social force and to ask whether sacrifice is a central religious performance in the construction of social order and the authority of city-states, or at least these particular city-states.

The Aztec pattern stimulates this general reflection on cities and aggression for two reasons: First, Mesoamerica was the site of one of the most profound social transformations in world history, the process known as primary urban generation. Only five or perhaps six other culture areas managed the evolution of social life from the world of villages to the urban landscape. Second, as we shall see, a major strand of Mesoamerican mythology is associated with this evolution, driven by sacrifice, even monumental sacrifice. My asking about the general symbiosis of ritual violence and the city is reflected, in part, in these Mesoamerican patterns.

Sacrifice was a way of life for the Aztecs, enmeshed in their temple and marketplace practices, part of their ideology of the redistribution of riches and their beliefs about how the cosmos was ordered, and an instrument of social integration that elevated the body of the ruler and the potency of the gods. Ritual slaughter within the ceremonial precincts of Aztec life was the instrument, in part, for educating adolescents about their social future, communicating with the many gods, transmitting cosmological convictions, as well as directing social change in the form of imperial expansion. In my mind, this growing awareness led to an alteration of René Girard's claim that "Violence is the heart and secret soul of the sacred"[1] to the possibility that in Tenochtitlan the public heart and soul of the sacred was the ritual killing of human beings who were first turned into gods! My sense of the power and significance of religious violence changed that day when Matos showed me the children's remains, and this book traces the discoveries and images that have animated my research and teaching since.

The dimensions of shock and fascination that ritual violence in sacred landscapes brings became clearer to me over the last decade while lecturing on Aztec and Maya religions in the United States, Europe, Mexico, and Japan. After I lectured at Stanford University on Aztec sacrificial practices inspired by myths of cosmic creation, a graduate student nearly accosted me physically for my use of the term *cosmos,* which in his words means "order, peace, and harmony in the Greek sense and has nothing to do with your lecture." He then bumped me as he brushed past me, exclaiming, "Thanks for giving the Casper Weinberger lecture in the history of religions." This awareness of the difficulties that religious violence presents to the public and to the academy continued when my essay "The Templo Mayor: The Aztec Vision of Place" was refused for publication by *Parabola* magazine because I failed, and then later refused, to insert a disclaimer about the theme of human sacrifice. Published elsewhere, the article won a scholarly writing award, but the message had been sent—religious violence is a very difficult topic for scholars to face, especially for those interested in religion. But the topic has a curious fascination for both the scholarly and lay public. I noticed that audiences were larger when the topic of sacred violence was advertised. Somewhat later, responding to pressures from audiences in post-lecture discussions, I did insert a disclaimer at the beginning of a lecture on ritual violence: that I was not defending this brutal practice, that it was difficult to turn to these texts day after day, and that seeing the remains of sacrificed children while working at Aztec shrines was particularly challenging in understanding the nature of the ancient city-state. But these comments brought reactions from the other side. Didn't I realize how sacrificial the Christians were; how brutal the Inquisition was; how hungry for martyrdom the Muslims are; how militant the State of Israel is; how devastating the atomic bombing of Hiroshima and Nagasaki were; how widespread, in military terms, human sacrifice is? I realized that ritual violence troubles, fascinates, and stimulates people to think about their own cultural traditions and religious practices. It also became clear that examples provided by Mesoamerican cultures could help scholars examine the relationships between cities and violence in world religions.

Understanding the relationships between sacred spaces, urban settings, and ritual killing is especially important when we remember that contemporary history is increasingly filled with prodigious acts of violence that take place within or in primary relation to symbolic sites, sacred shrines, and temples. Troubling events, such as the suicide bombings in Tel Aviv, gunshots at the Wailing Wall, gassings in Tokyo, the massacre of people in the Oklahoma bombing, Balkan deportations, rapes and murders within cities or in relation to urban populations, and numerous acts of fanatic violence in sanctified places like churches in El Salvador, criticize our comfortable claims about how sacred places and stories and theologies of hope and prophetic discourses operate at the heart of religious traditions to invigorate and heal human cultures. Ritual violence, tinged and often pulsating with religious cosmologies, national theologies, and cultural mythologies, fill our media representations every day.[2]

This book is based on essays I wrote over the last two decades, representing, in part, linked studies in the evolution of my thought about the history and imagination of religion. It is organized by three major concerns that should be on the mind of any student of religion and culture: (1) the symbolism of human settlement, (2) the integrative/ destructive powers of ritual performances of violence, and (3) the creative hermeneutics of the history of religions. These concerns reflect my interest in developing a dynamic model of religious performance organized by attention to center and periphery relations. I approach the dynamics of centers and peripheries through reflections on two types of *orientatio*—meaning the "fundamental process of situating human life in the world. Fixing the human place in existence in a significant way is a religious act when it orients a human being toward the sacred."[3] In this book, I extend the meaning of *orientatio* to include both the discovery and organization of central place and the sacrificial performances that have the power to reorganize, redistribute, and regenerate the central place as a culturally and politically meaningful environment. A great deal of scholarship in the history of religions has been concerned with understanding how myths, hierophanies, sacred spaces, and rites help human beings experience and achieve orientation.[4] But not enough attention has been given to the supreme sacred places and sites of total social orientation that I am referring to as cities. The traditional cities of Mesoamerica were the sites of permanently established social hierarchies whose asymmetries were embedded and symbolized in all social, political, economic and imaginary aspects of social life. It has been difficult for historians of religions to realize what urban ecologists have made clear, namely, that the urban way of life was not a system contained within the city's walls, or formal boundaries, but rather it spread far beyond the limitations of the built form. Tenochtitlan in particular was a monumental and socially stratified way of life, crystallized in the great ceremonial center but containing organizational capacities extending way beyond its physical limits. As Paul Wheatley has cogently noted in his comparative analysis of primary urban generation, ceremonial cities were the instruments for the creation of "effective space"—that is, the integration of political, social, economic, and symbolic spaces into coherent social worlds. In my view, the urban nature of Tenochtitlan is not to be contrasted with the social world of the countryside but with the pre-urban society that existed over two thousand years earlier and continued to exist on the margins of urbanized social systems. The overall orientation of Tenochtitlan and other Mesoamerican capitals was achieved through the city's primary export: control. The capacity to control peoples, goods, relationships, meanings, and human lives was expressed in the centripetal and centrifugal powers of the capitals. In this way, the elites maintained the upper hand in dealing with the diversities and challenges of the peripheral societies and kingdoms. Most important for understanding the orientation achieved in the Aztec capital is the acknowledgment of the various cosmo-magical formulas made of traditional symbolic, cosmological frameworks imprinted in the physiognomies of capital cities.

As my exposure to the history and morphology of Mesoamerican cities increased, I was continually confronted with the ways ritual violence in the forms of warfare and especially human sacrifice functioned to establish, maintain, and renew widespread social and symbolic *orientatio* for the capitals and the way of life for their inhabitants. The archaeological evidence, as well as the extensive descriptions of ritual killing, always coordinated in the Aztec city, or *altepetl*,[5] by a closely watched calendar system, indicates that the dynamic daily life of Tenochtitlan was reconstructed as a religiously meaningful landscape, in part, through the sacrifice of *teotl ixipitlas,* or deity impersonators, in public ceremonial gatherings. These human sacrifices,[6] always performed in religious precincts, had profound and detailed political purposes as well, often dramatizing the tensions of center-periphery geopolitical relations. Ritual violence, and especially the increase in human sacrifices, became a way of managing, from within the sacred enclaves of the capital, the unstable social and symbolic dynamics between the imperial center and the allied and enemy periphery.[7] At one level, the flux of political history, fortunes, and uncertainties was handled through the immense tribute system by which nearby and peripheral communities demonstrated their dependence upon and servitude to the capital by paying large quantities of goods on a regular basis, always threatened with the pain of human sacrifice or military attack. At another level, this management of center and periphery was symbolized in the ritual systems of debt payments in the form of human sacrifices to the gods and under the authority of the god kings. One important point for the reader to understand is that, according to the descriptions of these sacrifices, much more effort was put into dancing, singing, moving in procession, sometimes long-distance walking, and changing costumes than into the actual act of killing people. The act of ritual death, while centrally important, was not all that these ceremonies were about. A ceremonial landscape is marked and re-marked and is being brought to life at the same time a deity impersonator is being prepared for an ultimate transformation. The Aztec problem of symbolic and political orientation takes on two significant dimensions—orientation through the monumental city and orientation through ritual human sacrifice— and as we shall see in reviewing the mythological and historical record, often *monumental* human sacrifice. The present study cannot explore the full implications of these patterns of violence, and I plan to take up two troubling dimensions of this sacrificial society in a later study, namely, the cultivation of cruelty and the institutionalization of hatred, which, in part, animated Aztec warrior society. The cycles of rage, grief, and hatred that appear to motivate some of the exchanges between rival city-states are briefly explored in chapters 4 and 5, but much more work needs to be done with the primary sources in order to effectively elucidate emotional hatreds and political cruelties in Tenochtitlan.

These dimensions of Mesoamerican history, when turned back on the history of theory about ritual sacrifice, constitutes something of a scandal in religious studies—namely, that all significant theories of ritual sacrifice, from Robertson Smith through Hubert and Mauss, René Girard, Walter Burkert, Adolph Jensen, and J. Z. Smith, *com-*

pletely ignored the most thorough record of real, historical human sacrifice while favoring either distant reports of animal sacrifices or *literary sacrifices* from Western Classics![8] Why does the physical, pictorial, ethno-historical, and sometimes eyewitness evidence of actual ritual human slaughter provoke so little interest among the major theorists of ritual violence? How can each theory parade right on by the sacrifice of Tezcatlipoca, Spanish soldiers, and horses, and the dismemberment of teenage warriors, adolescent girls, and infant children while constructing general principles of interpretation about human aggression? More recently, Nancy Jay has written a justly celebrated work positing a feminist theory of human sacrifice that almost completely ignores the most vivid evidence available anywhere in the historical record for evidence of the patriarchal sacrifices she criticizes. I am forced to ask why is there such a lack of interest in the Mesoamerican cases while Christian and Jewish literary exemplum serve as "classic" cases? In the Aztec case, violent sacrifices performed the city.

THE DEPTH OF CITIES IN HUMAN LIFE

> . . . the city says everything you must think, makes you repeat her discourse . . .[9]

The expansion of my view of the city as a performance space also developed while working with students in courses on the Mesoamerican city in comparative perspective. This not only exposed me to complex sets of performances that animated cities, but also with the ways in which cities were religio-political performances themselves. City after city that my students and I examined unfolded their histories as dramaturgical landscapes in which the major ideas, economic exchanges, political ideas, religious beliefs, personal tragedies, and hopes of the populace were acted out through ritual and daily life. Furthermore, it became evident that performance spaces and cultural performances did not just re-present city values but also functioned to re-generate and re-make the cities as meaningful landscapes. The ceremonies brought the city to life.[10]

   While the essays in this book do not explore in detail comparisons with other urban traditions, I do work as a historian of religions interested in useful comparisons and analogies that can draw light to the Mesoamerican cases and then take them from Mesoamerica into broader discussions. In courses I have taught, I have followed Clifford

Geertz's insistence about the reconfiguration of social thought that "theory . . . moves mainly by analogy"[11] and constructed a series of resemblances that relate social theory and the city. Each analogy brings influential thinkers into contact with both the analogy and each other. These include but are not limited to (1) city as cosmological symbol (Otto von Simson, Mircea Eliade, and Paul Wheatley); (2) city as religious community (Fustel de Coulanges and Emile Durkheim); (3) city as fulcrum of political power (Max Weber and Clifford Geertz); and (4) city as center of economic exchange (Raymond Williams and David Harvey). And now, the city as performance.

These comparative exercises in social thought and the city led me to appreciate the city as both the general term for a particular hierarchical patterning of social life and as an opulent trope for the ways in which social differences (class, ethnic, and racial) were subsumed under images and symbols of common if pyramidal cause. In the process, I have made use of Italo Calvino's positions in *Invisible Cities,* where he shows that the city is as much a metaphysical force in our lives as a material one and in the end escapes from the confines of our series of analogies. On the one hand, the city has the power of redundancy, reiteration, and recreation for it inhabits our minds, or in Calvino's words about one of the invisible cities of Kublai Khan's empire, "the city says everything you must think." The city becomes, especially in those great capitals, the sum of all wonders that "makes you repeat her discourse, and while you believe you are visiting Tamara you are only recording the names with which she defines herself and all her parts." But these repetitions do not exhaust the power of cities to re-create meaning or open ways to incorporate new meaning, stories, and power, for as with a primordium or ideal type, our discourse falls short of the parts that make up the whole. "However the city may really be, beneath this thick coating of signs whatever it may contain or conceal, you leave Tamara without having discovered it."[12]

As my students and I realized, this redundancy of wonders and concealment of meanings is what is often performed as well as symbolized in some of the grand monuments of cities. Who can doubt that the church Santa Maria della Salute, which for centuries greeted the ships coming in off the Adriatic Sea into the Grand Canal of Venice and the gondola travelers who ventured to its base, is a performance of Venetian art, religion, and political pride? The drama of

Venice's canals, houses, colors, gondolas, churches, moods, and curving vistas drove Charles Dickens to write in his *Pictures from Italy* that "opium couldn't build such a place and enchantment couldn't shadow it forth in vision . . . I've never before visited a place that I am afraid to describe."[13] And consider Henry James's observation of the spectacle of the Salute during one of his fourteen visits to the city. The monument that towers over the entrance to the Grand Canal is described as a grand actress on a stage in which the drama of an arrival, greeting, and encounter between complex forces is about to unfold.

> The classic Salute waits like some great lady on the threshold of her salon. She is more ample and serene, more seated at her door, than all the copyists have told us, with her domes and scrolls, her scalloped buttresses and statues forming a pompous crown, and her wide steps disposed on the ground like the train of a robe. This fine air of the woman of the world is carried out by the well-bred assurance with which she looks in the direction of her old-fashioned Byzantine neighbor; and the juxtaposition of two churches so distinguished and so different, each splendid in its sort, is a sufficient mark of the scale and range of Venice.[14]

I was also stimulated to understand how a city may perform its social hierarchy and royal pathology linking sex, death, and inflated authority when reading Bruno Bettelheim's *Freud's Vienna and Other Essays*. As Vienna grew to dominate the intelligentsia of the Hapsburg empire, its city fathers not only arranged for the World's Fair of 1873 so that *it* could perform *their* empire, but also constructed the Ringstrasse, the monumental avenue that circled the inner city and "was intended to outshine the world-famous Haussmann boulevards of Paris, because the buildings on the Ringstrasse would be even more splendid than those gracing the Paris avenue."[15] In this case, the performance is an inter-capital one, with rulers, elites, and architects competing with each other for spectacle and spectacular statements of political or cultural imperial leadership. In this view of the city as a performance, the house of Freud, the intimidations leading to his flight, and the museum that his house has become were all ceremonies of Viennese metamorphosis. I am reminded of the intense competition of Maya city-states during its glowing classic culture, when ceremonial cities competed publicly to perform the most powerful and extravagant ceremonial festivals to call the gods down (or up) into their midst and draw the populace into their markets.

The performance of the psychological depth and power of British cities is illustrated in the work of Raymond Williams, especially in his *The City and the Country*. Reading a wide series of literary works, Williams shows how the city and the novel of the city combine to reveal the "true significance of the city," which is the revelation of the "double condition" of humankind. When he comments on Charles Dickens's ability to create a new kind of novel after many false starts, lapses, and versions, Williams notes that London brought together in unique ways "the random and the systematic, the visible and the obscured which is the true significance of the city, and especially at this period of the capital city, as a dominant social form."[16]

The city as a sum of all wonders was most of all a place of new kinds of in-depth human experiences of "unknown and unacknowledged relationships, profound and decisive connections, definite and committing recognitions and avowals" that were brought into contact and exchange. In the city of mutual friends and competitors, enemies and outcasts, "what was important or even decisive could not be simply known or simply communicated, . . . it had to be revealed, to be forced into consciousness,"[17] or we can say performed into consciousness.[18] It is this performing into consciousness and framing consciousness that is also at work in the *orientatios* and ritual violence of cities in general and Mesoamerican cities in particular.

THE ARCHÈ OF THE CENTER

In exploring the capacity of cities to perform culture, communicate cosmo-magical meanings, and direct processes of social, political, and symbolic change and metamorphosis, I am reminded of Charles H. Long's claim that for students of religion, especially in the Americas, the world-wide history of colonialism constituted a "new archè," a fundamentally new *orientatio* for humankind. Long constructs the rationale for a "new archè" and the importance of linking colonialism to religious studies by first praising and then going beyond Mircea Eliade's concept of "archaic consciousness." Long shows regard for Eliade's creative hermeneutic because "instead of explaining originary constitution (i.e., the constitutions of human life and culture) as only an internal ordering of consciousness, Eliade always related this constitution to something other than itself."[19]

This "other than itself," as interpreted in *Patterns in Comparative Religion,* was the structures and forms of nature such as the sky, the sun and moon, the earth, stones, trees, water, and plants and animals whose presence, actions, bodies, and patterns stimulated the human mind to open its doors of perceptions and work to employ meaning, powerful ideas, myth, ritual, and ritual specialists to recreate and redirect relations with cosmic beings and entities. In Long's view, humankind underwent and is still undergoing *an other* internal ordering of consciousness, through the violence, significations, and processes of colonialism carried out over the last five hundred years to constitute *the environment* for the human condition in the postcolonial, postmodern world. Comparing his move with Eliade, Long writes,

> In an analogous manner I shall attempt to raise the issue of the constitution of religion and human consciousness but instead of seeking for an arena of primordiality, I shall locate this arena within the time and space of the formation of new extra-European cultures, the new mercantilism and the ensuing relationships that took place during the modern period of imperialism and colonialism.[20]

In my view, the power of this insight, that the social processes of colonialism constitute a new environment for the constitution of religion and human consciousness, should be extended and tested against the history and power of cities to shape society and thought. We can imagine that the city, as humankind's most powerful artifact, has, like the patterns of nature and the processes of colonialism, worked to orient and reorient human thought and culture. The city, playing with the present scheme, would constitute the *middle archè* or, to push the matter further, the *archè of the center and periphery* of human history. The patterns of nature as Eliade perceived them constitute the *archè of the beginning,* while Long's insight suggests the *archè of globalization.*

In Italo Calvino's *Invisible Cities,* the traveler Marco Polo attempts through words, exaggerated gestures, complex signs, and wonders to show to the ruler of the empire, Kublai Khan, the nature of his kingdom. Calvino writes, "Kublai Khan did not necessarily believe everything Marco Polo says when he describes the cities visited on his expeditions, but the emperor of the Tartars does continue listening to the young Venetian with greater attention and curiosity than he shows to any other messenger or explorer of his."[21] I realize that I am playing something like Marco Polo to the reader's Kublai Khan and do not expect you to believe all that I explore and say about the city as *the ecology* of humankind or the performances of Aztec cities. But I hope that like the emperor of that narrative, you will give great attention to these pages about the city of sacrifice. It is impressive to me, an explorer of urban settlements in the narratives of the Aztec world, that the very last section of the *Florentine Codex* reiterates the primordial, political, and economic importance of the city in the lake for both the Aztec and the conquering Spaniards. On the last page of the twelve-volume encyclopedia, collected over a period of four decades in the Basin of Mexico in the sixteenth century, we read that one of the surviving Aztec priests remembers the days when the capital was the sum of all Mexica wonders and demands Cortés's attention to this view. "May the nobleman, our lord the Captain, hear! When there was yet Moctezuma, when there was a conquest, the Mexicans, the Tlatilucans, the Tepanecans, the Acolhuans moved together. All the Tepanecans, all the Acolhuans, and those of the floating gardens—all of us moved together when we conquered."[22]

The priest recalls how the conquered peoples would return to their cities and bring to Tenochtitlan their riches, tribute as signs of submission.

> "And later came the people of the cities, the people already conquered. They brought their tribute; their goods went to become the victor's, the green stone, the gold, the precious feathers, and still other precious stones, the fine turquoise, the lovely cotinga, the roseate spoonbill. They gave it to Moctezuma. It arrived there together."[23]

And then the speaker concludes, showing Cortés, and now us, that this story is preeminently a story of the capital city and its performances. As though both remembering and masking the treasures buried in that greatest container of the stage that was Tenochtitlan—the Templo Mayor—the speaker to Cortés reports, "All the tribute, the gold was together there in Tenochtitlan." We end in the center, in the city.

Significantly, in Nahuatl, the narrative ends with a different word, one that forefronts not the city, but a vein in the earth on which the city sits and from which its gods emerge and leave their traces. The sentence reads *"ca umpa, ualmocemaci, in tenuchtitlan in ixquich tlacalaquili in teucuitlatl."* The final word, *teucuitlatl*, is not the name of the capital but the term for gold, which in the native vernacular was "the excrement of gods." Gold was the trace of the divine's presence in the earthly spaces beneath and around the human settlements. It was extracted in Aztec times, in part, in response to conquests. Now, led by the "lord" Captain Cortés, a new style of violence, a mass-sacrifice society, swept into the city to extract it, the gods who made it, and all that was Tenochtitlan. With cannon, fire, and Spanish and Indian bodies flung against the city's walls, temples, palaces, people, and barricades, all justified by a new religious vision, the invaders literally blew the city away, and then built their city, which eventually became today's Mexico City, the largest city in the world, on its ruins. Performing the Colonial City.

CHAPTER I

City as Symbol in Aztec Thought
Some Clues from the Codex Mendoza

> In the ceremonial centers of pre-Columbian Mesoamerica it is also possible to discern the plastic expression of a series of mythical or cosmic conceptions, although the implications of these symbols have not yet been elucidated in all their complexity.
>
> Paul Wheatley, *The Pivot of the Four Quarters*

> I could tell you how many steps make up the streets rising like stairways, and the degree of the arcades' curves, and what kind of zinc scales cover the roofs; but I already know this would be the same as telling you nothing. The city does not consist of this, but of relationships between the measurements of its space and the events of its past.
>
> Italo Calvino, *Invisible Cities*

One of the most significant developments in recent decades in the study of Mesoamerican cultures has been the realization that the Aztec society encountered by the Spaniards in the sixteenth century was a world dominated by that form known as the traditional city. This realization has been the outgrowth of long-term debates on the "nature" of pre-Columbian peoples and the eventual rejection of the anthropological theory that "the pueblo of Mexico" was, according to Lewis H. Morgan, peopled by "ragged Indians" living in the "middle status of Barbarism."[1] The Aztecs, said Morgan, were the Iroquois of the south, and their loosely organized social institutions were proof of "how distant yet were the conceptions of a state or nation among the aborigines of Mexico. . . . They were still a breech cloth people, wearing the rag of barbarism as the unmistakable evidence of their condition. . . . There was neither a political society, nor a state, nor

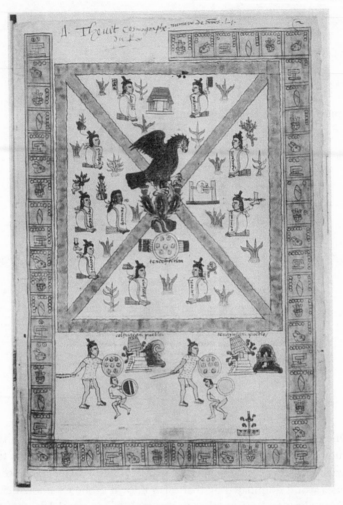

The first image in the *Codex Mendoza* depicts the founding of Tenochtitlan as
a performance of authority and war as well as a model of cosmological order.
In the center of the four sections of the city is the large image of the Aztec god
Huitzilopochtli landing on the blooming cactus growing from a rock in the
lake of Mexico. Notice the ten male leaders, the skull rack, the ceremonial
building, and the vegetation distributed around the central section. The human
action below shows the Aztec conquests of towns on the periphery of the
capital. The entire image is surrounded by calendar signs. (Folio 2 of the
Codex Mendoza. Courtesy of the Bodleian Library, Oxford, U.K.)

any civilization in America when it was discovered, and excluding the Eskimos, but one race of Indians, the Red Race."[2]

A series of impressive studies by archaeologists and cultural anthropologists following the groundbreaking work by Paul Kirchhoff have radically revised our understanding of Mesoamerican cultures and identified patterns of settlement, bureaucratic systems, and cultural order that, taken as a whole, represent urbanism as a dynamic way of life.[3] Whether investigated in terms and terminology of the stimulus for the rise of stratified societies,[4] of the cultural evolution of civilizations,[5] or as sacred theaters for the rites of kings,[6] the underlying question is no longer whether Mesoamericans constructed cities and states, but what kinds of urban settlements did they invent and dwell within and in relation to.[7] In spite of the new focus on the urban character of the ancient Mesoamerican world, there has been until recently very limited attention given to the relationship between cosmological symbols, sacred space, and the development of the monumental ceremonial centers and regional capitals that directed and dominated Mesoamerican cultural life for nearly two thousand years.[8] Only in the last decade have really insightful studies of the cosmic symbolism of major temples and precincts been carried out by scholars working on the site-planning principles, cosmology, and religious symbolism of Classic Maya and central Mesoamerican ceremonial centers.[9] Those scholars who have emphasized symbolic structures and religious forms in their studies of ancient Mexico have spoken passionately and sometimes brilliantly about the religious symbols within the Aztec city but not very much about the Aztec city itself as a religious form.[10]

In what follows, I begin to lay out my own approach to the prodigious expressions of sacred space in the Aztec world by focusing on the multivalent character of the imprint of cosmo-magical thought on the ritual and spatial physiognomy of the Aztec capital, Tenochtitlan, which was founded around 1325 and brought under Spanish military control toward the end of 1521. I use this chapter as an overview, in spatial terms, of the central ordering symbols that permeated and organized Aztec ceremonial centers, trade, warfare, sacrifice, cannibalism, astronomy, and selected cosmological ideas.[11] As an initial strategy, I focus on the frontispiece and other selected folios of the *Codex Mendoza* and show how these images, themselves reflections, in part, of pre-Hispanic thought, contain clues about the religious imagination of the Aztecs and more specifically about the conception of their city as a cosmic symbol. I hope to show through a new reading of selected images from the *Codex Mendoza* how the city was a symbol of dynamic relationships between, in part, myths, measurements, history, rulers, nobles, centers, and peripheries. The Aztec version of the conquest of Tenochtitlan, articulated a generation after the city fell to Spanish cunning and aggression, reflected the persistence of their cosmo-magical view of the world. We will see how several pre-conquest cosmological ideas were meaningful enough to enter into a symbiosis with their experience of the conquest, thus ensuring their endurance for at least several generations.

THE *CODEX MENDOZA* AS A SPATIAL STORY

> What the map cuts up, the story cuts across.
>
> Michel de Certeau, "Spatial Stories"[12]

I choose images from the *Codex Mendoza* because they serve to raise themes, problems, and hermeneutical opportunities I want to emphasize in this study of Mesoamerican religions. The *Codex Mendoza* as a whole and the opening scene[13] in particular can be used, contrary to what most commentators think,[14] to *initiate* the study of such religious dimensions as sacred space, ceremonial centers, mythology, ritual renewal and human sacrifice, and archaeoastronomy and the calendar, all of which are discussed in later chapters. This single image of the founding of the city also reflects the important issues of center/ periphery dynamics, the performance of head collecting and warfare, as well as the mixed cultures of the colonial period. The frontispiece and many of the other folios constitute something of what Michel de Certeau calls "spatial stories," narrative structures that order and regulate changes and movements through space. De Certeau explores two primary spatial projects, or *spatial practices,* that produce geographies of action: the tour and the tableau. The tour presents an itinerary that organizes movements through space, through a spatial landscape with emphases on direction, velocities, and time variables. The tableau, which depends on a fixed vision, presents territory as a locative space, emphasizes the static moment, and communicates the knowledge of an order of places. De Certeau claims that these spatial projections represent contraries, and that visual symbols and images tend to give priority to either the tour or the tableau. But, as we shall see, the frontispiece of the *Mendoza* combines the tour and the tableau in a single description. It is the last move in the tour of migration and the first tableau of the tour of empire![15] My project seeks to illustrate more of the social and symbolic relationships of the Aztec capital by focusing on how some of the symbols and related narratives locate the sacred *and* cut across social locations. A number of these images are also spatial stories that map out a ceremonial landscape.

Another reason for choosing the *Codex Mendoza* is that it provides access to two kinds of *orientatio* fundamental to understanding Aztec cosmological and social topography: (1) an understanding as to how they represented their discoveries, achievements, and practices of a cosmo-magical orientation prior to *and* after the European invasion, and (2) our orientation as students interested in developing a method for understanding the vibrant religious dimensions of the Aztec world.

The discussion begins with a description of the creation of the codex and then focuses on the religious dimensions of its many images.

THE CREATION OF THE *CODEX MENDOZA*

One of the leading patrons of the native artists in New Spain was the viceroy of Mexico, Don Antonio de Mendoza, who has been called an enthusiastic collector of native "curios." Labeled by one scholar a "Renaissance Maecenas," Mendoza noted how the ravages of the conquest had destroyed countless native artifacts and had effaced the craft traditions that generated them. He was ordered by the Spanish crown to provide evidence of the Aztec political and tribute system, and he responded by inviting trained artists and scribes, who were being schooled at the Franciscan college in Tlatelolco, to gather in a workshop where they could recreate, under the supervision of Spanish priests, the document for himself and the King of Spain[16] that became known as the *Codex Mendoza*. One of the most beautiful and revealing pictorial documents composed under his patronage was the *Codex Mendoza* (1541–1545), consisting of seventy-one folios on Spanish paper but done largely in the native style and currently bound at the spine in the manner of European books. As Kathleen Stewart Howe writes in her study of the manuscript, "The *Codex Mendoza* was a hybrid, a European commission grafted onto an indigenous tradition."[17] Picture pages carrying short annotations alternate with pages containing Spanish commentaries and extensive annotations. Together, they provide an all too rare example of how natives and Europeans worked together to tell a story and to present a panorama of a city's life that was at once old and new. The document is divided into three sections, with the first two appearing to have been copied from earlier pre-Columbian pictorials, now lost: (1) the pre-Columbian history of the Aztec capital of Tenochtitlan, beginning with its foundation and the recounting of the wars and conquests of its kings, through to 1523 (on nineteen pictorial pages); (2) a colorful account of the tribute paid to the capital by the four hundred towns in the five regions of the empire (on thirty-nine pictorial pages); and (3) a pictorial account (on fifteen pages) of some aspects of the daily life, education, warfare, priestly training, crime and punishment, and social stratification of Mexica society. The document was originally composed for the King of Spain, Charles I (also called Emperor Charles V), known as "the king of two worlds, whose address was Spain," as an example "of the strange and the rare, of the arts of the natives of the new world, to explain Mexico to their King across the sea."[18]

The codex was probably painted by the *maestro de pinturas* Francisco Gualpuyogualcal, who likely copied the first two sections of it from one or several pre-Columbian manuscripts "now lost." The Spanish annotations appear to have been written by one of three individuals: the priest Juan González of the cathedral of Mexico, a *nahuatlato*[19] of great repute; J. Martin Jacobita, a student of Sahagún, who had attended the Colegio de Santa Cruz de Tlatelolco, the school set up by the Franciscans to train Indians in Spanish classical education; or the pioneer Friar Andrés de Olmos.[20] The interpretation of the pictorial material was full of elaborations, as the Spanish translation includes a great deal of information not directly communicated by the pictures. It is also clear that the informants interpreting the pictograms and ideograms argued over some images, because the commentator noted that controversy left him only ten days to complete the manuscript prior to the ship's departure for the Spanish court. Alas, this high destiny was rudely interrupted by French sailors who attacked the Spanish ship on the high seas and took, among other things, the codex and turned it over to the French court, where it became, prior to 1553, the possession of André Thevet, the royal cosmographer. Thevet was so excited by the document that he wrote his name and title on it five times, as if trying to make it his companion. After 1587, he became friends with the English navigator Richard Hakluyt, who purchased the codex from him for twenty French crowns. After Hakluyt's death in 1616, Samuel Purchas acquired the *Mendoza* and translated and published the first section of it in 1625 in *Hakluytus Posthumus, or Purchas, His Pilgrimes,* calling it "the choicest of my jewels." Finally, it came into the possession of John Selden, the English jurist who donated it to the Bodleian Library at Oxford, where it sits today.

THE IMAGE OF CITY AND SYMBOL

> Still another type of Early Colonial space exists, and it, too, has its native precedents. We shall call it "panel space". . . . This kind of space results in a composition that is a single unit filling a single page with a strongly centralized symmetrical pattern. Subordinate elements may be a part of the larger design-year signs, for instance, but they are subject to the over-all unity of the formal pattern much more than in scattered-attribute space. In the Colonial Period panel space is often used as the underlying principle of rather formalized and stylized maps, or it is used as in the Codex Mendoza as a sort of frontispiece.
>
> Donald Robertson, *Mexican Manuscript Painting*
> *of the Early Colonial Period*[21]

Our eyes are drawn to the opening folio of the codex, described by Donald Robertson as a map or symbolic representation of the Aztec capital, Tenochtitlan.[22] Actually, it is more than a spatial image or the fixed-panel space referred to previously. It is a spatial story and contains an implicit narrative of the mythical action and performance of the Mexicas founding their city of Tenochtitlan as well as the historical action of warfare, conquest, and transference of magical power from enemy warriors to Aztec warriors. This single image is rich in individual images and symbols that convey information on Aztec cosmological thought, the ideology of warfare, the dynamics of political relations between urban centers and their peripheries, and a sense of monumentality associated with the cult of Huitzilopochtli. Thus, it serves well to provide clues to remedy the neglect, mentioned at the outset of this chapter, of understanding the complex urban character of Aztec society by revealing the formative role performed by religious symbols and cosmo-magical thought remembered even through the devastating experience of military conquest and the cultural subordination of the capital. In other words, I see this image depicting a series of relationships that include spatial, social, and symbolic relations vital to the Aztec city. In general, I can see the relations of (1) myth to history and the colonial memory of both, (2) ruler to nobles and their control of social space, (3) the dominant patron god who guided the Aztecs to, and legitimated, the new spatial order and story of the settlement, and (4) center to periphery, including the initial process of political expansion. What is especially evident is the dynamic relationship between the history and mythology of the warrior god and the founding and formation of the city's ceremonial landscape. The frontispiece is both a map and a pictorial event, several strobe light shots of ongoing action combined into one image. This dynamic quality is reflected in the telltale speech glyph of the ruler communicating not only that this is the Chief Speaker, but that the Chief Speaker is speaking! He is having a conversation, apparently a one-way conversation, with the places, people, god, and other signs in the space of the opening folio, performing an illocutionary art of ordering, announcing and, as will be seen in subsequent folios, making things happen according to his semi-divine will. This conversation of mythical center to historical periphery is elaborated again and again in other images within the first part of the *Codex Mendoza* where various *tlatoanis* are pictured, often with speech glyphs, in relation to conquered towns. The economic implications of this authoritarian conversation are reflected in Part Two of the *Mendoza,* where we see the painted list of tributes paid to the capital and the elites.

Framed by Time Signs

Beginning with the borders, we see that temporal signs, in a series of blue boxes, frame the city and the significant acts depicted below it. Thevet's extravagant signature and title fill the gap at the top left. The year count begins with the sign for "2 House" immediately to the left of the signature. It continues down and around in a counterclockwise fashion, mixing thirteen numbers, presented as dots, with the four year-signs—House, Rabbit, Reed, and Flint Knife—and ends at the top with the year-sign "13 Reed." As the Spanish commentary states, "each little compartment . . . figured in blue . . . means one year."[23] We know that the life of the society was likewise framed and animated by intricate intermeshing calendrical systems, and this pattern will be discussed in a later chapter.[24] For now, suffice it to say that this aspect of the frontispiece is critical to understanding the cosmovision of the city and the Mexica representation of place. Places, like actions, derived part of their power and meaning from their relationship to temporal images. They were *places and actions in time* and in this case, a sacred place, the city, appears in particular segments of mythical and historical time.

The Central Place
Within this temporal frame, the city appears as a large square that was, in the words of the commentator, "divided in the form of St. Andrew's Cross" with stylized blue borders representing the waters of Lake Texcoco. Two blue intersecting lines, apparently representing canals, divide the island city into four quarters. Within these four parts, we see a number of human, vegetal, and cultural images that, while appearing simple in design and size, tell us essential things about the Aztec city and its symbols. In the upper quadrant is an important ceremonial building, perhaps an early version of the temple dedicated to the patron god Huitzilopochtli (Hummingbird on the Left).[25] It is also possible that this structure was the *tecpan*, or nobles' house, or a *cabildo*, a townhouse used for community rituals and meetings.[26] In the right-hand quadrant close to the central image is a *tzompantli*, or skull rack, with a single large skull.[27] This structure grew to become a prominent part of Aztec ceremonial life and it is significant that it is part of the founding iconography and located so close to the central image. It is interesting that an axis of cultural symbols appears in the central region of the page. The great images of temple/Huitzilopochtli/blooming cactus/rock/shield form the vertical arrangement. Looking horizontally, we see a series of images, including Tenoch the Chief Speaker/Huitzilopochtli/cactus/rock/shield/skull rack. This central cluster combines a sacred center, war, ceremonial structures, and rulership.

Within the four quadrants sit ten males, nine identically dressed and one more prominently attired, who were the leaders of Mexica society. Nine of these men appear with a white *tilmatli* snugly wrapped around their bodies and are seated on bundles of green reeds, with their hair worn in the warrior hairstyle known as *temillotl*, or "pillar of stone," signifying achievements as warriors. It is important to emphasize the appearance of these nine men because it is reminiscent of the nine lords of the night who accompany many cosmic images and appear, albeit in a different arrangement, in the cosmic image of one of the most impressive surviving pre-Hispanic codices, the *Codex Fejérváry Mayer*. The tenth man, immediately to the left of the large cactus in the center, is the most prominent leader. He is distinguished by a blue speech glyph in front of his mouth, signifying that he is the *tlatoani*, or speaker. The Spanish annotation refers to him as being "especially gifted with leadership abilities."[28] The mat on which he sits is finely woven to signify that he is the "lord of the mat" and occupies the place of authority.[29] His elevation above the others is further marked by his black body paint (signifying his priestly status), smears of blood on his temple and right ear, indicating bloodletting, and loosely tied hair, showing that he was a priest. His name is expressed by the thin line attached to the sign above and behind him, which is a blooming cactus growing from a stylized rock. This image translates as "Tenoch," written *"tenuch"* (stone-cactus fruit) on the front of his white garment. It seems significant to me that his quadrant contains the largest number of original leaders, in fact four, who became an important governmental group in the subsequent history of the community.[30] Several different kinds of vegetation also are distributed throughout the four quadrants.

All these signs surround the huge central image, which shows an eagle with extended claws perched on a blooming prickly pear cactus growing from a stylized rock. This entire image, appearing in a number of colonial documents and as a part of the national emblem for Mexico, is the *place-event sign* for Tenochtitlan. Strictly speaking, the place sign is the cactus growing from a rock. This sign of orientation in space metamorphoses into an event sign with the presence of the eagle. What was *tableau* is topped by the sign of *tour*.[31] The eagle represents the sun, and the god Huitzilopochtli and his posture and location on the cactus signify the arrival of the Aztecs, led by their god of war, into the valley of Mexico. It appears that the rock out of which the cactus is growing is also a stylized human heart. Below this sign of the city's place and origin, almost supporting the rock, is a large Aztec war shield with seven eagle-down feathers and six spears attached. We are presented with a complex sign with several layers of meaning. The image of the shield and arrows refers, in part, to the Nahuatl term *in mitl in chimalli* (the arrow, the shield), which is a metaphor for war.

When the circular down balls, or *ihuiteteyo* design (with four circles around a central feather, signifying cosmic order), are added to the shield, it becomes a symbol of sacred conquest. This image communicates the idea that Tenochtitlan's power and authority derive at the moment of its foundation from warfare, the war god, and the warrior. This idea is also reflected in the attacking posture of the giant eagle's claws. The entire central image can be translated to express *The Aztecs arrived, led by their war god Huitzilopochtli, and Tenochtitlan was the seat of conquest and authority.*

The Periphery: War and Expansion
The geographical, social, and military implications of this central emblem deepen when we look at the signs, postures, and actions portrayed in the bottom third of the frontispiece. Below the scene of the founding of the capital are two episodes of Aztec conquest. These conquests take place outside the city and ceremonial center in a peripheral location to the central emblem. Away from the city, but still within the cosmo-temporal frame of the fifty-one-year count, the Mexicas carry out conquests against the communities of Colhuacan (Curved Hill) and Tenayuca (Rampart Hill). What impresses me is the fact that this military action reflects the painter's concern for *place,* and even the *religious orientation of place,* as well as the presentation of Mexica monumentality at the periphery of the city. In fact, we see the first signs of center-periphery dynamics. Historically, both sites were located on the periphery of the island, with Tenayuca on the northern edge of the lake and Culhuacan on the southern edge. The two place glyphs are prominent features attached to temples, both of which are tipped and burning. The standard glyph in the codex for the conquest of a community—a tipped and burning temple—highlights a central feature of the religious dimensions in the manuscript that is seldom remarked upon by most commentators. The main images by which Tenochtitlan is represented link military power and political authority with religious symbols and sacred places. What would otherwise (for modern secular interpreters) be seen as geographic or socioeconomic relations in space here become religiously oriented, denoted, and interpreted. The tipped and burning temple signifies that the structure, symbols, gods, energy, and "essences" of a community have been destroyed. In a sense, this is a simple religious image of a total destruction.

The expression of Mexica dominance is illustrated by the posture, costumes, and especially the size of the two pairs of warriors. As Frances Berdan and Patricia Anawalt comment in their description of the scene,

> All four warriors wear *ichcahuipilli*, the standard Mesoamerican armor of thick quilted cotton. In keeping with the greater glorification of Tenochtitlan, only the armor of the Mexica warriors is detailed, showing marks of the quilting. Both of these conquerors wear their hair in the "pillar of stone" style and carry the *ihuiteteyo* shield, symbolizing their city. One carries the *maquahuitl*, the obsidian-inset warrior club; the other wields a wooden battle stick, the *huitzoctli*.[32]

What is impressive is the emphasis on the size and martial readiness of the Mexica warriors. They not only dwarf the enemy warriors and symbolically subdue them by forcing them to crouch by pushing their shields on their heads, they are also the tallest figures on the entire page, certainly larger than the ten leaders, including Tenuch (Stone Cactus Fruit), and even taller than the great eagle image of Huitzilopochtli in the center of the page. If we focus on the warriors' shields subduing the head of the enemy, another possibility comes into view. The Aztec warrior may also be gripping the *temillotl* (the sacred shock of hair) of the enemy as an act of ritual dominance. In Aztec thought, grasping another's *temillotl* was equivalent to capturing the *tonalli*, one of the essences or souls of the person. This reflects still another religious dimension to the folio's actions. Whether or not the size factors are a post-conquest or pre-Hispanic device, the impression is that the Mexica warriors were monumental figures and, through the temple imagery, war was seen as an action with religious meanings crucial to the foundation and expansion of the city. This nexus was reiterated by the fact that the nine assistants to Tenuch were warriors. As will be seen later in this book, the collection of nine warriors, deities, or levels of the cosmos had profound cosmological significance in the geometry of the universe. And the image of the city's founding rests on the interaction of images of sacred place, war, and ideal, giant warriors. The Spanish commentator reflected this interaction of images by saying,

> In the course of some years, the inhabitants were multiplying and so the city was named Mexico, a name derived from the Mexicans, naming it

the place and site of the Mexicans. And as the people had developed as daring and warlike, they gave vent to their spirit by overcoming their neighbors. Thus by force of arms they manifested (their power) by subjecting as vassals and tributaries two towns near Mexico called Colhuacan and Tenayuca . . . [33]

The spatial relations of these various images have not received the comment they deserve. The connections between the center and periphery are reflected in the images of warriors captured at the edge of the city, which are linked to the image of their destiny, in part, as skulls on the *tzompantli* located close to the center of the settlement. The cosmo-magical significance of the warrior is reflected in the military expansion of the city and symbolized in the founding of the ceremonial center through the linked images of the warrior/god/eagle Huitzilopochtli and the shield. The entire image presents a series of give-and-take relationships—the Aztecs gave their best military- and deity-ordained shots to the periphery and took control of temples, warriors, and tributary goods. And again, we see the interplay of tour and tableau. The scene within the blue lines signifying the lakes signals the end of a tour as it also celebrates the tableau of Mexica authority and ceremonial city. The action of conquests below, signaling the expansion of Mexica power into new territories, reflects the tour of warrior cults. In this way, we are witnessing an image that is both tableau and tour, and the itinerary for the future is signaled in these spatial relationships that were also the cues for stories.

The Periphery and the New Fire

The frontispiece image yields still more clues and pointers about the city that became a symbol of so many Aztec myths and institutions. Focusing again on the marginal calendar count, which falls one short of the fifty-two-year cycle, or *xiuhmolpilli* (bundle of reeds), we note that one calendar date, 2 Reed, in the bottom right-hand corner, draws special emphasis. A fire-drill glyph rises from the year-sign, attached by a single thread, showing that this was the year of the famous New Fire Ceremony, one of the most profound and inclusive ceremonies of the Mexica world. Since this ceremony is interpreted in chapter 3, suffice it to say here that once every fifty-two years at the culmination of the interlocking permutations of the 365-day calendar and the 260-day calendar, the New Fire Ceremony was held at the sacred site of the Hill of the Star, beyond the limits of the Aztec capital. After household goods were destroyed and all fires extinguished, the populace waited in the darkness and watched in anticipation for the new fire to be lit on the chest of a sacrificed warrior. This fire was then taken down the mountain to the center of the city and placed in the shrine of Huitzilopochtli, from whence it was then distributed to all parts of the empire. This path of the New Fire indicates that the Mexica were redistributing their cosmo-magical power, in the form of a fire generated out of the sacrifice, from the capital (the main center of all redistribution) to the periphery.

It is important that the spatial relationships between the capital and the periphery of the Hill of the Star and the other communities, which were joined during the New Fire Ceremony, parallel the peripheral location of the New Fire Ceremony glyph in the right-hand corner of the frontispiece. My point is that this bottom section of the frontispiece, combining the Mexica conquests and the sign of the New Fire Ceremony, tell us that the page is much more than a "symbolic map of the founding of Tenochtitlan." It is a spatial story of several major rituals and social practices of domination, astronomy, and cosmic renewal—a very cosmological image indeed. One of the most meaningful patterns is the spatial sense of the interconnectedness of the ceremonial structures (temple of Huitzilopochtli, skull rack) and the alleged enemy communities of the Aztec world.

Finally, it is important to remember that this image was painted long after the Aztec empire's rise to extraordinary heights and twenty years after its collapse. Its symmetry, its sense of centeredness, and the signs of expansion, all circumscribed only by the cosmic signs of calendrical passage and renewal, combine to suggest not only the tableau of foundation but the future tour of the boundless Aztec empire, a place that became, through ritual and political metamorphosis, the performance of imperial success.

Now, as a way of gaining a significant advantage into the cosmological and social meaning of this rich image of Aztec origins and spatial order, I will utilize Paul Wheatley's discussion of city and symbol in traditional urbanism.

SACRED SPACE AND COSMO-MAGICAL THOUGHT

Since Paul Wheatley wrote his remarkable essays and magisterial books on the origins of urban ecology, a number of scholars have utilized, applied, and challenged his model.[34] While some of these responses are discussed in subsequent chapters, it is appropriate to outline aspects of his cosmo-magical model here. According to Wheatley, cosmo-magical consciousness was generally expressed in a worldview that (1) saw the "real" powers of the cosmos as transcending "the pragmatic realm of textures and geometrical spaces," and (2) demanded that human beings, if they wished to participate in that reality, strive to bring the human social order into coordination and harmony with the divine society of the gods, and vice versa. Wheatley's perceptions were initially developed out of sustained reflection on the evidence about urban symbolism in traditional China and were then honed through a series of comparative exercises with other areas of primary urban generation. The construction of capitals, which functioned as "ideal types" for their cultures, was achieved not only through the imitation of archetypes, but through processes of discovery and analysis of the patterns of nature and the construction of a model of this discovery and analysis. More than imitation is at work here. Human beings in the ancient city understood their society to exist within a mythic-cosmic setting,[35] and what we call politics, social organization, economic exchange, and ritual performance took their cues, profounder meanings, and reasons for existence from the gods, ancestors, and forces they understood to emerge and fold back into that mythic cosmic setting on a continuous, regenerative schedule. In what I consider to be one of the most succinct statements of the paramount importance of studying urban settlements as a means of understanding religion and culture, Wheatley writes,

> It is the city which has been, and to a large extent still is, the style center in the traditional world, disseminating social, political, technical, religious and aesthetic values, and functioning as an organizing principle conditioning the manner and quality of life in the countryside. Those who focus their regional studies on peasant society to the exclusion of urban forms are—as I have stated elsewhere—as deluded as Plato's prisoners (or in another sense, Beckett's) who mistake flickering shadows on a wall for reality. They, too, are turning their backs on the generative force of ecological transformation and seeking the causes of the great tides of social change in ripples on the beach of history.[36]

The integrating mechanism for traditional cities was the cosmo-magical conviction, consisting of a complex of ideas that held that in those religions where "human order was brought into being at the creation of the world, there was a pervasive tendency to dramatize the cosmogony by constructing on earth a reduced version of the cosmos, usually in the form of a state capital."[37] Wheatley, who utilizes the works of Mircea Eliade and René Berthelot in this regard, is eager to point out the sense of confidence that early urban societies displayed in being able to regulate a tight fit between the patterns of the heavens and the patterns of society. He notes,

> It must be emphasized at the outset, albeit perhaps supererogatively, that the various models of this kind which provided frameworks for the evaluation of spatial significance in the past were not simple-minded attempts by unsophisticated men of an earlier age to explain the causality of natural and human phenomena, but rather protosciences whose central objective was to demonstrate the unity of all existence. They were not "primitive" in the sense of undifferentiated thought systems as Lévy-Bruhl employed that term, but offer magnificent exemplars of associative, or coordinative thinking, utilizing a logic no whit less rigorous in its own way than that of contemporary science. Nor were the intellectuals who elucidated and elaborated them fanciful dreamers. Rather they were organizers of knowledge, codifiers, builders of systems, men who shared a corporate consuming passion for distinction, definition, and formalization, who conceived a universe order so precisely that, to borrow a metaphor from one of the Chinese exponents of this style of thought, one could not insert a hair between the parts.[38]

This pattern of thinking, with its confidence in tight parallelism, was expressed in at least three aspects of spatial organization in the traditional city, (1) the symbolism of the center, (2) its cardinal axiality, and (3) its architectural parallelism between macrocosmos and microcosmos. Wheatley notes that in the seven areas of primary urban generation there was a tendency to dramatize the cosmology by reproducing on earth a reduced version of the cosmos in which "terrestrial space is initially generated by and subsequently structured about, an existentially centered point of ontological transition between cosmic planes," an *axis mundi*, a center.[39] This central point becomes the quintessential sacred precinct and is usually marked by the construction of a series of special ritual buildings. In this ritual construction and in a ritual return to this central point, people gain access to the source and flow of "reality" in the world. This symbolism of the center, or "center oriented construct" as S. J. Tambiah[40] terms the ancient city, is joined to techniques of spatial orientation that attempt to align the major causeways, thoroughfares, or sections of a capital city with the cardinal compass directions of the universe, "thus assimilating the group's territory to the cosmic order and constructing a sanctified living space or habitabilis within the continuum of profane space."[41] These four guiding highways that emerge from the central ceremonial precinct, the theater of sacred ritual, act as centripetal and centrifugal guides, magnetizing the sacred and social energies into the center and diffusing the supernatural and royal powers outward into the kingdom. This centering and cardinal orientation, these attempts to coordinate supernatural forces and social forces, are also elaborated plastically, that is, when a city or its ceremonial center not only "marks the spot" and controls the lines of force, but actually represents and signifies in its design and structure a cosmic struggle, a myth or divine drama.[42]

Though I work with the pattern of center and periphery a great deal in later chapters, I want to emphasize here the centripetal and centrifugal forces generated by the interaction of ceremonial centers and marketplaces situated within the limits of major urban settlements. Some of the most impressive forces at work in favor of urban settlements are the magnetic economic institutions and power relations that draw travelers, pilgrims, merchants, artisans, rulers, and military units into their confines. As we shall see in this study of the first two parts of the *Codex Mendoza*, all the meaningful activities, including warfare and trade, were pictured in terms of the "central zone," or "effective space," of the city. The point here is to emphasize that the symbols of cities need to be explored for the dynamics of their centripetal and centrifugal power and not only for their power to denote and fix locations in space.

The magnetic abilities of ceremonial complexes, like the one pictured in the *Mendoza*, are twins to the centrifugal, extensive needs of urban settlements to saturate the spaces, minds, technology, and symbol systems of other communities and geographies with their styles, messages, and authority. Wheatley's work on the cities and symbols of the traditional world shows how rulers and their cosmo-magical systems thrive, in part, on the exercises of the diffusion of authority, power, and symbolic dominance. Italo Calvino has a clear way of referring to centrifugal forces, "The city says everything you must think, makes you repeat her discourse . . ."[43]

TENOCHTITLAN: THE FOUNDATION OF HEAVEN

With these elements of cosmo-magical thought in hand (the symbolism of the center, cardinal axiality, centripetal forces, and centrifugal drives), I now turn back to the *Codex Mendoza* and related contextual material in order to widen and deepen our perceptions of how Tenochtitlan was an effective symbolic space. Several later chapters elaborate on the way cities act (and lead urban dwellers to act) as places of cosmo-magical, political, and economic relationships.

As an Aztec lyric poem reveals, the capital city of Tenochtitlan was considered the material expression of the Mexica conviction that they had come to occupy the axis of the cosmos.

> From where the eagles are resting,
> from where the tigers are exalted,
> the Sun is invoked.
> Like a shield that descends,
> so does the Sun set.
> In Mexico night is falling,
> war rages on all sides.
> Oh Giver of Life!
> war comes near. . . .
>
> . . . Proud of itself
> Is the city of Mexico-Tenochtitlan
> Here no one fears to die in war
> This is our glory
> This is Your Command
> Oh Giver of Life
> Have this in mind, oh princes
> Who would conquer Tenochtitlan?
> Who could shake the foundation of heaven?[44]

The city was eulogized as a proud, invincible place, the center of the vertical structure of the cosmos that linked the human world with the commands of the supreme deity Ipalnemohuani ("he by whom we live"), or the Giver of Life.[45] Before commenting on the key phrase, the city as "foundation of heaven," it is important to note the parallels between the clues from the frontispiece of the *Codex Mendoza* and the couplets, *difrasismos*, and images in these stanzas. The opening three lines refer to the Sun God, Huitzilopochtli, and the phrases "where the eagles are resting" and "the sun is invoked" refer at once to both the celestial resting place of the Sun God *and* his alignment on the blooming cactus in what will be the heart of Tenochtitlan. This celestial/terrestrial possibility is supported by the next two lines, which speak of the sun descending from the sky and sinking into the earth! The reference to the "shield" and the "rages" of war reminds me of the Aztec shield of war and authority and the battles, simply presented below the scene of the city's foundation, in the *Codex Mendoza*. The poetic images where "war rages on all sides" and soon "comes near" parallel the spatial relations in the pictorial image where warriors are captured outside the city but whose skulls end up on the skull rack near the central shrine. These are pictorial and poetic expressions of the centripetal relations I am emphasizing. This parallelism is followed by the boastful order/question,

> Have this in mind, oh princes
> Who could conquer Tenochtitlan?
> Who could shake the foundation of heaven?

Tenochtitlan's glory must (like Calvino's cities) be kept in mind for it is the unconquerable "foundation of heaven." The song ends with a reiteration of the *Mendoza* claim that the city, from its very foundation, existed through arrows and shields.

My interpretation of this verse turns on the significance of the Nahuatl phrase *in itlaxillo in ilhuicatll*, which León-Portilla renders as the "foundation of heaven" and Bierhorst translates as "the prop of heaven." Another usage of this term appears in Book 12 of the *Florentine Codex* as a description of warriors as *itlaxilloan altepetl*, meaning "they (the warriors) are the mainstay of the city." León-Portilla's translation points to the cosmological significance of the great social order, which was eulogized in poem and frontispiece. The reference to the city as a *ground* of the celestial world becomes more acceptable when we realize that the Aztecs conceived of their cosmos as containing three superimposed sections: the heavens, the surface of the earth, and the underworld. An ensemble of pictorial and written sources, including the *Codex Vaticano Latino 3738*,[46] shows us that the vertical ordering of the cosmos consisted of thirteen celestial layers rising above the earth, culminating in the realm of Omeyocan, the "Place of Duality," and nine layers below the earth, ending in Mictlan, the "Place of the Dead." This dense vertical column was joined by the central region, Tlalticpac, the "Earth Surface." The lynchpin was the city of Tenochtitlan.

At the time of the Spanish contact, thirteen deities inhabited the thirteen levels, which were designated the "Sky of the Paradise of the Rain God," the "Sky of the Star-Skirted Goddess," the "Sky of the Sun," the "Sky of the Salt-Fertility God," the "Sky Where Gyrating Occurs," the "Sky That Is Blackish," the "Sky That Is Blue-Green," the "Place That Has Corners of Obsidian Slabs," the "God Who Is White," the "God Who Is Yellow," the "God Who Is Red," and the "Place of Duality." The layers below the earth had such names as the "Place for Crossing the Water," the "Place Where the Hills Crash Together," the "Obsidian Mountain," the "Place of the Obsidian Wind," the "Place Where the Banners Are Raised," the "Place Where People Are Pierced with Arrows," the "Place Where People's Hearts Are Devoured," the "Obsidian Place of the Dead," and the "Place Where Smoke Has No Outlet."[47] The underworld is subject to interpretation later in this book, but I can say here that the claim that Tenochtitlan was the "foundation of heaven" demonstrates that it was considered to be the *groundwork*, or fundamental place of social and ritual work to prop up the heavens and serve as a passageway into the underworld.

This claim that the capital was the *axis mundi* of the cosmos takes on horizontal and historical significance in the various accounts of the peregrination of the Mexicas through a landscape of ordeals before arriving, under the tutelage of their patron god Huitzilopochtli, in the Basin of Mexico. Most stories of their journey tell that the Mexicas had left their primordial home, Aztlan, the "Place of White Reeds," and Chicomoztoc, the "Place of the Seven Caves," and taken a long, arduous journey in search of a new home. Several pictorial manuscripts present a detailed itinerary of their adventures and hardships. They discover the new site of their city through the appearance of an omen.

The key image of this omen is, of course, the giant eagle landing on the blooming cactus growing from a rock. While a number of versions of this foundation story exist,[48] Diego Durán's account found in Doris Heyden's recent translation of *Historia de las indias de Nueva España e islas de tierra firme* is one of the most vivid and emotional available to us. Durán's native informants told him the story of how Huit-zilopochtli, the Hummingbird God of War, appeared in a dream to the shaman priest, Cuauhtlequetzqui, who later recounted the appa-rition. The scene is described in rich detail. After stating all these things, Cuauhtlequetzqui cried out,

> Know, O my children, that this night our god Huitzilopochtli appeared to me. Remember, on our arrival in this valley . . . Our enemies drove us from that region, but Huitzilopochtli commanded us to kill Copil and this we did, taking out his heart. And standing in the place where the god commanded, I threw the heart into the reeds: it fell upon a rock. Ac-cording to the revelation of our god when he appeared to me this night, a prickly pear cactus standing upon a rock has grown from this heart and has become so tall and luxuriant that a fine eagle has made his nest there. When we discover it we shall be fortunate, for there we shall find our rest, our comfort, and our grandeur. There our name will be praised and our Aztec nation made great. The might of our arms will be known and the courage of our brave hearts. With these we shall conquer nations, near and distant, we shall subdue towns and cities from sea to sea. We shall be-come lords of gold and silver, of jewels and precious stones, of splendid feathers and of the insignia. We shall rule over those people, their lands, their sons and daughters. They will serve us and be our subjects and tributaries.
>
> Our god orders us to call this place Tenochtitlan. There will be built the city that is to be queen, that is to rule over all others in the country. There we shall receive other kings and nobles, who will recognize Te-nochtitlan as the supreme capital. And so, my children, let us go among these marshes of reeds, rushes, and cattails, as our god has indicated. Everything he has promised us has come true; thus we shall now find this place for our city.[49]

The phrases "rule over all others" and "who will recognize Te-nochtitlan as the supreme capital" show that for the informants of Durán, years after the conquest, Tenochtitlan was remembered as the *axis mundi* of the wider society, subduing others, gathering wealth, and exercising its magnetic political authority, ". . . we shall subdue . . . from sea to sea . . . become lords of gold and silver . . . of splendid feathers and of the insignia . . . to rule over all others in the country . . . [and] we shall receive other kings and nobles." The text goes on to say that when the people found the prickly pear cactus and saw Huit-zilopochtli in the form of the eagle "with his wings stretched out toward the rays of the sun," they humbled themselves, and the god "humbled himself, bowing his head low in their direction." The Mexicas "marked the site," rejoiced, and rested. Their first community action was the construction of a shrine to the god, the shrine that, as we will see in the next chapter, became the Great Temple of Tenochtitlan. The site of this city and temple was not only discovered through a vision, it came to embody the Aztec vision of place, par excellence.

Another version of the city's founding tells that one of the priests who saw the eagle then dived into the lake and disappeared. When he failed to surface, his companions thought he had drowned and they returned to their camp. The priest soon returned and announced that he had descended into the rain god Tlaloc's underworld, communicated with the deity, and was granted permission for the Mexica to settle in this sacred place. This shows that a true *axis mundi,* an opening to both the celestial and underworld realms, was ordained by the sun god and the water god of the earth. It was to be, as the place sign suggests, the center of authority on the horizontal plane as well as the vertical.[50]

THE FOUR-QUARTERED CITY

Our principal image from the *Codex Mendoza* shows that the space of the city was divided into four parts, suggesting that it was laid out to conform to the cosmo-magical principle of cardinal axiality.[51] One of the main goals of this chapter is to illustrate the profound commitments the Mexicas developed to an overall urban design and sense of cosmic *orientatio* in their geography. The four-quartered orientation of the city appeared to the conquistador Hernán Cortés during his reconnaissance and entrance into the lakes of the Basin of Mexico. In the Second Letter to King Charles I, his report suggests further evidence of a cardinal orientation of Tenochtitlan, here referred to as Temixtitan: "The great city of Temixtitan is built on the salt lake, and no matter by what road you travel there are two leagues from the main body of the city to the mainland. There are four artificial causeways leading to it, and each is as wide as two cavalry lances. The city itself is as big as Seville or Cordoba."[52] Fortunately, Cortés ordered a map made of the entire island city (published in Nuremberg in 1524), which presents in cartographic terms the image of the city organized into five major sections with extended artificial causeways leading out from an enormous ceremonial center. In his article "The Internal Structure of Tenochtitlan," Edward E. Calnek summarizes the present archaeological consensus on the spatial layout of the Aztec capital, stating that "Tenochtitlan (but not Tlatelolco) was divided into four great quarters, marked off by four avenues that extended in the cardinal directions from the gates of the ceremonial complex."[53] According to the extensive legendary account in Diego Durán's *Historia*, this spatial division was dictated by the deity who founded the city, Huitzilopochtli. The text reads that after the Aztecs had labored over the construction of their god's temple, Huitzilopochtli spoke to his priest, saying, "Tell the Aztec people that the principal men, each with his relatives and friends and allies, should divide the city into four main wards. The center of the city will be the house you have constructed for my resting place. And let each group build its part of the city as it wishes."[54] The divine command was to lay out the new settlement on the five-part model of the horizontal cosmos, assimilating the form of the city to the form of the four quadrants and the center, which constitute the cosmos. This spatial order was formerly achieved following the coronation of the first Aztec King, Acamapichtli, "Handful of Reeds," when the Aztec elites gave their four sectors the name Nauhcampa, meaning the "Four Directions of the Wind." It is clear from archaeological evidence and other relevant maps that the city was divided by four major highways that crossed at the foot of the Templo Mayor and drove straight out of the heart of the city, passing through a great platform surrounding the entire sacred precinct.[55] Recent studies have shown that the intersection of the four great causeways was located at the foot of Huitzilopochtli's shrine at the Templo Mayor and not in the central axis joining his temple to Tlaloc's.[56]

It must be emphasized that these symbolic roads had a crucial impact on life in the city. As Jorge Hardoy, an urban geographer who has studied this city, notes, "These two streets, converging on the solid ground of the original island, were continuations of the causeways which served the dual purpose of crossing the lake and avoiding the swampy chinampa areas. The causeways not only connected the city with the mainland towns but also acted as dikes to contain floods, and to determine the direction of the city's major streets and canals."[57]

While it is evident from extensive archaeological work in Meso-america that the practice of four-quartered orientation of settlements varied a great deal, it is also clear that the Aztecs were drawing upon the traditional ordering of a capital city, developed as far back perhaps as the Teotihuacan era but certainly by their royal predecessors, the Toltecs.[58] In the tenth-century Toltec capital of Tollan, located fifty kilometers north of Tenochtitlan, from which the Aztecs claimed their legitimate right to rule Mexico, we find the construction of major ritual buildings modeled on the cardinal points of the compass.[59] The relevant text reads, "He the Prince, 1-Reed Quetzalcoatl, built his house as four: house of turquoise, house of redshell, house of whiteshell, house of precious feathers. There he worshipped, did his penance and also fasted."[60] Another extended description of the cere-monial buildings in Tollan states,

> Wherefore was it called a Tolteca house? It was built with consummate care, majestically designed: it was the place of worship of their priest whose name was Quetzalcoatl. It was quite marvelous. It consisted of four (abodes). One was facing east: this was the house of gold: for this rea-son it was called house of gold: that which serves as the stucco was gold plate applied, joined to it. One was facing west, toward the setting sun: this was the house of green stone, the house of fine turquoise. For this reason was it called the house of green stone. One was facing south, to-ward the irrigated lands. This was the house of shells or of silver. . . . One was facing north, toward the plains. . . . this was the red house: red be-cause shells were inlaid in the interior walls, as those stones which were precious stones were red.[61]

One reliable interpreter of these descriptive phrases, Leonardo López Luján, argues that they refer to a cosmological model, an archetypal Tollan, and not actual buildings in the historical city of Tollan. He notes that in the *Historia de los Mexicanos por Sus Pinturas* there is a sim-ilar description of the four houses of Tlaloc around a central patio, which refers to a celestial place and not architectural buildings.[62]

Aztec cosmology and the city that symbolized it derived their general plan, or at least shared their principle features, from a wider Mesoamerican paradigm of the cosmos. The finest image we have, which has a strong resonance in the colonial production of the *Codex Mendoza*, is the opening page of the pre-Conquest divinatory manual known as the *Codex Fejérváry-Mayer*, in which the cosmos is divided into five precisely defined sections of space organized by sacred trees, deities, birds, and appropriate colors.[63] This paradigmatic image, combining a calendar, body parts, gods, colors, and ritual objects, presents the cosmos as four trapezoidal-shaped quarters of the universe surrounding the central image of a great warrior with weapons whose blood is streaming into the four quarters of the universe. One prominent orientation feature of the *Fejérváry-Mayer*, which shows up again in the *Mendoza* image, is that each of the four quarters is centered by an identical type of image with three parts, that is, a blooming tree growing out of a cultural image (temple, sacrificial bowl, celestial spirit, or earth deity) with a sacred bird on top. This pattern of orientating the four quarters is repeated in the central image of the *Mendoza*, that is, the stylized rock (heart), blooming *nopal,* and eagle. Further, Tenochtitlan's four-quartered organization surrounding the militant god (in both the *Mendoza* and actual architectural order) is in a fashion similar to the *Fejérváry-Mayer*, which has the war god bleeding and poised for battle in the center.[64]

Archaeology and the study of colonial maps have shown that each of the city's four quarters was a replication of the larger image of centeredness, in that each quarter had its own central temple complex that housed the deities of the groups who inhabited that quarter of the city. Durán's informants said, "Huitzilopochtli commanded them to distribute the gods among them (the four districts) and that each barrio choose a special place where these deities might be revered. Thus, each neighborhood was divided into many small sections according to the number of idols it possessed."[65] A marketplace and administrative center were part of each quarter's central precinct. Thus, each quarter had its own sacred pivot, reproducing the image of the center that dominated the city as a whole.

This pattern of centering was further duplicated and miniaturized in the many barrios of each quarter, each of which had a local ceremonial precinct consisting of a temple, a small market, and a school. Calnek writes,

> The barrios—conceived as territorial units—were marked by a structure that housed the patron deities of the group. This structure was evidently part of a large complex that also included a telpochcalli (young man's house) and in most or all cases, a plaza or market. . . . In addition to providing the locus for public and private rituals dedicated to local deities, the temple was also the meeting place for barrio elders and the focal point for large ceremonials organized by occupationally specialized groups. It

provided, in short, a kind of civic center in relation to which the social identities of the greater part of the urban population were most immediately expressed, and additionally, where a great variety of activities essential to the urban neighborhood were conducted.[66]

Center and Periphery

Returning to the abundant images of the *Codex Mendoza*, it is possible to see the traces, if not the actual outlines, of centrifugal and cardinal orientation in sections of the manuscript, which are often ignored as resources for studying the religious dimensions of the Aztec city. I am reminded of Edward Shils's observation that central value systems and their authoritarian ideologies have a powerful tendency to saturate the social and mental space of every society. Place after place within the society is visited, penetrated, and changed by the symbols and values of the "central place" even as local communities work to adapt them to local conditions. One of the most intense concerns of the painters of the *Mendoza* is the reiteration of the importance of place and place signs. All the action of the first two sections of the manuscript, especially warfare and trade, is presented in relation to the category of place and place names.[67] Page after page of the conquest section is a pictorial interplay between the combined images of the particular Aztec ruler with his war shield and the series of place signs and tipped and burning temples of the conquered towns. The underlying pattern of the first part of the *Codex Mendoza*, which Elizabeth Hill Boone shows to be "a victory chronicle" rather than a secular history of the city, is the pattern of the expanding frontier of the main settlement through the practice of warfare.[68] For instance, when we view the successive mappings of the territorial expansions of each ruler's conquests in the work of Berdan and Anawalt, we are witnessing not just a victory chronicle but a chronicle of imperial expansion and the saturation of central Mesoamerica by the sacralized military power of Tenochtitlan.[69] The expanding interplay of centrifugal and centripetal force begins with the very modest *four* conquests of Acamapichtli (1376–1396) in the nearby southern region of the lakes, to Huitzilihuitl's (1397–1417) *eight* conquests further east and north, to Chimalpopoca's (1418–1427) paltry *two* conquests to the south and north, to Itzcoatl's (1428–1440) explosive *twenty-three* victories largely in the western and southern regions, through Motecuhzoma Ilhuicamina's (1441–1469) *thirty-three* further to the south and the east, and Axayacatl (1470–1481) with *thirty-six* conquests reaching further toward the eastern coast and the conquest of the sister city of Tlatelolco. This is followed by Tizoc's (1481–1486) disappointing *fourteen* to the south, west, and north, and Ahuitzotl's (1487–1502) *forty-five* conquests on the borderlands, which expanded the empire's territorial reach to unprecedented limits. Ahuitzotl's military campaigns reached into the Tehuantepec and Xoconochco regions along the Pacific and deep into Oaxaca. Finally, we arrive at the *forty-four* victories of Motecuhzoma Xocoyotzin (1503–1520), which focused on consolidating conquests within the boundaries established by his predecessor. It is significant that his campaigns led to

> an escalation in the flowery wars with Tlaxcala and its allies. During his reign, massive campaigns against the Tlaxcalans were conducted in earnest, although the stalemate between the two powers continued. Moctecuhzoma's forces conquered numerous towns to the south, east, and north of Tlaxcala; this may reflect a strategy of isolating Tlaxcala from potential allies and material resources. The flower war had become a serious war. [Author's note: Moctecuhzoma, Motecuhzoma, and Motecuzoma are variant spellings of Moctezuma.][70]

Boone's innovative interpretation of Part 1 of the *Mendoza* links the victory chronicle of the expanding central authority of Tenochtitlan to the pattern of tribute payments and shows how centrifugal forces were tied to centripetal capabilities of the elites of Tenochtitlan. The expansion of the city's power outward is always reintegrated back into the substance of the capital, that is, economic gain and redistribution in the capital. When we review the bright series of folios depicting the tribute payments of scores of towns and cities to the capital, we witness, in material and symbolic terms, the Aztec pattern of urban control over the peripheries. Boone writes about the relations of the conquest and tribute sections of the *Codex Mendoza*:

> It presents only the reigns of the Mexica rulers and the towns they claimed to have subjugated, omitting mention of other events—such as natural climatic phenomena, building programs, religious celebrations, and the births of rulers—found in other pictorial histories. *This focus on the monarchy and its conquests may have been selected for the first* Codex Mendoza *section as a way of preparing the reader of the codex for the tribute list that follows, for the dynastic conquests were fundamental in creating the tribute empire:*

> *either tribute-bearing provinces entered the empire by conquest or they entered vol-*
> *untarily but under the threat of conquest. Certainly Part 1 stresses the strength of*
> *the Aztec empire.*[71] (italics mine)

In my view, the victory chronicle gives us important clues to not only the strength of the Aztec empire, but the pulsating expansion of central-place symbols and policies and the collection of goods and symbols into the center as it constantly redefined its peripheries and alliances. The centripetal powers of the capital, for example, are brilliantly portrayed in the largest section (thirty-nine folios), Part 2, which is an accounting of Aztec imperial tribute. These stunning pages are full of the orderly presentation of symbols and images of tribute collected by a militarily dominant state from its conquered regions. A full listing is impossible here except to note that great care was taken by the artist to depict large quantities of cacao, *piñol,* mantas and mantillas, warriors' costumes of over thirty styles, shields, feathers, bins of corn, *chia,* beans, and amaranth, plus gourd bowls, native paper, mats, bulrushes, seals, maguey syrup, limes, tunics, beans, plants of wood, firewood, loaves of salt, jars of honey, unrefined copal, strings of greenstones, copper axes, scallop shells, gold tablets, gourd bowls of gold dust, earthen pans of yellow varnish, masks of rich blue stones, loads of cane mouth perfumes, carrying frames, deerskins, quetzal feathers, red feathers, turquoise feathers, crystal and amber lip plugs, bird skins of specific color, jaguar skins, bales of cotton, live eagles, and many other objects in various and often tremendous quantities.[72] These payments, and their illustrations and displays, served a symbolic as well as a material purpose. They symbolized the expanding dominance and magnetic control over the production of the outlying communities and provided revenues for the capital, "underwriting its complex political structure" and stimulating the production of "specified goods in conquered areas."[73]

The work of Johanna Broda suggests that the Aztec practice of tribute collection was influenced, or at least organized, by principles of cardinal orientation. The entire city, and certainly the well-being of the capital's elites, was sustained by the tribute payments. In her seminal article "El tributo en trajes guerreros y la estructura del sistema tributario mexica," Broda utilizes the abundant evidence (found in Part 2 of the *Codex Mendoza*) concerning the patterns in sending warriors' uniforms to Tenochtitlan to demonstrate that the Mexica

organized their tribute system into five great regions corresponding
to the five major directions (north, west, south, east, and the center).
Here again we find conformity to the cosmic order. Thus, it is particularly important to note that the victory chronicle and the tribute roll
may reflect more of the fundamental cosmic orientation of the elite
planners and leaders of Tenochtitlan than previously noted.[74]

Other images in the *Codex Mendoza* suggest that the cardinal orientation of the city and the authority and performance of royal life
were intimately linked. For instance, the image of the palatial structure of Moctezuma shows that it was divided into five principal
rooms, with Moctezuma's larger chamber sitting on a higher level. I
agree with Broda that this organization reflected the influence of
cosmo-magical orientation in the very house of government.[75] The
tie between a vision of the cosmos and political history is also reflected in the corresponding annotations placed over various rooms.
The central room is labeled "Throne and Dais of Motecuhzoma
where he sat in audience and to judge." The room on the left of the
tlatoani was the guesthouse where visiting lords from Tetzcoco and
Tlacopan, partners in the Triple Alliance, stayed when visiting. The
room on the right was for the lords of Tenayuca, Chiconauhtla, and
Colhuacan, "friends and allies of Motecuhzoma." Below two courtyards are two other grand rooms, the Council Hall of War and Motecuhzoma's Council Hall. This image also shows that the apex of
Aztec government consisted of Motecuhzoma at the center of power
with four judges, "Learned Men," assisting his royal judgments. It appears that the Aztec perception of their universe as a four-cornered
cosmos significantly influenced not only the spatial structure of their
city, but also the order of their tribute system, the image of the royal
palace, and the organization of their government.

ARCHITECTURAL PARALLELISM OF
MACROCOSMOS AND MICROCOSMOS

... Mexico City ... city of fixed sun, city ancient in light, old city cradled among birds of men ... city in the true image of gigantic heaven.
Incandescent prickly pear.

Carlos Fuentes, *Where the Air Is Clear*[76]

The third spatial element of cosmo-magical thought is the parallelism
between the microcosmos, in the form of architectural assemblages,
and the macrocosmos expressed in the myths about the realms of the

gods and their associated conceptions. This cosmo-magical parallelism is often expressed in the monumental ceremonial centers of imperial and regional capitals. We see the persistence of this mode of architectural organization reflected in the Map of Tenochtitlan published by Friedrich Peypus of Nuremberg in 1524. The map is a woodcut thought to be based upon a drawing ordered by Cortés as part of his reconnaissance of the capital. It shows that the entire city, as well as the swampy lake, was dominated spatially by the oversized ceremonial precinct located at the heart of the settlement.

Consider this eyewitness description of the ceremonial structures in the city by Cortés in his second letter, which, incidentally, was published along with the woodcut map.

> There are, in all districts of this great city, many temples or houses for their idols. They are all very beautiful buildings, and in the important ones there are priests of their sect who live there permanently: and, in addition to the houses for the idols, they also have very good lodgings. . . . Among these temples there is one, the principal one, whose great size and magnificence no human tongue could describe, for it is so large that within the precincts, which are surrounded by a very high wall[,] a town of some five hundred inhabitants could easily be built. All round inside this wall there are very elegant quarters with very large rooms and corridors where their priests live. There are as many as forty towers, all of which are so high that in the case of their largest there are fifty steps leading up to the main part of it: and the most important of these towers is higher than that of the cathedral of Seville. They are so well constructed in both their stone and woodwork that there can be none better in any place, for all the stonework inside the chapels where they keep their idols is in high relief, with figures and little houses, and the woodwork is likewise of relief and painted with monsters and other figures and design. All these towers are burial places of chiefs, and the chapels therein are each dedicated to the idol which he venerated.[77]

Cortés is describing, among other structures, the huge, 500-meter square ceremonial center surrounded by "the very high wall" that occupied the heart of the capital. When we turn to the map he had drawn up of the city, we see the prominence of the ceremonial area that covers (obviously an exaggeration by the mapmaker) an area that is one-quarter of the size of the entire island city! While the ceremonial precinct was not that large in relation to the capital, its prestige was enormous. Within the precinct we see temples for human sacrifice, the *tzompantli* skull rack, a headless person, and an image of the Great Temple with the sun peeking out between the two shrines. During the two hundred years of the city's existence, an elaborate ceremonial center flourished around these shrines. It consisted of numerous monumental structures, which included schools, a ball court, a skull rack, temples to major deities, and several administrative buildings, all surrounded by a ten-foot-high platform. Fortunately, we have a partial list and description of these "towers" and the "idols," or supernatural entities, who inhabited them in Book 2 of the *Florentine Codex*.[78] A review shows some of the cosmo-magical commitments materialized in the precinct and crudely reflected in the Cortés map. These attempts at parallelism between the demands of heaven and the ritual labors on earth included places of prayer, numerous temples for sacrificial killing, dancing platforms, ritual springs, palaces for visiting rulers, dormitories for priests, and fasting temples. In addition to the monumental temple pyramid dedicated to Huitzilopochtli and Tlaloc, which is examined in the next chapter, there was "Tlalocan," a fasting temple in "honor of the Tlalocs," and "The Temple of the White Cinteotl," where captives with skin sores were sacrificed, and "The Temple of Mixcoatl," where victims were killed like deer. Especially revealing of the centripetal forces of the Aztec capital was the "Coacalco" where the "gods of (foreign) cities dwelt. Whenever the Mexicans conquered, they took (the gods) captive" and guarded them in this temple.[79] There was Quauhxicalco, the place where Titlacauan blew his flute and deposited incense, and Uitztepeualco, where the offering priests scattered the thorns they used in autosacrifice, and the Tzompantli, or skull rack, where "they strung up the severed heads of captives whom they had cast into the fire," which was not the same as the "Uey Tzompantli," or Great Skull Rack, and the Netotiloyan, where those victims under the sign 9 Wind danced before they died during the first month of the year, Atl Caualo. A related structure was Atempan, where the child sacrificial victims called "human paper streamers" were assembled before their deaths. There was a structure called Yopico, where many captives were slain during the Feast of the Flaying of Men, and various *temalacatl*, a circular round stone to which the victim was tied and attacked by a series of Aztec warriors before the heart was extracted. And there was "Tzonmolco Calmecac," a school where the fire god Xiuhtecuhtli was kept until the ruler Motecuhzoma took the flame, when he offered incense before the new fire was made each year, and "Tlamatzinco Calmecac," where the fire priests lived and offered incense.[80]

These architectural representations, developed after the founding event depicted in the *Mendoza*, show us that the "foundation of heaven" and the four-quartered universe of the city eventually received their most eloquent cosmo-magical expression in the material form of the huge sacred space that housed the Aztec gods, served as a theater for the acting out of appropriate rituals, and functioned as an expanding model of celestial archetypes.

OMENS AND SYMBOLS OF THE FALL OF THE CITY

> And this woman, after she had returned to life, then went to converse and speak with Moctezuma about what she had seen. She informed and said to him: "For this reason have I returned to life: I have come to tell thee that thou art come to the end. With thee the reign of Mexico ceaseth; for in thy time the city of Mexico will end. They who come, lo, these have come to subjugate the land; these will occupy Mexico."[81]

It is the experience of the conquest of Mexico to which, having come full circle, I now return. When informants of the Franciscan priest Bernardino de Sahagún reported their version of the fall of Tenochtitlan decades after the event, they displayed the persistence of their cosmo-magical thought and its tie to their city in a vivid and pathos-filled manner. Their valuable reports show that, as in the foundation of Tenochtitlan so in its fiery end, omens communicated a divine destiny. Just as the city was promised by divine forces, so was its end. And this linkage between omens and the tableaus and tours of Mexica history cannot be overestimated. Some scholars have made much of the apparent ex-post-facto generation of omens, and no doubt the Mexicas sometimes used the reports of omens to reshape their understanding of events as afterthoughts. But it is also clear that omens were a way of anticipation, preparation, and prophecy. For instance, Book 5 of the *Florentine Codex* is dedicated to a series of omens that were standards among the Mexica, and the presence of omens at the beginning of the account of the fall of Tenochtitlan points to their major importance in Mexica sacred histories. Tours and tableaus *needed* omens in order to have plausible meaning.

This sense of cosmic destiny is illustrated in the first chapter of Book 12 of the *Florentine Codex*, which tells of the appearance of omens of great portent in Mexico. "Here are told the signs which appeared and were seen, when the Spaniards had not yet come here to this land, when they were not yet known to the natives here. When the Spaniards had not arrived by ten years."[82] It is important to note that this text places the omens prior to the presence of Spaniards in Mexico because it suggests that the Aztec understood their collapse to be marked by the arrival of celestial signs, not just the arrival of the Spaniards. These signs were apparently seen and feared by the populace of the city, for we are told, "This great marvel caused so much dread and wonder that the people spoke of it constantly." Of the many omens that appeared, I will focus on three to end the discussion.[83]

The first omen is described as a "fiery signal, like a flaming ear of corn, or the blaze of daybreak; it seemed to bleed fire, drop by drop, like a wound in the sky." The series of signs opens with the threatening image of a rip in the Aztec universe (Dibble and Anderson translate the passage as "piercing the heavens")—a rip of bleeding fire that suggests the beginning of death in the cosmos that encloses and is centered on the city. Then, however, a more direct hit is described.

> The Temple of Huitzilopochtli burst into flames. It is thought that no one set it afire, that it burned down of its own accord. The name of its divine site was Tlacateccan (House of Authority). . . . The flames, the tongues of fire shoot out, the bursts of fire shoot up into the sky. The flames swiftly destroyed all the woodwork of the temple. . . . and the temple burned to the ground.[84]

The temple of their patron god, who had led them through hardship and appeared at the center of their new landscape, is destroyed, reflecting the image of the burning and falling temple that symbolized the fall of a city so central to the "conquest narratives" of the *Codex Mendoza*.

Other celestial omens appear that illustrate how the conquest is clearly placed within a cosmo-magical setting in the Aztec mind. Following Motecuhzoma's death and near the end of the Spanish siege of Tenochtitlan comes the following scene. Just before the surrender of the city, we read:

> At nightfall it began to rain, but it was more like a heavy dew than a rain. Suddenly the omen appeared, blazing like a great bonfire in the sky. It wheeled in enormous spirals like a whirlwind and gave off a show of sparks and red hot coals, some great and some little. It also made loud noises, rumbling and hissing like a metal tube placed over a fire. It circled

the wall nearest the lake shore and then hovered for a while above Coyonacasco. From there it moved out into the middle of the lake where it suddenly disappeared. No one cried out when this omen came into view: the people knew what it meant and they watched in silence.[85]

They knew that the magic of their cosmos had turned against them. This is a striking example of how cosmo-magical consciousness could interpret and sustain an Aztec sense of order long after it had been shattered. Thirty years after the conquest, in a Spanish-run society, Aztec survivors poignantly reaffirm the cosmological conviction lodged in their minds: The collapse of their central city was influenced not primarily by Spanish arms and intentions, but by the pattern of their heaven.

It is important to note that Mexico City has been the center of a nation for over five hundred years, making this sacred location the oldest continuous capital in the Americas. Carlos Fuentes refers to it as "city of fixed sun . . . city ancient in light . . . witness of all we forget . . . old city cradled among birds of omen . . . city in the true image of gigantic heaven."[86] It was a gigantic image of heaven and earth, sun and water, magnet of the people and heart of the empire that, in spite of upheavals, betrayals, immense migrations over centuries, and periodic earthquakes of geological and political natures, has periodically resurfaced as a reminder, as a "witness of all we forget."

There is an ironic persistence, a haunting, of all this today, for the center of Mexico has once again magnetized the glances of Mexico's citizens and archaeologists around the world. The most prominent structure of the entire capital, Coatepec, or the Templo Mayor, has been excavated and transformed into a museum that is visited by over a million people each year. As Eduardo Matos Moctezuma, the director of excavations, said recently, reflecting my concerns about centers and models, "Our efforts have focused on excavating this single ceremonial precinct as a means of understanding the entire Aztec empire." The task of this chapter has been to explore the cosmo-magical symbols and spatial stories through which the Mexicas organized and interpreted their urban-centered world. It is to this quintessential material center, the quintessential collecting place and symbol of that "vision of place," the Great Temple of Tenochtitlan, that we can now turn with a greater ability to appreciate its cosmological-religious dimensions.

CHAPTER 2

Templo Mayor
The Aztec Vision of Place

> To us, it seems an inescapable conclusion that the *religious man sought to live as near as possible to the Center of the World*. He knew that his country lay at the midpoint of the earth; he knew too that his city constituted the navel of the universe, and, above all, that the temple or the palace were veritably Centers of the World. But he also wanted his own house to be at the Center and to be an *imago mundi* . . . to reproduce the universe.
>
> Mircea Eliade, *The Sacred and the Profane*

> More can be said for the thesis that all orders and forms of authority in human society are founded on institutionalized violence.
>
> Walter Burkert, *Homo Necans*

When the Spaniards arrived in the Basin of Mexico and first saw the Aztec capital of Tenochtitlan in 1519, they were startled by its architectural order, social complexity, and spatial organization. Bernal Díaz del Castillo, a sergeant in Cortés's troop, left us this memorable first impression of the Aztec capital:

> During the morning we arrived at a broad causeway and continued our march towards Iztapalapa and when we saw so many cities and villages built in the water and other great towns on dry land and that straight and level causeway going towards Mexico, we were amazed and said that it was like the enchantments they tell of in the legend of Amadis, on account of the great towers and cues and buildings rising from the water, and all built of masonry. And some of the soldiers even asked whether the things that we saw were not a dream. Gazing on such wonderful sights, we did not know what to say . . . and the lake itself was crowded with canoes and in the causeway there were many bridges at intervals and in front

of us stood the great City of Mexico . . . we went to the orchard and garden, which was such a wonderful thing to see and walk in, that I never
tired of looking at the diversity of the trees, and noting the scent which
each one had, and the paths full of roses and flowers, and the many fruit
trees and native roses and the pond of fresh water . . . and all was cemented and very splendid with many kinds of stone (monuments) with
pictures on them, which gave much to think about.[1]

Compare that reverie with one of the last impressions the Spaniards
had of the Aztec city before the conquest. During the ferocious Spanish siege of Tenochtitlan, the Aztecs made a desperate sacrifice of
captive Spaniards to their sun and war god, Huitzilopochtli, whose
shrine sat on top of the Great Temple, the Templo Mayor, located in
the heart of the ceremonial center,

When we retreated near to our quarters and had already crossed a great
opening where there was much water, the arrows, javelins and stones

The Coyolxauhqui Stone depicting the dismembered body of the warrior
goddess Coyolxauhqui was discovered at the foot of the stairway leading up to
the top of the Templo Mayor of Tenochtitlan. Notice the blood flow, with
jewels attached, just above her left knee. Each elbow and knee wears the mask
of a death god. The human figure is Maria Luisa Franco, curator. (Courtesy of
the Moses Mesoamerican Archive.)

could no longer reach us. Sandoval, Francisco de Lugo and Andrés de Tapia were standing with Pedro de Alvarado each one relating what had happened to him and what Cortés had ordered, when again there was sounded the dismal drum of Huichilobos and many other shells and horns and things like trumpets and the sound of them all was terrifying, and we all looked towards the lofty Pyramid where they were being sounded, and saw that our comrades whom they had captured when they defeated Cortés were being carried by force up the steps, and they were taking them to be sacrificed. When they got them up to a small square in front of the oratory, where their accursed idols are kept, we saw them place plumes on the heads of many of them and with things like fans in their hands they forced them to dance before Huichilobos and after they had danced they immediately placed them on their backs on some rather narrow stones which had been prepared as places for sacrifice, and with some knives they sawed open their chests and drew out their palpitating hearts and offered them to the idols that were there, and they kicked the bodies down the steps, and the Indian butchers who were waiting below cut off the arms and feet and flayed the skin off the faces, and prepared it afterwards like glove leather with the beards on, and kept those for the festivals when they celebrated drunken orgies and the flesh they ate in *chilmole*.[2]

These radically different impressions of Aztec life and religion, one emphasizing the peaceful mood, architectural order, and natural delights of a capital city, and the other lamenting the horrifying human sacrifices of Spaniards at the Great Temple, reflect the incongruous and enigmatic image of Aztec life that has troubled modern readers for centuries.[3] For students of American Indian religions and cultures, this fractured image raises questions of the most profound and emotional sort. For instance, how could a people who conceived of and carved the uniquely marvelous Calendar Stone,[4] and developed one of the most accurate calendrical systems in the ancient world, spend so much energy, time, blood, and wealth in efforts to obtain and sacrifice human victims for every conceivable feast day in the calendar?[5] Why did a people so fascinated by and accomplished in music, sculpture,[6] featherwork, astronomy, craft industries, poetry,[7] and painting become so committed to cosmic regeneration through the thrust of the ceremonial knife? Why did the people who understood themselves to occupy the center of the world appear desperate in relation to their peripheries? The Aztec image that glares at us through the texts is an image of startling juxtaposition of Flowers, Songs/Blood, Cut!

We may come to a greater understanding of the Aztec situation by focusing our attention on the Aztec "vision of place," that is, the way they conceived the character of their cosmos and their vital and pressured role within it. By knowing a culture's sense of its own place and position in the cosmos, through a reading, in part, of its creation myths, we can become familiar with the central and dominant concepts, paradigms, and enigmas of that culture.[8]

In fifteenth- and sixteenth-century Mexico, the city of Tenochtitlan was the place upon which a vision of empire was founded. This capital, and especially its amazing ceremonial center, was the place where the Aztec vision of cosmic order and dynamics was expressed in stone, wood, color, sound, myth, ritual, and the drama of sacrificial rites. From this ceremonial theater, Aztec symbolic language, social character, and political authority flowed outward to influence over four hundred towns and cities in central Mesoamerica.[9] But the power of the city worked in the reverse direction as well. The magnetic pull and prestige of this grand settlement made it the gathering place of central Mesoamerican pilgrims, luxury items, ambassadors, traders, gods, gifts for the gods, diplomats, and nobles, all of whom were periodically located and constrained within the boundaries of this island community. The Aztecs intended that everything powerful, beautiful, and meaningful would flow into the ceremonial landscapes of the city. As the second quotation from Díaz del Castillo, earlier in this chapter, suggests, the quintessential example of Aztec symbolization of cosmological order and imperial intention within the larger precinct was the Great Temple, which dominated the ceremonial center. In fact, numerous other references to the rituals performed at the Great Temple during Aztec times,[10] plus the amazing discoveries at the excavations of the temple's base in Mexico City,[11] demonstrate that this shrine was not only the axis of their universe, it was the *imago mundi*, the architectural image of their cosmic order and sense of political destiny. The mythology, shape, sculpture, and ceremony associated with the Templo Mayor reveal that more than any other single structure, it embodied the Aztecs' vision of their place in the world. But this supreme sense of emplacement was characterized by immense aggressions, death by obsidian knife, and signs of anxiety, hatred, and fear of the outsiders. When we examine the mythic expressions of this vision of place, we find that the whole language of symbols and social structure that followed were filled with messages of religious violence, sacrifice, and even monumental sacrifice of enemies, slaves, women, and children. This is an important point for historians of religions concerned with understanding how sacred spaces, throughout the traditional world and especially in Mesoamerica, oriented the political order of societies. It appears that these *imago mundis* were permeated with and expressive of religious patterns of violence, conquest, and extreme brutality. As Walter Burkert showed in *Homo Necans,* the ties between religio-political authority in its most sophisticated expressions and institutionalized violence (not just eccentric violence) are foundational and inextricable. The evidence from Mexico City suggests that the matter of extreme violence in the center of the world is due to both cosmogonic myths of its foundation and to eccentric relations with the peoples, lands, and forces beyond the confines of the Aztec island. In this chapter, I expand my previous discussion of spatial stories to talk about "storied spaces of sacrifice," or the stories that give us a vivid sense of the sacrificial meaning and purpose of the vision of this *imago mundi* that attracted the ritual activities of the Aztecs and so fascinated and terrorized the Spaniards. I also want to complicate the Aztec image of their own supreme centrality and the prestige of the category of the symbolism of the center by uncovering the symbolic objects and rebellious forces of the Mexica peripheries buried in the floors of the Great Temple and disguised in the myths of the birth of the gods of the sun.

HERMENEUTICS AND THE TEMPLO MAYOR

The ruins of the Great Temple were excavated during the intense archaeological period of 1978–1982. Today, small localized digs and analyses continue at the site, which has been turned into one of the finest teaching museums in the Americas.[12] The excavation is extremely important for students of Indigenous American Religions because it uncovered the foundation and treasures of a structure that reflected the Aztec sense of cosmic and political order, military expansion, religious inspiration, and authority. Unlike the majority of texts available to us about the Aztecs, which were painted or written during the conquest or colonial period and reflect that crisis situation,[13] the Templo Mayor is a pre-Columbian expression, and it can be viewed as the Aztecs' statement of their worldview. But its decipherment has demanded well-thought-out methodological approaches, including attention to social and symbolic exchanges between the center of the society and its social and geographical peripheries.

When I first visited the excavation in 1978, I saw the massive, intimidating carved stone of the goddess Coyolxauhqui, whose dramatic death is told in the myth of the birth of the Sun God Huitzilopochtli. During the next twenty years, I witnessed the uncovering of the foundation of the great shrine, which almost daily yielded offerings of masks, statues of deities, animal and human sacrifices, and treasures from distant towns under Aztec control. I saw the seven rebuildings of the shrine (there were seven complete rebuildings and five extra additions to the main facade), far more than anyone imagined had taken place. I realized I was witnessing the exhumation of the essential ceremonial center of a city and empire.[14] My previous interest in the centripetal and centrifugal function of central shrines in Mesoamerica was rewarded by having more evidence, literally at my feet, than I had ever dreamed of. But there was something of perhaps even greater significance. Over 80 percent of the offerings being unearthed contained materials from natural landscapes, cities, and towns beyond the core area of the Aztec realm, including many communities with unstable relations with Tenochtitlan.[15] It seemed likely that the Aztecs were making special efforts to gather and integrate the objects of peripheral cities and places into their city's center, holding them together in unique arrangements below the surface of everyday life. This forced me to ask, "How can we pay so much attention to the Symbolism of the Center without giving equal attention to the Symbolism of the Periphery and the dynamics between the capital and the rest of the Aztec empire?"[16] The effective category of the "Center" has been too narrowly discussed, with not enough attention to dynamic, unstable, and periodically threatening exchanges that take place between exemplary sacred ceremonial centers/capitals and the shifting allegiances, alliances, and edges of the cosmos. For example, one influential formulation that represents this interpretive problem is Clifford Geertz's eloquent discussion of the "Myth of the Exemplary Center," worked out primarily in relation to the Balinese state of the nineteenth century. He writes,

This is the theory that the court and capital is at once a microcosm of the supernatural order—an image of . . . the universe on a smaller scale—and the material embodiment of political order. It is not just the nucleus, the engine, or the pivot of the state, it *is* the state. . . . it is a statement of a controlling political idea—namely that by the mere act of providing a model, a paragon, a faultless image of civilized existence, the court shapes the world around it into at least a rough approximation of its own excellence. The ritual life of the court, and in fact the life of the court generally, is thus paradigmatic, not merely reflective, of social order. What it is reflective of, the priests declare, is supernatural order . . . [17]

From analyzing the relevant pictorial and written texts and the evidence from the excavation, it is clear to me that the Aztecs saw themselves, their shrine, city, and empire as the center of excellence in the universe. The Aztecs felt a profound "cosmic security" that was expressed in grandeur and aggressive pride. However, careful analysis of the data shows, surprisingly, that the Aztecs also suffered a "cosmic paranoia," a haunting sense of cosmic insecurity, social instability, and cultural inferiority associated with threats posed by kingdoms of the Aztec periphery and sacred histories of the past.[18] This combination of the capital and the temple as symbols of the "faultless image" and the "image with a fault" may be used to both apply and alter the theory of the exemplary center as expressed in Geertz and other influential writers. The "rough approximation" of the world that was represented at the Templo Mayor reflected rebellions (sometimes successful), droughts, the combats of the gods, and attacks from the periphery. It also appears that there is a direct link between this unstable center/periphery social world and the extraordinarily violent vision of place that animated Aztec social and symbolic life. In what follows, I focus on the evidence associated with the Great Temple in order to show how the Aztec vision of place was directed not only toward founding and maintaining a magnificently ordered cosmos held firmly at the capital and shrine of Huitzilopochtli, but it was also directed toward dealing with the threats, limitations, and weaknesses that were identified with peripheral places, objects, and peoples.[19] I hope to show that the Aztec expressions of their exemplary center and *imago mundi* as represented in a series of myths and ritual practices both conforms with and departs from Geertz's understanding. My strategy is to interpret the Aztec vision of place exemplified in the Templo Mayor through drawing the lines of coincidence between

Aztec mythology, understood in the light of the history of religions, and the two dimensions of *orientatio* at the Templo Mayor reflected in the opening quotations—*monumental* ceremonial space and *monumental* ritual death—and to suggest that both types of monumentality were stimulated by historical crisis. Specifically, I approach this coincidence through a direct interpretation of two major mythic episodes in the Aztec tradition, the myth of Huitzilopochtli's birth at the mountain of Coatepec and the cosmogonic myth of the Creation of the Fifth Sun at the sacred city of Teotihuacan.[20]

IMAGINATION AND THE TEMPLO MAYOR

I must note the tentative nature of this chapter because the Templo Mayor is not only a paradigm of the postclassic Mesoamerican world, but continues to be, for modern scholars, at least two other things—a puzzle and a scandal. It is a puzzle because it contained so many bits, pieces, parts, and shapes of the Aztec world arranged according to a plan that we have still only partially discerned. There are an enormous number of questions raised by the groups of masks, rebuildings, chronology, child sacrifices, strange deity images, Teotihuacan and Toltec symbolism, pervasiveness of Tlaloc imagery, and absence of images of the young, vital war god Huitzilopochtli. It will take several decades to figure out the full design of this puzzle. The scandal of the Templo Mayor resides in its pre-Hispanic use as a theater for large numbers of human sacrifices of warriors, children, women,[21] and slaves. Although we have been aware of this shocking practice (for us) for almost half a millennium, the scholarly community has been remarkably hesitant to explore the evidence and nature of large-scale ritual killing in Aztec Mexico. As I discuss in later chapters, *all major theories of sacrifice and human sacrifice have ignored the most compelling record available.* Something repulsive, threatening, and apparently mind-boggling about the increment in human sacrifices has confounded theologians, anthropologists, and other scholars in their consideration of Aztec ritual.[22] The exemplary, puzzling, and scandalous nature of this temple and the excavation demands an approach similar to the one articulated by Peter Brown in his essay on imaginative curiosity, "We must ask ourselves whether the imaginative models that we bring to the study of history are sufficiently precise and differentiated, whether they embrace enough of what we sense to be what it is to be human, to enable us to understand and to communicate to the others the sheer challenge of the past."[23]

In my view, the imaginative models of the history of religions do provide a useful approach to the "sheer challenge of the Aztec past" and its great temple.

THE TEMPLO MAYOR AS *IMAGO MUNDI*

The most imposing and powerful structure in the grand ceremonial center of Tenochtitlan was the Templo Mayor. Early colonial depictions, such as the one found in the *Códice Durán*, emphasize the monumentality of the Templo Mayor.[24] There it is presented as a four-sided pyramid resting on a large base. The pyramid actually consisted of two vertical structures, each with a separate stairway, joined down the middle and leading to the two shrines on top. The commentator of the *Códice Durán* notes, "On top there was a platform supporting two temples adorned with merlons. The god Tlaloc was in one temple and Huitzilopochtli was in the other. Leading up to their shrines was a double stairway down which were thrown the bodies of sacrificial victims."[25] Its sustained importance as the sacred center of the capital is reflected in the fact that it was enlarged frontally twelve times during the less than two hundred years of its existence. Its size and the imperial vista it provided were described by Bernal Díaz del Castillo,

> We stood looking about us, for that huge and cursed temple stood so high that from it one could see over everything very well, and we saw the three causeways which led into Mexico, that is the causeway of Iztapalapa by which we had entered four days before, and that of Tacuba, and that of Tepeaquilla [Guadalupe], and we saw the fresh water that comes from Chapultepec which supplies the city, and we saw the bridges on the three causeways which were built at certain distances apart through which the water of the lake flowed in and out from one side to the other, and we beheld on that great lake a great multitude of canoes, some coming with supplies of food and others returning with cargoes of merchandise; and we saw that from every house of that great city and all of the other cities that were built in the water it was impossible to pass from house to house, except by drawbridges which were made of wood or in canoes; and we saw in those cities Cues and oratories like towers and fortresses and all gleaming white, and it was a wonderful thing to behold; then the houses with flat roofs, and on the causeways other small towers and oratories which were like fortresses.[26]

At the supreme moments of Aztec political expansion within and beyond the Basin of Mexico, which usually involved the wars of coronation required of Aztec kings, the temple was enlarged to symbolize, celebrate, and sanctify the political and military manipulation and inclusion of peoples, territories, goods, gods, and meanings. The excavations of the shrine's base and surrounding area have uncovered a stunning example of the architectural attempt to translate into a single ceremonial structure one of the great cosmogonic acts that inspired and legitimated the central conceptions and rituals of Aztec life and authority. And this cosmogonic act turns on the violent tensions between gods located at the center of the world and gods who attack them after an arduous journey from the periphery. The result of this violent tension appears in one monumental piece of sculpture.

In February 1978, electrical workers excavating a pit beneath the street behind the National Cathedral uncovered a massive oval stone more than ten feet in diameter with the mint-condition image of a contorted Aztec goddess carved on it. The image consists of a decapitated and dismembered female goddess whose blood streams are depicted as precious fluid symbolized by jewels attached to the blood. Her striated head cloth, stomach, arms, and legs are circled by serpents, usually two-headed serpents, and a skull serves as her belt buckle. She has earth-monster faces on her knees, elbows, and ankles. Her sandals show that she is a royal figure and the iconography shows that this is the Aztec moon goddess Coyolxauhqui, the sister of the Aztec war god Huitzilopochtli who dismembered her in battle.[27] As a result of this incredible discovery, Proyecto Templo Mayor was initiated to excavate the foundation of the entire structure, which has resulted in the most expensive and most intensely excavated single structure in the Americas. One of our most important aids in understanding how this stone represents key elements of the Aztec vision of place is a surviving *teocuicatl*, or divine song, that was recorded in the Aztec capital soon after the conquest.

The Song of Huitzilopochtli

Earlier in this chapter, I pointed out the value of identifying a people's vision of place, in particular the mythic dimensions of that vision. We learn a great deal about the Aztec mythic vision from the *teocuicatl*, or divine song about Huitzilopochtli's birth,[28] for this story was the sacred history about the Great Temple, the god, and ritual sacrifice. At the beginning, middle, and end of this song, we see that the place of the war god Huitzilopochtli's birth, called Coatepec (Serpent Mountain), is the center, axis, and symbolic "navel of the earth." It is the place where the ferocious god is conceived and born. A closer look at the story and its relationship to the evidence from the excavation shows that the temple of Tlaloc and Huitzilopochtli was an *imago mundi*, an image of the monumentality of the violence of Aztec society.

In order to gain an interpretive perspective on these complexities, the myth is read in six parts, which reveals the dramatic progression of a violent conflict that weaves together the center and the periphery of the Aztec cosmos: (1) the cosmological setting of the story; (2) the miraculous pregnancy of Coatlicue, the Mother Goddess; (3) the ferocious preparation for war by the four hundred children at the periphery of the Aztec world; (4) Huitzilopochtli's birth and the massive killing of his siblings; (5) the mythical escalation of sacrifice; and (6) the historical epilogue.

The Cosmological Setting

The narrative begins, "The Aztecs greatly revered Huitzilopochtli, they knew his origin, his beginning, was in this manner . . . " The cosmological setting of Huitzilopochtli's birth is emphasized in the story. We are immediately told that the Aztecs had great reverence for the god and remembered "his origin, his beginning" in detailed form. The combination of reverence and creation reflects the cosmogonic prestige of the story. This is not just a story about the god—it is the story of his creation. As the narrative continues, we hear of two major places of religious significance in the Aztec landscape—Coatepec, or Serpent Mountain, and Tula,[29] which was the capital of the Toltec empire. We are told that the action to come takes place near Tula on the great mountain. This location of the action repeats a pattern in many Mesoamerican sacred histories, in which the movement from action in the heavens to action on earth passes through, or in relation to, the paradigmatic kingdom of Quetzalcoatl (quetzal = feathered, precious and coatl = serpent, water snake) whose seat of power and authority was in Tollan, also called Tula. The proximity to the Toltec tradition is a sine qua non of Aztec authority, as my previous work on Quetzalcoatl demonstrated. In terms of the history of religions, this combination of Coatepec, Tula, and the prestige of origins reflects a "mythical geography," a geography that transcends but influences the political geography of the singers and storytellers. Association with Tula and its beginnings sanctifies action and individuals related with it.[30] In this case, the Aztec poets have created a prestigious space for Huitzilopochtli's birth by linking the Toltec capital, source of the sanctity of kings and cultures, with Coatepec, the source of their own god, and then casting this linkage in the setting of *in illo tempore*, his creation, his beginnings. At the center of this landscape, at the *axis mundi*, where the origin of Huitzilopochtli was revealed, the Mother of the Gods, Lady of the Serpent Skirt, is sweeping the temple. She is identified as the mother of "the four hundred gods of the south," especially one, Coyolxauhqui, by name.

The Miraculous Pregnancy of Coatlicue, the Mother Goddess

The narrative continues, "there fell on her some plumage." Following the narration of the cosmological setting comes a short episode of the miraculous impregnation of the Mother Goddess by a small ball of "fine feathers" that fell from above. This form of engendering a god reflects a common Mesoamerican pattern. In this case, the divine semen descends from the sky in the form of white feathers, replicating what López Austin calls the "process of the descent of divine semen into the earthly sphere to create new beings."[31] It is significant that the meeting point of heaven, in the form of the fine feathers, and the earth, in the form of the Mother Goddess, is the hill Coatepec. The joining of sky and earth symbols in this simple way represents a *hieros gamos*, a sacred union of the above and the below in order to produce a deity.

The Four Hundred Children Prepare for War

Hearing of their mother's pregnancy at the sacred mountain, her four hundred children "were very angry, they were very agitated, as if the heart had gone out of them. Coyolxauhqui incited them, she inflamed the anger of her brothers, so that they should kill her mother." The third and longest episode in the myth details the ferocious preparation for war at some distant location, at the periphery of the Aztec world, and the march to Coatepec. The episode is one of dramatically shifting scenes between center and periphery, important dialogues between the unborn Huitzilopochtli and his mother and uncle, a military march and a crescendo of motion leading to the ascent of the mountain. The entire action is laced with a ferocity of the divine warrior cultivated by Coyolxauhqui. The episode reveals, among other things, the martial ideal par excellence of the Aztec warrior who builds himself up into a berserk mode of being through ritual array and communal incitement. It is also revealing that this berserk response to the pregnancy at the temple on the mountain begins at the periphery of the mythical geography and moves toward the center.[32] This movement is especially important for understanding the increment in human sacrifice that took place at the Templo Mayor.

The episode begins with the report that the four hundred gods of the south were insulted by Coatlicue's pregnancy, and Coyolxauhqui exhorts them with "My brothers, she has dishonored us, we must kill our mother" and the inquiry of who fathered "what she carries in her womb." The scene abruptly shifts to the mountain, where Coatlicue becomes very frightened and saddened by the threat from her children. Then Huitzilopochtli, still in her womb, calms her with the promise "Do not be afraid, I know what I must do." The action then shifts back to the four hundred gods of the south who decide to kill their mother because of this disgrace, "they were very angry . . . very agitated . . . Coyolxauhqui incited them . . . she inflamed them." They respond to this mounting anger by attiring themselves "as for war." While they dress and groom themselves as warriors, one of the four hundred, named Cuahuitlicac, sneaks to Coatepec and reports every movement and advance toward the hill to Huitzilopochtli, who, still speaking from the womb, instructs his uncle, "Take care, be watchful, my uncle, for I know well what I must do." The text bears repeating at this point.

> And when finally they came to an agreement, the four hundred gods determined to kill, to do away with their mother, then they began to prepare, Coyolxauhqui directing them. They were very robust, well equipped, adorned as for war, they distributed among themselves their paper garb, the anecuyotl, the nettles, the streamers of colored paper, they tied little bells on the calves of their legs, the bells called oyohaulli. Their arrows had barbed points. Then they began to move.

As they move, the informing uncle periodically leaves the encampments and reports their advance to Huitzilopochtli, who listens carefully from the womb, "Now they are coming through Tzompan-titlan . . . Coaxalpan . . . up the side of the mountain . . . now they are on the top, they are here." Coyolxauhqui is leading them.

Huitzilopochtli's Birth

At the climactic moment of their ascent, "Huitzilopochtli was born . . . he struck Coyolxauhqui, he cut off her head . . . Huitzilopochtli pursued the four hundred gods of the south, he drove them away, he humbled them, he destroyed them, he annihilated them." The entire song has been building toward this dramatic devastation, not just of the sister Coyolxauhqui, but of the entire warrior population that attacks the mountain. When Coyolxauhqui arrives at the top of the mountain, Huitzilopochtli is born fully grown, swiftly dresses himself as a great warrior, and dismembers his sister with a serpent of fire. The text is specific not only about her head being cut off, but about her body falling to pieces as it rolls down the hill.

Now we gain a fuller understanding of the meaning of Coatepec in the drama. The Templo Mayor was called Coatepec by the Aztecs and consisted of, as noted earlier, a huge pyramid base supporting two temples, one to Huitzilopochtli and one to Tlaloc.[33] Two grand stairways led up to the shrines. The Coyolxauhqui stone was found directly at the base of the stairway leading up to Huitzilopochtli's temple. On both sides of the stairway's base, completing the bottom of the stairway's sides, were two large grinning serpent heads and numerous others jutted out from the different walls of the pyramid. The image is remarkable. The Templo Mayor is the architectural image of Coatepec, or Serpent Mountain. Just as Huitzilopochtli triumphed at the top of the mountain, while his sister was dismembered and fell to pieces below, so Huitzilopochtli's temple and icon sat triumphantly at the top of the Templo Mayor with the carving of the dismembered goddess far below at the base of the steps. This drama of sacrificial dismemberment was vividly repeated in some of the offerings found around the Coyolxauhqui stone in which the decapitated skulls of young women were placed. And it appears from surviving descriptions of sacrifice that the bodies of victims toppled down the steps and landed on the stone below. The suggestion is that there was a ritual reenactment of the myth at the dedication of the stone sometime in the latter part of the fifteenth century.[34]

Mythical Escalation of Sacrifice

Most interpretations of this myth end with the dismemberment of Coyolxauhqui and the realization that the Templo Mayor and the architectural arrangement of Huitzilopochtli's temple and the Coyolxauhqui stone replicated this cosmogony. However, a further reading of the myth holds a major key to the significance of this vision of place.

Following Coyolxauhqui's dismemberment, there is a total reversal in the location of berserk, ferocious action—away from the attacking warriors onto the person of Huitzilopochtli. Before, it was Coyolxauhqui who generated the ferocity of battle and transmitted it to her siblings. Now, it is Huitzilopochtli who embodies enormous aggression and attacks. We are repeatedly told about his aggression, but, most important, that he attacks and sacrifices *nearly all* the other deities in the drama. *It is a myth not just about one sacrifice, but about a sudden increment in human sacrifices to include innumerable warriors who come to the Templo Mayor/Coatepec from the distant regions of the Aztec world.* Consider the text. Huitzilopochtli "was proud" and drove the four hundred off the mountain of the snake, but he did not stop there, "He pursued them, he chased them, all around the mountain . . . four times." Here we see reference to the symbolic number four representing directions, but also perhaps to the four previous cosmogonic ages. The text is emphatic regarding this ritual combat and the aggressions of the god, "with nothing could they defend themselves. Huitzilopochtli chased them, he drove them away, he humbled them, he destroyed them, he annihilated them."

The text does not end there but continues to portray this ritual aggression in more vivid terms, "they begged him repeatedly, they said to him, 'It is enough.' But Huitzilopochtli was not satisfied, with force he pushed against them . . . stripped off their gear [their ornaments]." The aggression of Coyolxauhqui and her four hundred siblings dissolved before this one great warrior who did more than defeat and kill them, he obliterated their existence. Finally, he took their costumes, their symbols, and "introduced them into his destiny, he made them his own insignia." In this act of symbolic possession, Huitzilopochtli transformed their obliteration into his own power, integrating the ritual array, the spiritual forces of their costumes, into his own design. This is a remarkable act of paradigmatic value because, as the excavation has shown, over seven thousand ritual objects from conquered and allied communities were literally collected, integrated, and arranged according to Aztec cosmic symbolism into the base of the Templo Mayor.[35]

The Historical Epilogue

Following Huitzilopochtli's victory, "the Aztecs venerated him, they made sacrifices to him . . . and his cult came from there, from Coatepec, the Mount of the Serpent." The myth ends with a direct reference to the paradigmatic role this action played in Aztec religion. We are told that Huitzilopochtli was a "prodigy" who was conceived miraculously, "he never had any father," and that sacrifices were made to him in exchange for his rewards. In this final section of the song, we are taken out of the mythic realm of the story into the socio-historical purpose of the divine action—to practice the religion of Huitzilopochtli and his manner of birth. As at the beginning, we are solidly placed on the peak of Coatepec, which is identified as the origin of not only the god, but also his cult of incremental human slaughter.

The narrative ends, "and his cult came from there, from Coatepec, the Mountain of the Serpent as it was practiced from most ancient times." What we learn from this Aztec statement about myth, sacred space, and sacrifice is that *Coatepec was the vision of place, the mythic place where a god was born who sacrificed—not sacrificing just one god, but ferociously sacrificing an abundance of gods as his first act of life.* We are also instructed that this place and these actions were the source of a cult, a religious practice of many sacrifices, many ascents, and many ritual combats.

Reference to the practice of this cult appears in the reports of Diego Durán, whose informants told him that the events at Coatepec were performed every year in the national festivals of the Aztecs during the month of Panquetzaliztli (Banners Are Raised). This ceremony was highlighted by a foot race called Ipaina Huitzilopochtli (the haste, velocity, or swiftness of Huitzilopochtli). Durán's comments reveal the relation of the myth and the theme and activity of the ceremony: "Thus was named this commemorative celebration because while the god was alive he was never caught, never taken prisoner in war, was always triumphant over his enemies, and, no matter how swift he goes, none ever caught up with him. He was the one who caught them. Therefore this feast honored his speed."[36] It is as though the swiftness of his birth and transformation into an adult warrior, followed by his pursuit and execution of warriors in the last episode of the myth of Huitzilopochtli, become the model for this attitude in the ritual. The Templo Mayor and related actions located at the heart of the city and empire represent the dramatic cosmic victory of Huitzilopochtli and the Aztecs over celestial and terrestrial enemies. When victims ascended the Great Temple dressed in plumes, were forced to dance in symbolic ecstasy, and were sacrificed before being thrown down the steps of the temple, a ritual repetition was being performed to reenact a mythic beginning that told of the systematic, violent destruction of gods from the periphery. This song provided a model of violence for the institution of ritual authority that resided at Coatepec.

CENTER AND PERIPHERY

Until now, we have seen abundant evidence that the Aztec city was structured by a series of meanings and activities associated with the "Symbolism of the Center." It is apparent to me that the usual way in which some historians of religions and anthropologists conceive of the category of the center does not constitute a thorough interpretive approach for understanding the Templo Mayor's history and meaning. A people's vision of place reflects their strategies, mechanisms, and performances for integrating their potent symbols with their social organization and historical developments, their theology, ontology, and social ambitions. In this regard, it is vitally important, at least in the Aztec case, to be aware of not only the integrating powers of the *axis mundi*, but also to acknowledge and interpret the impulses of expansion of a sacred center and the results. The previous chapter showed how this process of the expansion of Aztec sacred space paralleled the development of Tenochtitlan from the site of the *nopal* to the shrine of Huitzilopochtli and spread to the four quadrants of the city and eventually the organization of tribute payments for the empire. But it is also necessary to understand the historical, social, and symbolic tension that developed between the centripetal character and centrifugal tendencies of both the capital and its main shrine. For example, Edward Shils has shown that great centers are ruled by elites whose authority has "an expansive tendency . . . a tendency to expand the order it represents towards the saturation of territorial space . . . the periphery. Rulers, simply out of their possession of authority and the impulses it generates, wish to be obeyed and they wish to obtain assent to the order they symbolically embody."[37]

Yet these impulses of expansion will inevitably lead to involvement in peripheral and competing traditions of value, meaning, and authority, which sometimes results in tentative and fragile arrangements of power and authority between the center and the periphery. Though peripheral systems and their symbols may be weaker within a hierarchy of an empire, they nevertheless have the potential to threaten the center with disbelief, reversal, and rebellion. It is within this kind of situation that W. B. Yeats's famous line has direct relevance, "Things fall apart; the centre cannot hold." Although I will not go into the Mesoamerican pattern in detail here, it is evident that some ancient Mexican kingdoms were arranged similarly to what Stanley Tambiah calls "pulsating galactic polities," that is, kingdoms in which the capital cities, designed as *imago mundis,* were in constant tension and antagonism with the surrounding allied and enemy settlements. In these "pulsating" kingdoms, the "exemplary centers" are sometimes deflated by rebellion and disputes with unstable factions that threaten to bring about processes of disintegration on a large scale. In Southeast Asia, this resulted in the continual relocation of capital cities and an eccentric and unstable understanding of authority.[38] While Mesoamerican polities did not relocate capitals as often as did cultures in Southeast Asia, the disintegration and relocation of imperial centers (Teotihuacan, Tollan, Azcapotzalco, Tenochtitlan) did take place in significant numbers. This is an important point, because it suggests that centers not only dominate and control peripheries, but peripheries influence and sometimes transform centers, even a center as aggressive and dominant as Tenochtitlan.

With this pattern in mind, we can turn back to the evidence uncovered at the Great Temple to see the impact of peripheral territories on the capital city. We will see that threats from the Aztec past, as well as from the competing traditions of their contemporary world, transformed the Templo Mayor and the city it sanctified.

SYMBOLS FROM THE PERIPHERY

Ahuitzotl then requested that the royal officials have the majordomos, administrators, and treasurers of all the provinces bring the royal tribute to him . . . in gold, jewels, ornaments, fine feathers, precious stones, all of great value and in quantity. There were countless articles of clothing and many adornments, both for men and for women, of great richness, and an amazing quantity of cacao, chiles, pumpkin seeds, all kinds of fruit, fowls, and game.[39] As noted earlier, the Templo Mayor was the symbolic gathering place of the great tribute network of the Aztec empire.[40] Not only was it the material expression of Aztec religious thought, it was also, as Proyecto Templo Mayor has clearly shown, a ritual container of sacred, symbolic gifts from many parts of the unstable, shifting political geography of the empire. Over 7,000 ritual objects were found in the 131 burial caches, and about 80 percent of them came from distant towns and city-states. Leonardo López Luján's excellent synthetic study shows, for example, that the many animal remains spread throughout the offerings include species whose "natural habitats lie a considerable distance from Tenochtitlan. The animals identified came from four different ecological zones; the temperate zone of the Central Plateau, the tropical forests, the coral reefs, and the coastal estuaries and lakes."[41] Thus far, over two hundred species within eleven zoological groups have been identified as originating from distant ecosystems. Just considering the fish buried at the Templo Mayor, biologists are impressed by the predominance of specimens from the waters and reefs of the Gulf of Mexico.[42] And it appears that selective fishing was used in choosing which fish and elasmobranchs were offered to the gods in the capital.

But the burial of these objects within the floors and rooms of the Great Temple incorporated more than just natural habitats. They were also expressions of short- and long-distance social relations. The complex and vulnerable social world the Aztecs strove to control within and well beyond the Basin of Mexico consisted of small local states, called *tlatocayotl*,[43] in constantly shifting alliances and rebellions with one another. These city-states consisted of small, agriculturally based, politically organized territories under the control of a city that was the seat of government, ceremonial center, and home of a ruling class that claimed descent from the gods. Conflict and warfare were constant, and the conquest of one *tlatocayotl* by another resulted in the imposition of significant tribute on the conquered people. As the Aztec conquests proceeded to incorporate scores of these city-states into their empire, tribute payments to Tenochtitlan became enormous. The city's prestige and wealth depended to a large degree on these enormous amounts of tribute payments, which flowed into the capital and insured economic superiority for the royal house, the nobles, and the common citizens. A symbolic portion of these payments, collected by the workers and specialists of these outlying societies, were brought to the capital and ritually buried at state ceremonies. In this way, the social and natural habitats of peripheral communities were symbolically contained at the *axis mundi*.

López Luján's work on the offerings of the Templo Mayor reveals that the ritual specialists of the capital were concerned with the "management of inner space" of the caches, a management guided by a symbolic language that was developed to establish effective communication with the living and dying gods, vital forces, and sacred entities who dwelled within the great shrine.[44] This language, claims López Luján, is akin to writing but was not expressed in writing. He notes,

> The information . . . shows that archaeological contexts have a great similarity to ritual syntax and to verbal language. If this is correct, we will find two kinds of archaeological syntax: an "internal" one, corresponding to the distribution of objects within a container or receptacle, and an "external" one, related to the arrangement of the offerings with respect to architectural structures. In this sense, we could speak of a "language" of the offerings that resembles the basic principles of writing—a language not only expressed in signs and symbols, but also with grammatical (or contextual) rules.[45]

There was also an abundance of fabricated goods in the offerings, the greatest percentage of which were from peripheral communities. These included Mezcala-style objects, including around 160 masks and 200 anthropomorphic, full-size figures as well as scores of greenstone, obsidian, and animal and plant representations. Overall, there was a striking diversity of objects, symbols, and meanings that reflect the pattern of centripetal forces in relation to the tribute section of the *Codex Mendoza* as discussed in the previous chapter. López Luján notes that "the most common offerings assembled very diverse materials (for example, bone awls, copal, quail, beheaded skulls, alligators, shells, braziers, and images of Tlaloc) occasionally reaching a total of up to 364 elements grouped in 29 different categories."[46]

If we follow López Luján's suggestion about the religious, gift-giving language of the offerings, we can say that the grammatical or contextual rules evident in the offerings reveal two types of idioms: a cosmological language and a complex social, center-periphery idiom. For example, there are many offerings dedicated to the rain god Tlaloc that symbolize, among other things, the distant sacred landscapes of his mountains, paradise, caves, and seas.[47] This suggests that the Templo Mayor was not only the replica of Hutizilopochtli's birth mountain, but also of Tlaloc's paradises associated with the earth, which spread out far beyond the city. The priests at the Templo Mayor collected into the shrine's architecture the powers of Tlaloc, making it a vivid image of Tlaloc's sacred landscape. In this manner, the language is one of cosmological incorporation; the sacred peripheries of the cosmos come to the center of the Aztec capital. Many of these objects display the cosmic themes of creation and relations with supernaturals. But the second idiom of the management of inner space reflects the social, horizontal relations of conflict, conquest, and sacrifice. Throughout the ethno-historic sources, we read of the dynamic and rebellious rulers and peoples of other towns who challenge the exemplary Aztec capital, sometimes forcing long-distance military campaigns and large expenditures of goods and men that resulted in victories and defeats. This combination of a balanced cosmology with a disruptive social history may alter Geertz's formulation of the exemplary center continually poised to dominate with the illusion of effortlessness. As Stanley Tambiah rightly notes in his criticism, Geertz's model paints "all kings at the summits of exemplary centers as still points, immobilized into passivity and reflective trances. The higher their position and the greater their kingdom's glory and prosperity, the more they were reduced to 'mere signs among signs.'"[48]

In Aztec history, still points alternate with seismic disruptions. We witness constantly shifting, shrinking, bulging lines of an empire harshly contained. Aztec rulers were always either mobilized for war at the perimeter, on the brink of armed conflict within the realm, or at war near and far. During the reign of Ahuitzotl (1486–1502), the provinces of Tecuantepec, Xolotla, Izhuatlan, Miauatlan, and Amaxtlan, located far from the royal capital, decided to "block the way to Aztec merchants who came each year to milk the regions of its riches." Typically, hundreds of merchants from the Basin of Mexico would sack the natural and luxury items of these regions. The Aztec ruler responded by launching a major war that, in this case but not all cases, succeeded in destroying the rebellious armies and multiplying the amount of rich tribute that came into Tenochtitlan. The account of the conflict includes telling words about the social and political significance of tribute. "All of this opulence was directed toward demonstrating Tenochtitlan's greatness and magnificence, also to please the allied lords, to make them favorable to Tenochtitlan, and to have them at this city's orders when the need came."[49] If the court, capital, and temple of Moctezuma reflect the supernatural world, which they surely do, they also reflect the political struggles of center/periphery; the center is *engorged* with tribute from the border communities that periodically rejected its authority, usually with catastrophic results. But whatever the results, the Aztecs felt compelled to display and incorporate foreign symbols into their public rituals and burials. The Aztec capital and the Templo Mayor are then both an exemplary center and an exemplary periphery!

This integration of peripheral places is elaborated in one of the most stunning discoveries to date, the offerings of Chamber 2, at the base of the stairway in front of Tlaloc's shrine, in which a large number of finely carved masks were mixed with images of the gods Tlaloc, Xiuhtecuhtli, and Chalchiuhtlicue, a sacrificed puma, and other greenstone images in one burial. The three layers of offerings contained, among other items: 3,997 conch shells; 2,178 greenstone beads; 98 sculptures and 56 masks from the Mezcala region; and a puma's skeleton covering the eastern side of the deposit.[50] The Mezcala sculptures and masks are particularly indicative of center/periphery relations, as the Guerrero region of Mexico always had unstable, flimsy political relations with the Aztec capital. These masks have distant, frightening, awe-inspiring faces that were carved in many different settlements under Aztec domination. They display different artistic styles, emphasizing different facial features, and were apparently offered as a special tribute to the Great Temple for some auspicious ceremonial event during the period 1469–1481. They are not only signs of sacred offering, but signs of subjugation. Valuable objects, perhaps symbolic faces of different allies or frontier communities, were buried at the world's axis.

There is also an important temporal aspect to some of the other caches that contained masks and objects associated with the ancient civilizations of Teotihuacan (100 C.E.–650 C.E.) and Tula (900 C.E.–1150 C.E.).[51] One of the most remarkable offerings was of a small, mint-condition, Olmec jade mask that was probably carved two thousand years before the first of the temple's eleven facades were constructed. In these precious ancient treasures we see the Aztec commitment to integrating the symbols of ancient civilizations into the shrine.

TWIN TEMPLES

One of the most puzzling aspects of the Templo Mayor is its twin temples. The pattern of crowning a pyramidal base with two temples appears to be an Aztec innovation, but an important debate has developed about the cause and significance of this style. The first group, elaborated by Esther Pasztory, argues that the magnificent cities of Teotihuacan, Tollan, and Chollolan, with their great pyramids, imposing stone sculpture, complex social structures, long-distance trade systems, religious iconography, and sacred genealogies for kings, intimidated and inspired the Aztecs to measure up to and integrate the classic heritage into their own art and politics.[52] For example, the truly monumental four-quartered city of Teotihuacan (Abode of the Gods) was revered as the place where the present cosmogonic era was created. Aztec kings periodically went to the ancient shrines to perform sacrifices and re-establish ties to the divine ancestors and sanctity that dwelt there. The subsequent Toltec civilization of the Great Tollan and the cult of Quetzalcoatl were viewed as the quintessential source of artistic excellence, agricultural abundance, and ritual renewal and the place where giants had perceived the divine plan for human society.[53] Pasztory argues that these cities "cast a giant shadow over the Aztecs who could not help feeling small and inferior by contrast."[54] Plagued by a sense of illegitimacy and cultural inferiority, the Aztecs, who had recently descended from the wandering Chichimecas, made shrewd and strenuous efforts to encapsulate the sanctified traditions of the past into their shrine. This is reflected in the fact that the Templo Mayor supported great shrines to the ancient god Tlaloc, as well as to the newcomer Huitzilopochtli. As the excavation of the Templo Mayor proceeded, several small temples were discovered immediately adjacent to it that were decorated with Tlaloc symbols associated with Teotihuacan architecture. On the obvious level, Tlaloc's presence represents the great forces of water and moisture that were absolutely critical for agricultural conditions of the lake and surrounding lands. Elaborate ceremonies were held, involving the sacrifice of children to Tlaloc, in order to bring the seasonal rains to the land.[55] But Tlaloc's prominence at the shrine displays another Aztec concern as well. Tlaloc was the old god of the land who had sustained the great capitals of pre-Aztec Mexico. He represented a prior structure of reality in a cultural and supernatural sense. He had given permission to the Aztecs to settle in the lake, and he was therefore the indigenous deity who adopted the newcomers. As a means of legitimating their shrine and city, the Aztecs were forced to integrate the great supernatural and cultural authority of the past into the Templo Mayor.[56]

Other scholars, such as Matos Moctezuma, argue that the symbolism of two temples is a "clear superstructural image of an economy based on agriculture and on tribute obtained by military conquests of other societies."[57] The widespread cults of farmers and warriors are joined at the center of the world to insure communal commitments, productivity, and mystification of their labors.

A third group argues that the twin temples are primarily reflective of the ancient and consistent cosmo-magical worldview of a series of *co-incidentia oppositorium,* including the oppositions and complements of sky/earth, dry season/rainy season, summer solstice/winter solstice, two cosmic/geographical mountains (Coatepetl/Tonactepetl), and cults of the gods Tlaloc-Tlatltecuhtli/Cihuacoatl-Coatlicue Coyolxauhqui.[58] This approach places the dual design not within the Aztec search for political legitimacy or economic balance, but within the traditional religious concepts shared with a large number of postclassic societies in the central plateau from whom the Aztecs derived parts of their cosmovision.[59]

However, as clearly shown by the richness of the data and the obvious entanglements of political power to mythology, it is a reduction to limit and fold the specific style of Mexico life into the general cosmo-magical plan in this manner. The prominence of Huitzilopochtli's story and shrine clearly and uniquely reflects Mexica history, inferiority, and rise to power. In addition, the Mexica's "dual identity" of being labeled, in their own day, as both civilized *and* primitive must be taken into account. In a sense, the twin temples reflect not only the twin cosmic mountains and their associated symbolism, but also the *ascent of Huitzilopochtli and his people up the social pyramid to his place of great prominence.*

The practice of integrating the images of the great cultural past is also reflected in the discovery of an elaborately painted Chac Mool in front of one of the earliest Templo Mayor constructions. This backward reclining figure, which was perhaps a messenger to the fertility gods, holds a bowl on his lap that was used to hold the heart of sacrificial victims. But Chac Mools were definitely not Aztec. They were Toltec figures who appeared in prominent ceremonial centers of the Toltec cities. The statue's surprising appearance at the Templo Mayor again suggests Aztec insecurity and concern to bring the superior cultural past into their mighty present.

TEMPLO MAYOR, PERIPHERIES, HUMAN SACRIFICE

When the completed edifice was considered to be perfect, the king sent his emissaries to the provinces and cities to invite all the rulers and nobles there to be present at the solemn festivity for the dedication of the temple. All were asked to bring slaves for sacrifice, as tribute, which was obligatory on these occasions. With these instructions, the ambassadors set forth . . . The rulers of those cities accepted the invitation and promised to take the prisoners they were obliged to give.[60]

The Templo Mayor was the scene of elaborate human sacrifices that increased to large numbers during the last eighty years of Aztec rule.[61] Human sacrifice was based upon a unique and complex religious attitude that is explored in detail in subsequent chapters. In brief, it was believed that the human body was the vulnerable nexus of vital cosmic forces and was filled with divine essences that needed periodic regeneration. One means to this regeneration was called *teomiqui*, to die divinely or "dying like a god dies," which meant human sacrifice. Specific parts of the human body, especially the heart, the head, and the liver, contained animistic entities that were gifts and presences of the gods and could be returned to them as gifts through ritual sacrifice. Offerings of the divine fire embedded in the head and the heart were especially crucial for the sun's continued motion through the heavens and the earth's subsequent renewal of time, crops, human life, and the divine forces of the cosmos.[62] In some of these sacrifices, human hearts were offered to the sun and the blood was spread on the Templo Mayor's walls (as well as on other shrines and god images) in order to coat the temple with divine energy. Other parts of the body were also ritually used, including hair, skin, limbs, and the skull. The Aztec rulers were, in general, in charge of this process and had the responsibility of obtaining human victims through war. As we have seen, one paradigm for this process of war, the acquisition of prisoners and escalating human sacrifice, was the myth of Huitzilopochtli's birth. But this myth alone does not account for the *quantity* of human sacrifice and the expansion of the Templo Mayor's role in this development.

Johanna Broda's analysis of ideology and the Aztec state provides valuable insights into the interrelationship of the Templo Mayor, the increase in human sacrifice, and the powers and roles of peripheral city-states.[63] We know that within the Basin of Mexico, the Aztec warrior and priestly nobility managed a high degree of centralization of agricultural schedules, technological developments, labor management, and ritual processes. But in all directions beyond the valley there was little continued success in peacefully controlling the internal organization of conquered or enemy city-states.[64] The Aztec capital, while expanding its territory and tribute controls, was repeatedly shocked by rebellions that demanded complex and organized military and economic reprisals. This antagonism between the core area and the surrounding city-states created immense stresses within all the institutions of Tenochtitlan, which contributed to the astonishing increases in human sacrifice carried out at the Templo Mayor between 1440–1521. For not only did the political order appear vulnerable, but also the divine right and responsibility of rulers and warriors to conquer and subdue all peoples and enemies seemed unfulfilled. The anxiety the Aztecs already felt about their universal order (after all, cosmic life was an unending war) was intensified to the point of cosmic paranoia. In this situation, the ritual strategy to feed the gods became the major political instrument to subdue the enemy and control the expanding periphery.

The Templo Mayor's role in this explosive process can be seen in at least three important events. First, during the reign of Moctezuma Ilhuicamina (1440–1469), the shrine of Huitzilopochtli received its first large reconstruction.[65] As a means of ensuring quality of workmanship and allegiance to the new temple, workers from a number of city-states under Aztec control were ordered to do the job. However, one independent community, Chalco, refused to participate and was declared in rebellion against the Aztecs. A ferocious war was launched and eventually the Chalcans were defeated. Their captured warriors were brought to the Templo Mayor and, along with the other prisoners of war, sacrificed at its rededication. This pattern of celebrating the expansion of the Great Temple with warfare and the sacrifice of enemy warriors was followed by subsequent Aztec kings who increased the sacrificial festivals as a means of controlling resistance and peripheral territories.

Second, in 1487, Ahuitzotl celebrated a major renovation of the Templo Mayor by ordering great quantities of tribute brought into Tenochtitlan. Newly conquered city-states were ordered to send their tribute in the form of sacrificial victims who were delivered to the capital, ritually prepared and transformed into gods, and slain at the inauguration.

It must be emphasized that these inaugurations were city-wide events and, in fact, extended well beyond the Mexica equivalent of city walls! All temples and schools

> were plastered and painted, and clusters of reeds and flowers were used to decorate streets and buildings. Meanwhile, the priest ordered sacrificial knives, ceramic incense burners, and devices of precious feathers, designed expressly for the occasion, to be made. The calpixque (stewards) for their part, collected tribute of food, animals, jewels, mantles, wood, and fuel.[66]

The responsibility for these preparations was also carried out by peoples from communities on the mainland, including Tlacopan, Acolhuacan, and Tlalhuacpan, who carried a series of divine images to the temples for the inauguration.

Curiously, at some of these ceremonies of massive human sacrifice, the kings and lords from allied and enemy city-states were invited to the ceremonial center to witness the spectacular festival, as is seen in chapter 5. The ritual extravaganza was carried out with maximum theatrical tension, paraphernalia, and terror in order to amaze and intimidate the visiting dignitaries who returned to their kingdoms trembling with fear and convinced that cooperation and not rebellion was the best response to Aztec imperialism. Consider this description of the elegant ritual process by which one allied ruler and his gifts of sacrificial captives are incorporated into the ritual dedication of the Templo Mayor. After being lodged in the royal palace, Nezahualpilli

> delivered his captives to King Ahuitzotl and spoke to him with elegant phrases, at the same time offering his goodwill and desire to serve the Aztec ruler. Water was then brought for his hands ... After he had washed, he was given the usual fare for royalty and a chocolate drink. Flowers and tobacco were given not only to him but also to his followers, great lords and chieftains, who were lodged in other chambers, according to their rank. With great care and courtesy, they were given everything they desired. The captives were turned over to the priest who would take care of them.[67]

Another imperial ritual of gathering the peripheries into the center took place during the reign of Moctezuma Xocoyotzin (1502–1520); this ruler ordered the construction of the Coateocalli, which held an image of Huitzilopochtli and all the images of gods worshiped in the imperial domain, especially those belonging to allied and enemy city-states. Before the dedication of the shrine, he ordered a war against a rebellious coastal city-state, Teuctepec. From this campaign, 2,300 warriors were brought to Tenochtitlan and, reflecting the two quotations that opened this chapter, they were sacrificed while the king initiated the ritual killing. In the Aztec case, the *imago mundi* replicated a violent cosmology that legitimated the institutional authority of the realm. The leaders of many allied and enemy towns were invited and forced to enter the capital to witness the sacrifices. Gods, images of gods, and the rulers they ruled, all gathered within the city for the ritual slaughter.

All this suggests that the profound tensions between the capital and peripheral towns, and the political threats and cosmic insecurities that Aztec elites felt as a result, contributed in a major way to the increase of human sacrifice at the Templo Mayor. As the foregoing shows, the exemplary center had repeated difficulties in conquering rebel rulers and rival city-states and when they did, it was equally difficult to dominate them. The chosen method of symbolic and actual domination was incremental, ritual human slaughter. In the long run, this increment served to strengthen *and* weaken the authority of Tenochtitlan. While many city-states were securely integrated into the Aztec sphere, some were alienated to the direction of other kingdoms, and the capacity for rebellion increased. So, when the Spaniards came, Indian allies were not hard to find and, in fact, played vigorous roles in the conquest of Tenochtitlan.

IN COSMIC DARKNESS: THE BIRTH OF THE FIFTH SUN
This discussion of the influences of Aztec cosmology and unstable peripheries on the Aztec vision of sacrificial place and ritual killing in relation to the Templo Mayor enhances our understanding of the pervasiveness of mythic thought and its interaction with social history in Tenochtitlan. In retrospect, we have already learned that this pervasiveness and interaction were also specifically lodged in the action of human sacrifice as revealed in the relationship between the myth of Huitzilopochtli's birth and the sculptural image and location of the Coyolxauhqui stone, plus the evidence in text and archaeology of human sacrifice at the Templo Mayor. We see that the question of the increment in human sacrifice is partially answered through the discovery within the myth that Huitzilopochtli kills not just one goddess, but that he annihilates many deities—his sacrificial aggression extends to the killing of almost *all the divine beings.* This significant discovery appears to be Aztec-specific; that is, the mythic structure of massive sacrifices seems to be particularly Aztec. As a historian of religions, sensitive to Mircea Eliade's emphasis on the overriding prestige of cosmogonic myth, however, I am encouraged to search out the texts further to see if any prior inkling or similar pattern appears in more ancient or more pervasive cosmogonic episodes in Mesoamerica. In fact, when we go in search of myths of origins, we find that the cosmogonic imperative for incremental massive sacrifice has an even greater primordiality of surprising proportions. Equally important, the movement of retrieval from the specific Aztec cosmogony of massive sacrifice to the more general and probably ancient Mesoamerican paradigm was a movement made by the Aztecs themselves! That is, the prologue that accompanies the text of Huitzilopochtli's birth in Sahagún's Book 3 tells us to move in the direction of *prior cosmogony* that unfolded in the mythic city of Teotihuacan. Within this act of mythic retrieval, we discover not only the ancient symbols of

city, sacrifice, and fire, which constitute the *imago mundi*, but also the indications of an apocalyptic view of the universe in which order, place, and stability cannot be achieved without the abundant sacrifice of the gods.

This movement and discovery is suggested in the short but rich prologue to the sacred song of Huitzilopochtli's birth commented upon earlier in this chapter. Prior to the statement of Aztec reverence for the "beginning" of Huitzilopochtli, we are told that the entire chapter of Book 3 of the *Florentine Codex* is concerned not with Huitzilopochtli's beginning but with "how the gods had their beginnings."[68] This statement about the creation of the gods is accompanied by the acknowledgment that "where the gods began is not well known." This ignorance of place, indicating either a non-Aztec or older tradition, is in sharp contrast to the specific place and proximity of Coatepec and Tula, which organized the mythic geography of Huitzilopochtli's birth. Reference is then made to the prestigious capital of Teotihuacan (Abode of the Gods) as the location of the primordial gathering of the gods in the cosmogonic darkness. As in the myth of Huitzilopochtli's birth, a gathering of gods takes place to bring forth "the sun," and this creation involves the destruction of all the gods. The text suggests the weight of this creative/destructive process was in the minds of the deities, for they "debated who would bear upon his back the burden of rule, who would be the sun." The scene is impressive in its cosmogonic opaqueness. In the darkness, the deities have gathered in the great ceremonial center to struggle together to create a new universe. Then the prologue to Huitzilopochtli's story ends with the remarkable statement that "all the gods died when the sun came into being. None remained who had not perished."[69]

The discovery made in the Huitzilopochtli myth appears once more—the massive killing of gods brings about, or is part of, the cosmogonic act of creation—only in this episode, it is not just the birth of one god that matters, it is the passage from darkness into the brilliant light of the universe and cosmological order that is accomplished. The larger universe within which Huitzilopochtli, Coyolxauhqui, the Centzon Huitznahua, and the Fifth Age existed, is what is created in Teotihuacan. The gods gather to live at the center of the universe, and violence is unleashed, which has a *creative* result on earth.

This short prologue tells us that even in the Aztec mind, *a primordiality behind Tenochtitlan's primordiality* was the authentic stage of origin. Fortunately, we have a long and vivid account of this cosmogonic act in Book 7 of the *Florentine Codex*. The more detailed version of the cosmogonic prologue to Huitzilopochtli's birth tells us that for fifty-two years following the end of the four ages, the world was in darkness. "When no sun had shown and no dawn had broken," the gods gathered at Teotihuacan to create a new age. They asked, "Who will carry the burden? Who will take it upon himself to be the sun, to bring the dawn?" Following four days of penance and ritual, all the gods gathered around a divine hearth where a fire had been burning for the duration. Two gods, Nanauatzin (the Pimply One) and Tecuciztecatl (Lord of Snails), prepared to create a new sun by hurling themselves into the fire. After they dressed themselves for the ceremonial suicide, Tecuciztecatl approached the fire several times but became frightened. Then Nanauatzin was ordered to try. The text begins,

> Onward thou, O Nanauatzin! Take heart! And Nanauatzin, daring all at once, determined-resolved-hardened his heart, and shut firmly his eyes. He had no fear; he did not stop short; he did not falter in fright; he did not turn back. All at once he quickly threw and cast himself into the fire; once and for all he went. Thereupon he burned; his body crackled and sizzled . . . Tecuciztecatl . . . cast himself upon the fire . . . It is told that then flew up an eagle, [which] followed them. It threw itself suddenly into the flames, it cast itself into them . . . Therefore its feathers are scorched looking and blackened. And afterwards followed an ocelot, when now the fire no longer burned high, . . . Thus he was only blackened—smutted—in various places, and singed by the fire. . . . From this event it is said, they took . . . the custom whereby was called and named on who was valiant, a warrior. He was given the name *quauhtlocelotl*. [The word] *quauhtli* came first, it is told, because, [as] was said [the eagle] first entered the fire. And the ocelot followed thereafter.[70]

It is important that within this cosmogonic myth the story of the creation of warriors stands out as the primary act of creation. On the one hand, Nanauatzin's daring, hard heart and surrender to the fire is the paradigmatic attitude of the primal warrior. On the other hand, the result of self-sacrifice is the emergence of the eagle, who dives back into the fire, scorching himself and the jaguar, both of which become marked and darkened by the divine fire. When we remember that the

two great orders of warriors in Aztec society were the eagle and jaguar
knights, it appears that the Aztecs drew directly from this tradition to
legitimize the religious significance and power of their soldiers. The
text continues,

> Then the gods sat waiting to see where Nanauatzin would come to rise—
> he who fell first into the fire—in order that he might shine as the sun; in
> order that dawn might break. When the gods had sat and been waiting for
> a long time, thereupon began the reddening (of the dawn;) in all direc-
> tions, all around, the dawn and light extended, and so, they say, thereupon
> the gods fell upon their knees in order to await where he who had be-
> come the sun would become to rise. In all directions they looked every-
> where they peered and kept turning about. Uncertain were those whom
> they asked. Some thought that it would be from the north that (the sun)
> would come to rise, and placed themselves to look there; some (did so) to
> the west; some placed themselves to look south. They expected that he
> might rise in all directions, because the light was everywhere. . . . And
> some placed themselves so that they could watch there to the east.[71]

This original confusion about the sun's place of emergence in the
glowing dawn reveals the lack of clear orientation that existed in the
cosmos prior to the appearance of the sun above the horizon. It is
with the sun's clear appearance and passage that the universe becomes
organized. The text continues, "Thus they say that those who looked
there to the east were Quetzalcoatl: the name of the second was Ecatl:
and Totec . . . and the red Tezcatlipoca. . . . And when the sun came
to rise, when he burst forth, he appeared to be red; he kept swaying
from side to side."[72] This is the cosmic condition facing humans in the
Fifth Age of the Aztecs. The sun is "swaying from side of side," unable
to achieve stability, or find its place, or initiate a creative movement.
Even at the mythic level, the level at which cosmological order was
achieved, the sun has profound difficulty finding its place and orienting the world.

This unstable and threatening situation demands still more exer-
tion from the gods because the sun and moon "could only remain still
and motionless," that is, they could not travel upward and across the
sky. The gods then commit themselves to a course of action that will
have a profound influence on the Toltec and Aztec societies; they decide to sacrifice themselves to ensure the motion of the sun. "Let this
be, that through us the sun may be revived. Let all of us die." Then

Ecatl (the wind god) kills the remaining gods, but still the sun does not move. In his guise as Quetzalcoatl, Ecatl "arose and exerted himself fiercely and violently as he blew. At once he could move him, who thereupon went on his way."[73]

It is remarkable that upon finding the cosmogonic background for Huitzilopochtli's story, *we arrive at the same pattern*. Creation of the cosmos in Aztec and pre-Aztec Mesoamerica is directly tied to the sacrifice, not of one or a few deities, but to the increment in sacrifice that begins with one courageous warrior and spreads to annihilate all the gods who have gathered at the divine center of the world. The unstable cosmos that is created depends on massive ritual killing and an increment in divine death.

The cosmic pattern of massive sacrifices to energize the sun is repeated in a subsequent episode in which terrestrial warfare and human sacrifice is created by the gods to ensure their nourishment. In one version, the god Mixcoatl (Cloud Serpent) creates five human beings and four hundred Chichimec warriors to stir up discord and warfare. When the masses of warriors pass their time hunting and drinking, the god sends the five individuals to slaughter them. In this account, war among human beings is created to ensure sacrificial victims for the gods.[74]

PATTERNS OF HUMAN SACRIFICE

> This was done so those lords might secretly enter the city of Tenochtitlan together and to give them certain instructions so they would not be recognized . . . Their customary garments were changed in favor of those of the Aztecs and, in order to disguise them further, they were made to hold flowers, branches, and rushes, as though they were men who were coming to adorn the temple and the royal house. . . . All the lords from the provinces and all the enemies were watching from within bowers that had been built for this occasion. Prisoners from the lines began to mount the steps (of the Great Temple) and the four lords, assisted by the priest who held the wretches about to die by their feet and hands, began to kill.[75]

As is well documented in the ethno-historical and archaeological sources, the Templo Mayor was the scene of elaborate human sacrifices, which increased to incredible numbers during the last eighty years of Aztec rule.[76] The previous quote describes the efforts made to disguise the allied and enemy rulers who were smuggled into the capital to watch, behind screens of plants and flowers, the sacrifice of warriors, sometimes their own! The usual interpretation for this increment has been the belief that the Aztecs were feeding their gods in order to keep the cosmos in motion. Before looking more closely at some of these rituals in this and subsequent chapters, let us consider a short survey of the practice and paraphernalia of human sacrifice in order to demonstrate the basic pattern of ritual violence.

It must be understood that human sacrifice was carried out within a larger, more complex ceremonial system in which a tremendous amount of energy, wealth, and time was spent in a variety of ritual festivals dedicated to a crowded and hungry pantheon.[77] This bloody dedication is reflected in the many metaphors and symbols related to war and sacrifice. Blood was called *chalchiuh-atl* (precious water). Human hearts were likened to fine burnished turquoise, and war was *atl tlachinolli* (water and fire), another powerful duality. War was the place "where the jaguars roar," where "feathered war bonnets heave about like foam in the waves." And death on the battlefield was called *xochimiquiztli* (the flowery death).

The many ritual festivals were organized by at least five calendars, a divinatory calendar of 260 days, a solar calendar of 360 days with 5 "dangerous days" at the end, a 52-year calendar, an 8-year calendar, and a 4-year calendar, all of which were related to one another in Aztec calculations of time and ritual. The divinatory calendar appears to have organized the birthday festivals of the patron deities of the neighborhoods and local communities throughout the empire. The solar calendar marked the major festivals for the prominent deities of agriculture, including those of the sun, rain, and fertility. Some festivals included rituals dedicated to both local and major gods and dramatized the relationships between them.

As described in chapter 1, this crowded ceremonial schedule was acted out in the many ceremonial centers of the city and empire. Important variations of ritual activity were carried out at these temples, schools, skull racks, and bathhouses; however, the general pattern of human sacrifice was as follows. Most Aztec rituals began with a four-day (or multiples of four) preparatory period of priestly fasting (*nezahualiztli*). An important exception was the year-long fast by a group of priests and priestesses known as the *teocuaque* (god eaters) or the greatly feared *in iachhuan Huitzilopochtli in mocexiuhazcuhque* (the elder brothers of Huitzilopochtli who fasted for a year). This preparatory period also involved nocturnal vigil (*tozohualiztli*) and offerings of flowers, food, cloths, rubber, paper, poles with streamers, as well as incensing (*copaltemaliztli*), the pouring of libations, and the empowering of temples, statues, and ritual participants. Dramatic processions of elaborately costumed participants moving to music ensembles playing sacred songs passed through the ceremonial precinct before arriving at the specific temple of sacrifice. The major ritual participants were called *in ixiptla in teteo* (deity impersonators, or individuals or objects, whose essence had been cosmo-magically transformed into gods). All important rituals involved a death sacrifice of either animals or human beings.

The most common sacrifice was the decapitation of animals such as quail, but the most dramatic and valued sacrifices were the human sacrifices of captured warriors, women, children, and slaves. These victims were ritually bathed, carefully costumed, taught to dance special dances, and either fattened or slimmed down during the preparation period. They were also elaborately dressed to impersonate specific deities to whom they were sacrificed.

The different primary sources reveal a wide range of sacrificial techniques, including decapitation, shooting with darts or arrows, drowning, burning, hurling from heights, strangulation, entombment and starvation, and gladiatorial combat. Usually, the ceremony peaked when splendidly attired captors and captives sang and danced in procession to the various temples where they were escorted (sometimes unwillingly) up the stairways to the sacrificial stone. The victim was quickly thrust on the sacrificial stone (*techcatl*), held down by a group of four priests, and the temple priest cut though the chest wall with the ritual flint knife (*tecpatl*). The priest grasped the still-beating heart, called "precious eagle cactus fruit," tore it from the chest, offered it to the sun for vitality and nourishment, and placed it in a carved circular vessel called the *cuauhxicalli* (eagle vessel). In one case, the body, now called "eagle man," was rolled, flailing, down the temple steps to the bottom where it was skinned and dismembered. In several rites, the corpse was decapitated, the skull was removed, the brains taken out, and after skinning, it was placed on the Tzompantli (skull rack), which consisted of long poles horizontally laid and loaded with skulls. In Tlacaxipehualiztli, the Feast of the Flaying of Men, the captor was decorated, for instance, with chalk and bird down and was given gifts. Then, together with his relatives, he celebrated a ritual meal consisting of "a bowl of stew of dried maize called tlacatlaolli . . . on each went a piece of the flesh of the captive."

While this pattern of ritual preparation, ascent and descent of the temple, heart sacrifice of enemy warriors, dismemberment and occasional flaying of the victim, and (sometimes) ritual cannibalism was usually followed, it is important to emphasize the diversity of sacrificial festivals that involved variations and combinations of these elements. For example, during the feast of Tlacaxipehualiztli, a prisoner of war "who came here from lands about us" was taken by a priest called the "Bear Man" and tied up to a huge, round sacrificial stone (*temalacatl*) placed horizontally on the ground. The captive was provided with a pine club and a feathered staff to protect himself against the attacks of four warriors armed with clubs of wood and obsidian blades. When he was defeated, he was removed from the stone and short temple base, his heart was taken out, and he was flayed.

Offering a captive for sacrifice brought warriors an elevation in social prestige and a promise of reward in the next world. However, not only warriors offered sacrifices. Groups of peasants, hunters, midwives, merchants, and artisans would buy slaves and after ritually bathing them, ritually transform them into *teteo ixiptla* (living images of gods) and offer them to temples to be sacrificed.

Another distinctive festival was called Toxcatl, dedicated to the ferocious god Tezcatlipoca (Smoking Mirror). Elaborate efforts were made to find the perfect deity impersonator for this festival. The captive warrior had to have a flawless body, musical talents, and rhetorical skills. For a year prior to his sacrifice, he lived a privileged existence in the capital. He had eight servants, who ensured that he was splendidly arrayed and bejeweled, and four wives were given to him during the last twenty days of his life. Just before the end of the sacrificial festival, we are told that he arrived at a "small temple called Tlacochcalco . . . he ascended by himself, he went up of his own free will, to where he was to die. As he was taken up a step, as he passed one step, there he broke, he shattered his flute, his whistle" and was then swiftly sacrificed.

A very remarkable festival, celebrated on the first day of the month of Atlcahualo, involved the paying of debts to Tlaloc, the rain god. On this day, children (called "human paper streamers") with two cowlicks in their hair and favorable day signs were dressed in such colors as dark green, black striped with chili red, light blue, some set with pearls, and were sacrificed in seven different locations. The flowing and falling of the children's tears ensured rain.[78]

In addition to these theatrical ritual killings, everyone in the Aztec world participated in some form of self-sacrifice, or bloodletting. Bloodletting was either an offering or penitential rite involving the pricking of earlobes with maguey thorns or, in more severe circumstances, the drawing of strings through holes cut in the tongues, ears, genitals, and other fleshy parts of the body. Often, blood was placed on slips of paper and offered to the gods.[79]

The claim that this ceremonial system was developed to feed the gods is true;[80] however, my interpretation of the two cosmogonic episodes at Coatepec and Teotihuacan affirms that human sacrifice and incremental human sacrifice were acts of cosmic creation that functioned not only as a feeding ritual, but also as a ritual recreating Aztec dominance and power established in their sacred history. The Aztecs were re-establishing a mythic structure in order to legitimize the authority of their institutions to rule. And this was achieved, not by rational rhetoric, but by the public performance of ritual extremities, the descent of the knives, the explosions of blood, the rapid and total transformation of dancing, struggling, virile bodies into pieces and parts of divine images raised to the sun, displayed at the top of temple steps, cast down the stairways, and paraded through the streets.

The myths reviewed here show that the "flowers/songs" dimensions of Aztec religion are overwhelmed, at the height of these rituals, by the "blood/cut" dimensions. The vision that was created showed that sacralized male military aggression against the forces from the periphery created a new world—the world of Huitzilopochtli, or the cult of the Fifth Sun.

THE HEART OF THE ACTION

All this suggests that the tension between the capital and peripheral towns, and the political threats and cosmic insecurities that Aztec elites experienced as a result, contributed in a major way to the increase of human sacrifice at the Templo Mayor. The significant changes in Aztec religion between 1449, when Moctezuma I comes to the throne, and 1521, manifested prominently in increments of human sacrifice at the Templo Mayor, require further discussion here. One fact the excavation and ethno-historical analysis proves is that pervasive changes were taking place throughout Aztec society during the period of the rapid expansion and rebuilding of the Templo Mayor. Friedrich Katz, in his excellent general history of the Aztec state, reveals how the royal counselor, Tlacaelel, set in motion a number of innovations to ensure Aztec dominance in the face of the intense rebellions and threatening agricultural crises that periodically plagued the capital.[81] This flexibility and increment in the religious rituals of the Aztecs can be partly understood with reference to Roy Rappaport's work on the capacity of the sacred to assist a society in adapting to new social circumstances without weakening the cherished cultural conceptions of a people. We have long known, says Rappaport, that sanctity supports and conserves the social order. Traditionally, scholars have viewed adaptations and innovations as signs of secular advances and the break with conventional theologies and ideologies. Rappaport, however, uses Hockett and Ascher's formulation of "Romer's rule" to argue a different approach. This formulation "proposes that the initial effect of an evolutionary change is conservative in that it makes it possible for a previously existing way of life to persist in the face of changed conditions." Rappaport argues that the sacred can actually enhance the flexibility in social structure and symbolic organization to persist in the face of innovation and change. In other words, the threatening aspects of changed conditions can be somewhat neutralized by incorporation into sacred tradition. This ability to combine flexibility and rigidity derives from the fact that some elements of the sacred are not restricted in their meaning to specific social goals or institutions. Rappaport states,

> They can, therefore, not only sanctify any institution while being bound by none but can also sanctify changes in institutions. Continuity can be maintained while allowing change to take place, for the association of particular institutions or conventions with ultimate sacred postulates is a matter of interpretation, and that which must be interpreted can also be reinterpreted without being challenged. So, gods may remain unchanged while the conventions they sanctify are transformed through reinterpretation in response to changing conditions.[82]

Rappaport shows that sacred concepts communicate much more than information about temple activity. They convey information about the political arrangements and the regulation of society, and they imbue these arrangements with an aura of the sacred. Sanctity is infused in all systems and subsystems of society in order to maintain the fundamental order of social life. Sanctity allows the persistence of traditional forms in the face of "structural threats and environmental fluctuations."

From this perspective, the time-honored tradition (human sacrifice) underwent a significant innovation (large-scale human sacrifice in relation to conquered warriors) in order to maintain Aztec dominance in the face of threats (rebellions) and fluctuations (droughts). The increment in human sacrifice is an example of Romer's rule and not the expression of protein deficiency or merely a response to environmental pressures, as others have suggested. It was a religious strategy carried out to conserve the entire cosmogonic structure of the Aztec city-state.

There is a remarkable parallelism between these events and the mythic structure of Huitzilopochtli's song, where enemy warriors from distant and rebellious communities were slain with unceasing aggression at the sacred mountain. One important difference is that, within the myth, these killings intensified the power of the temple on the mountain and served as the origin of Huitzilopochtli's cult. In history, the increment of ritual killing served to both strengthen *and* weaken the authority of Tenochtitlan. Many city-states were securely integrated by terror into the Aztec sphere; however, some were alienated into the direction of other kingdoms and the capacity of rebellion increased. Nowhere is this pattern of social fission clearer than in the alliance-building process that Cortés directed as he traveled through the outskirts of the empire and met both vicious resistance and vital support from communities both loyal and disloyal to Moctezuma's capital. All the more reason then for the Aztecs to sacrifice those Spanish warriors at the Templo Mayor during their "rebellion" against the capital. In the eyes of the eagle and jaguar knights, the Spaniards were the threatening personification of the four hundred children who had come out of the darkness, marching from the periphery of the cosmos to destroy the deity, the temple, and the empire.

CHAPTER 3

The New Fire Ceremony and the Binding of the Years

Tenochtitlan's Fearful Symmetry

In the autobiographical work *My Life and Hard Times*, James Thurber describes a struggle he underwent while attempting to pass his undergraduate course in botany. Thurber tells that he never succeeded in passing botany because in spite of his instructor's guidance, insistence, and even emotional outbursts he (Thurber) "never once saw a cell through a microscope." Even though all the other students saw the mechanics of flower cells through the microscope, Thurber didn't and proclaimed, "It takes away from the beauty anyway"—a comment that drove his teacher into a fury. He was supposed to see a vivid, restless clockwork of sharply defined plant cells, but Thurber didn't, exclaiming, "I see what looks like a lot of milk." The instructor claimed this was the result of not having adjusted the microscope properly, so the instructor adjusted the microscope. Thurber states, "And I would look again and see milk . . . a nebulous milky substance—a phenomenon of maladjustment." This crisis of perspective reached a high pitch during his second year in lab. The teacher claimed grimly, "We'll try it, with every adjustment of the microscope known to man. As god is my witness, I'll arrange this glass so that you see the cells or I'll give up teaching."

Then one day, Thurber thought he saw what the teacher so much wanted him to see. He writes,

> With only one microscopic adjustment known to man did I see anything but blackness or the familiar lacteal opacity, and that time I saw to my pleasure and amazement, a variegated constellation of flecks, specks and

dots. These I hastily drew. The instructor noticing my activity came back
from an adjoining desk, a smile on his lips and his eyebrows high in hope.
He looked at my cell drawing. "What's that?" he demanded, with a hint
of a squeal in his voice. "That's what I saw," I said. "You didn't, you didn't,
you didn't," he screamed losing control of his temper instantly, and he
bent over and squinted into the microscope. His head snapped up. "That's
your eye!" he shouted. "You've fixed the lens so that it reflects! You've
drawn your eye."[1]

The New Fire Ceremony, held only once every fifty-two years, illustrated the
symbolic and ritual dynamics between the ceremonial center of the capital and
the expansive ceremonial landscape of the empire. Four high priests bring fifty-
two pieces of wood to be burned in the sacred fire. Notice on the right side of
the temple a woman enclosed within a granary and families huddled together
wearing masks. (*Codex Borbonicus.* After Laurette Séjourné, *El pensamiento
náhuatl cifrado por los calendarios* [Mexico, 1981], courtesy of Siglo Veintiuno
Editores, S.A.)

I begin this chapter with a story from an American humorist to illustrate a problem in the interdisciplinary attempts some of us are making to gain a clearer view of how "stargazing," or the practice of astronomy, and the sacralized character of this practice influenced the construction and experience of sacred space in the Aztec world. It is the problem of perspective, or rather perspective in the plural, and how perspectives can be in contact with one another.[2]

One of the most creative developments in the study of religious cosmology and sacred space, especially in Mesoamerican cultures, is the new discipline of archaeoastronomy. Some key insights of this new discipline have emerged out of a series of international meetings, especially the Oxford Conferences on Archaeoastronomy and several meetings in Mexico City. The leading spokesman for this new interdisciplinary orientation is Anthony Aveni, who defines archaeoastronomy in straightforward terms when he states that "archaeoastronomy is the study of the practice and use of astronomy among the ancient cultures of the world based upon all forms of evidence, written and unwritten."[3] Through the cooperative work of archaeoastronomers from Mexico, Great Britain, and the United States, archaeoastronomy has expanded from the study of "astronomical orientations of alignments at prehistoric sites in the British Isles and Central Europe" to the interpretation of multiple methods of indigenous "time reckoning" and the ways in which astronomy influenced architectural orientations, ritual performance, warfare, and social ordering in Mesoamerica, the Andes, and North American native cultures.[4]

In a way, seeing is what archaeoastronomy is largely about: seeing stars, seeing how the ancients saw stars, seeing alignments between human order and celestial patterns, and seeing to it, in the case of rulers, that alignments between celestial events and human society were created and maintained. In our different attempts to see with a native eye, or see how the natives saw things, or, in the case of ideological arguments, see how some natives wanted other natives to see things their way, we are often in the position of either Thurber or his teacher. We work hard trying to get others to see things according to the received ideas of how things ought to be done, or we "fix the lens of our discipline" so that we end up seeing our own eye and mistaking it for their visions.

In the teacher's case, in some teachers' cases, the gesture of persuasion becomes the gesture of coercion to have younger North American, Mexican, or European scholars see what they are supposed to see—the mechanics of flowers or, in the case of astronomy, the mechanics of stars, or mathematics, or symbolism. At the other extreme, we act like Thurber (who lost an eye when he was ten after his brother shot him with an arrow while they were playing William Tell) and only see, in fact, insist on seeing, reflections of our own eye, perspective, or discipline. In this case, "we reduce the difficult richness of the necessities before us."[5]

A simple example in the history of archaeoastronomy will illustrate part of the problem. In the fall of 1984, I had the opportunity to study with the archaeoastronomer Anthony Aveni while he was working in the Mesoamerican Archive in Boulder, Colorado. During our eight-week jointly taught seminar on the history of religions and archaeoastronomy, Aveni (who is not like Thurber's teacher) made several presentations on the history of scholarship about Stonehenge. He pointed out the parallel between cultural fashions and the Stonehenge fashion—how popular intellectual fads determined the way people understood Stonehenge for certain decades. He noted that when the fashion was observatories, computers, or eclipses, Stonehenge became an observatory, a computer, an eclipse marker. The point was, as Aveni quotes Jacquetta Hawkes, "Each generation gets the Stonehenge it deserves." The best illustration of this was the day Aveni brought to class the Thurberesque ad about the Stonehenge watch you could purchase through the mail that was made up of little stones on the dial that cast shadows according to the time of day.

APPROACHING HEAVENLY REGIMES

Aveni's observations about Stonehenge led me to ask, "Does each generation get the Tenochtitlan it deserves, the Jerusalem it deserves, the Banaras it deserves, the Copan it deserves, or the Palenque it deserves?" My work with Aveni also led me to ponder, "To what extent does archaeoastronomy contain an approach that enriches our understanding about the relationship of astronomy to a religious creativity?"[6] The exploration of these questions depends in part on what Aveni calls the "fundamental principle that archaeoastronomy is an 'interdiscipline-in-practice' and not simply a multidiscipline or collection of unrelated investigations, each emanating from different disciplines."[7] In a more focused way, one beneficial result of archaeoastronomy has been the new detail and depth of focus in celestial observations of recurrent patterns, which were crucial to the indigenous formation of world visions and the continual renewal of society and the cosmos through rituals and ceremony. For example, consider how archaeoastronomy can give increased substance to the claim of the urban ecologist Paul Wheatley about one of the fundamental characteristics of cosmo-magical thinking in the ancient world. In writing about the mode of thought that helped organize the social worlds in the seven areas of primary urban generation, Wheatley noted, "This mode of thought presupposes an intimate parallelism between the *mathematically expressible regimes of the heavens* and the biologically determined rhythms of life on earth, (as manifested conjointly in the succession of the seasons and the annual cycles of plant regeneration) . . . "[8] (italics mine) Archaeoastronomy, more than any other discipline I know, provides new tools for deciphering how the "mathematically expressible regimes of the heavens" were perceived, conceived, and applied to the earthly social order by various sky watchers of the ancient world. It also helps scholars discern the celestial sequences that guided the cosmo-magical formulas, ceremonial actions, and social order.

These new attempts at understanding how things interrelate, how religion plays a central role in these interrelationships, and how disciplines need to relate seem crucial in Mesoamerican studies, especially in light of Kent Flannery's claim that "Mesoamerican archaeology has absolutely no coherent and consistent theoretical framework by means of which ritual or religious data can be analyzed and interpreted."[9] Flannery, along with a handful of Mesoamerican specialists, has been exploring ways to construct the outlines of such a framework for the interpretation of formative and classical religious patterns. This framework is contextual in character and "ties religion to social organization, politics, and subsistence rather than leaving it on the ephemeral plane of mental activity."[10] Still, according to Flannery, when it comes to religion, most of us are "guessing" and, as Flannery states, anyone's guesses are as good as anyone else's.[11]

From Alignment to Symmetry

The reason for having many guesses is not only because each is as good as the next, but also because there are so many levels, angles, alignments, and points of view to guess about and from which to guess. As the poet Ovid noted, there are many heavens, the heaven of the astronomer, the heaven of the historian, the heaven of the priest, the heaven of the lover, and the heaven of the myth maker. If real interdisciplinary work is to intensify, at least a recognition of the abundance of the phenomena, the power of religion, and the inter-relatedness of the components is necessary. But the discovery of inter-relatedness has sometimes been thwarted by the ways in which scholars use the notion of alignment to explore everything from sight lines to pilgrimages to alliances. For example, I have long been bothered by the use of maps in books, for instance, that claim to trace the routes of processions, pilgrimages, war campaigns, and the like. We are presented with a series of alignments, usually dark, straight lines on the page, which show direct passages from town to mountain, city to battlefield, society to pilgrimage shrine. But actually try and travel these pathways and you'll find anything but straight alignments between these nodes of social action and meaning. The human experience of movement through the ceremonial, military, or agricultural landscape involves the human in turns, arcs, curves, hills and valleys, climbs and descents, and all the while exposes the traveler, through geography or a landscape of meaning, to a multiplicity of sights, sounds, symbols, challenges, social units, and diversities. No one moves in alignments, straight lines, or simple directions, whether marching, walking in procession, or thinking!

On a different plane, the search for inter-relatedness, or what Alfredo López Austin calls a "Mesoamerican world vision" in his watershed study *The Myths of the Opossum: Pathways of Mesoamerican Mythology*, is and will always be especially difficult in Mesoamerican studies.[12] Regardless of how long one studies, how expert in native and colonial languages one becomes, how new archaeological discoveries excite us, or breakthroughs in pictorial interpretation uncover new details and cognates, one obstacle that will always remain is the impact of colonialism on the pre-Columbian evidence and the difficulty of knowing what Mesoamerican peoples were up to, or thought they were up to, in their rites, myths, and stargazing between five and seven hundred years ago.[13] What Inga Clendinnen calls the problem of *finding out*—whether finding out the world vision, the general model, or the patterns of actions—will be with us, in various manifestations, for the duration. Deeply aware of the impact of colonialism on the indigenous record, she asks (while describing the thick Spanish gloss and competing visions of Mesoamerican peoples, the destruction of indigenous records, and the need for new questions), how are we to be able to "discover anything of the views and experience of a people whose voices were hushed to a murmur more than 400 years ago?"[14] The need, or as she says, "the trick is to strip away the cocoon of Spanish interpretation to uncover sequences of Indian actions, and then try to discern the pattern in those actions, as a way of inferring the shared understanding which sustains them."

One example of this difficulty, which teases us with such a high potential for providing access to the Aztec vision of place and symmetry, albeit in limited form, is the New Fire Ceremony that renewed the entire society and cosmos in a ritual conflagration every fifty-two years. If ever a massive ritual performance could give us access to the Aztec gestalt, or what Stanley Tambiah calls a "node of cultural structuring," it would be this spectacular ceremony. The problem of the difficulty of knowing is created, in part, when the surviving information is so limited. We know more about a number of the monthly rituals of limited importance than we do about the ritual of the cosmic fire! In Sahagún's crucial Book 7 of the *Florentine Codex*, for example, we have a paltry four columns of text and much of it out of sequence, and other documents are even less yielding with information. Alfredo López Austin, who investigated Sahagún's method of gathering information in each of the twelve books of the *Florentine Codex,* calls Book 7 a "personal failure" by the Franciscan priest. Sahagún's preface to this book is full of his own biases and prejudices against native cosmology, intelligence, and language. He calls them "vulgar" in their thinking, language, style, and intelligence without realizing that he missed a crucial opportunity to gain access to their cosmovision. López Austin responds,

> If he attacks the Indians for their low level of understanding, they must have felt the same way about his intelligence when confronted with ques-

tions they considered ingenuous in their lack of knowledge. If Sahagún had understood something about the clash of ideas, perhaps his book would be one of the best sources on the cosmic vision of the Nahuas, discussing the upper to lower floors, the course of the stars through them, the supporting trees—information that is seldom available from other sources.[15]

In my view, what was also lost was invaluable information about the imperial rite of cosmic renewal that would tell more about the "total" cosmic and social world than any other rite, building, moment, or idea in the Nahua imagination. Even so, with the help of new alliances between disciplines and new questions and applications of models, it may be possible to gain an enlarged understanding of how this ceremony worked to bind together not only the years, but all the spaces and peoples of the Aztec empire. I am not sure that Aveni's hopes for the interdisciplinary advances stimulated by archaeoastronomy have yet been met, and only time will tell if scientists, social scientists, and humanists within this movement will be able to learn from one another the disciplinary practices that will in fact lead to an effective interdisciplinary methodology. At this stage, I can only claim to draw upon several of the insights and leads of archaeoastronomy to explore a fresh way of understanding the Aztec ordering of sacred space as expressed through several major rituals that were guided by celestial events. Specifically, I will (1) replace the notion of alignment,[16] still influential in archaeoastronomy, with the notion of ritual symmetry,[17] and (2) compare the ritual uses of space within the New Fire Ceremony as reported in various sources with the ritual use of space in the description of the equinox sunrise at Templo Mayor.

By symmetry I mean the ways in which component parts of a ritual and its symbolic landscape were organized and interrelated around a major ceremonial axis. This will often involve natural and symbolic mountains (pyramids), astronomical events, ritual killing, and the rulers. With respect to these spaces and events, I want to suggest that the ceremonial order of Aztec life, what has been called the "Aztec arrangement,"[18] was a vigorous interplay between a locative view of the world, in which all things are sacred if they are in their place, and an apocalyptic view of the world, in which the sacred dissolves when things have no place or are out of place. The Aztecs observed stars, measured them, and calculated them into their social and agricultural cycles. This orientation toward a complex ordering system was periodically threatened by an assertion that the sun was unreliable, unstable, and wobbled at its original creation. Furthermore, I want to suggest that the Aztecs believed that their power and authority depended on their capacity to integrate certain major elements of their world, including kingship, astronomy, human sacrifice, trade and tribute, and royal and commoner sacred places, into a total and authoritarian symmetry. In its tantalizing opaqueness, the New Fire Ceremony suggests that the Aztecs took a series of social and celestial alignments organized by the new fire that appeared in the hills, plains, temples, and forests of the night and, in the terms of William Blake, they dared to frame them into a fearful symmetry.

THE NEW FIRE CEREMONY

On an evening in the middle of November in 1507, a procession of fire priests with a captive warrior "arranged in order and wearing the garb of the gods," including Quetzalcoatl and Tlaloc, walked slowly out of the city of Tenochtitlan toward the ceremonial center on the Hill of the Star. These were deity impersonators and the text uses the term *teonenemi,* or "they walk like gods."[19] During the days prior to this auspicious night, the populace of the Aztec world, "everywhere in the country round," participated together in the ritual extinction of fires, the casting of statues of gods and hearthstones into the water, and the clean sweeping of houses, patios, and walkways; "Rubbish was thrown out and none lay in any of the houses." In Book 7 of the *Florentine Codex,* entitled "The Sun, the Moon, the Stars, and the Binding of the Years," we are told that in anticipation of this fearful night, women were closed up in granaries to avoid their transformation into fierce beasts who would eat men, pregnant women put on masks of maguey leaves, and children were punched and nudged awake to avoid being turned into mice while asleep. For on this one night in the calendar round of 18,980 nights, the Aztec fire priests celebrated "when the night was divided in half," the New Fire Ceremony that ensured the rebirth of the sun and the movement of the cosmos for another fifty-two years. This rebirth was achieved symbolically through the heart sacrifice of a brave warrior specifically chosen by the king. We are told that when the procession arrived "in the deep night" at the Hill of the Star, the populace throughout the

Basin of Mexico climbed onto their roofs and terraces and "with un-wavering attention and necks craned toward the hill became filled with dread that the sun would be destroyed forever. All would be ended, there would evermore be night. Nevermore would the sun come forth. Night would prevail forever, and the demons of darkness would descend, to eat men."[20] It was feared that cosmic jaws would snap at human beings in a never-ending night. As the ceremony pro-ceeded, the priests watched the sky carefully for the movement of a star group known as Tianquiztli, or Marketplace, the cluster we call the Pleiades. As it made a meridian transit, signaling that the move-ment of the heavens had not ceased, a small fire was started with a *ma-malhuaztli,* or fire drill, on the outstretched chest of a warrior. The text reads,

> When a little [fire] fell, then speedily [the priest] slashed open the breast with a flint knife, seized the heart, and thrust it into the fire. Thus he fed, he served it to the fire. And the body of [the captive] all came to end in the flames . . . In the open chest a new fire was drawn . . . and when it came forth . . . and blazed, then it flared and burst into flames . . . and people could see it from everywhere.[21]

The populace cut their ears, even the ears of children in cradles, the text tells us, "and spattered their blood repeatedly toward the fire."[22] They also cut the ears of children confined to cradles and splattered the blood toward the fire. "Then it was said, everyone performed a penance."[23] The new fire was then taken down the mountain and in a choreographed sequence was distributed throughout the empire. First, it was carried to the pyramid temple of Huitzilopochtli in the center of the city of Tenochtitlan, where it was placed in the fire holder of the statue of the god. It was then transported down the tem-ple steps:

> before doing anything further, they brought and took it direct to the priests' house, the place named Mexico. Later, this was dispersed, and fires were started everywhere in each priests' house and each calpulli; whereupon it went everywhere to each of the young men's houses. At that time all of the common folk came to the flame, hurled themselves at it, and blistered themselves as fire was taken.[24]

Then messengers, runners, and fire priests who had come from every-where took the fire back to the cities and towns. Motolinía wrote about this dispersal, "waiting Indians from many towns carried the new fire to their temples. They did this after asking permission from the great chief of Mexico, their pontiff."[25] The sacred fire was then distributed, saturating Aztec social space according to a prescribed plan. Consider this description of saturation by fire of the neighboring and far away communities.

> This same all the village fire priests did. That is, they carried the fire and made it hasten. Much did they goad (the runners) and make them hurry, so that they might speedily bring it to their homes. They hurried to give it to one another and take it from one another; in this way they went alternating with one another. Without delay, with ease, in a short time they caused it to come and made it flare up. In a short time everywhere fires burst forth and flared up quickly. Also there they first carried and brought it direct to their temples, their priests, houses and each of the calpullis. Later it was divided and spread among all everywhere in each neighborhood and in the houses.[26]

As the fire spread rapidly throughout the capital and then the surrounding and distant towns where it moved from temple to schools to neighborhoods, "the common folk, after blistering themselves with the fire, placed it in their homes, and all were quieted in their hearts."

A Skillful Symmetry

These passages, which have only a few variants in sixteenth-century accounts, are rich in implication but short in detail. We see references to and relationships between astronomy, calendars, ritual theaters, human sacrifice, and even child rearing. It is helpful to look briefly at the entire Book 7 and especially the sections leading up to the description of the New Fire. These pages make it clear that the Nahua informants attempted to describe what they considered to be some of the most important, momentous, and sacred cosmic events in their world. They tried to describe the powerful forces in their celestial world, including the sun, "the soaring eagle, the turquoise prince," the cycles of time, the meaning of sunrise, eclipses, the phases of the moon, the birth of stars, the nature of Venus, the winds of the four directions, the Lord of Tlalocan, and the nature of hail, snow, and clouds, all of which led up to the short chapters on the greatest ritual of regeneration. The supreme moment of the New Fire Ceremony is indicated in the phrases referring to its relationship to the several cycles of temporal renewal of the calendar. It was the time when "the years were piled up," when they had been "added one to another and brought together." This rarest of moments when "one by one the four-year signs had each reigned thirteen years and when fifty-two years had passed," the once-in-a-lifetime (for most people) ceremony called the *toximmolpili*, the Binding of the Years, took place in which "once again the years were newly laid hold of."[27] It is a crucial change, when the Aztecs grasped the cycles of time that animated their existence, that draws my attention and causes me to seek new methods of interpretation. It is possible to gain an enlarged understanding of how this ceremony worked to bind together, not only the years, but the spaces, peoples, and central ideas of their religious imagination, because running through the data are two threads, partly hidden, that not only tie the description together but also provide clues to the underlying social and symbolic purpose of the ritual. These threads are the flow of Moctezuma's authority through all aspects of the ritual and the design of center/periphery dynamics in the saturation of space with sacred fire. Surprisingly, there are at least two *axis mundis* in the New Fire Ceremony, the Templo Mayor and the Hill of the Star.

The presence of these threads is more evident when we retrace *just* the physical actions of the description. The drama begins with Moctezuma in Tenochtitlan, even though he is not mentioned at the beginning of this account. But elsewhere in Book 7, we are told that months before the New Fire Ceremony, Moctezuma ordered that "indeed everywhere should be sought a captive whose name contained the word '*xiuitl*,'"[28] meaning turquoise, year, fire, grass, or comet—a symbolic name connoting precious time. A thorough search for a "well-born" captive was carried out in Moctezuma's reign and the right man, whose name was Xiuhtlamin, was found confined in Tlatelolco. It is a shame that more is not known of this captive and the process of identifying him for the great sacrifice. Once he is prepared as an *ixiptla*, or image of the god, and the day of the ceremony arrives, the ceremony begins when a procession of deity impersonators moves along a prescribed passageway, presumably seen and heard by masses of people along an extensive route before arriving at the Hill of the Star. In Motolinía, we are told that Moctezuma "had special devotion and reverence for the shrine" and the deity on the Sacred Hill.

Fortunately, we have a painted image of what may be the ceremonial center on the Hill of the Star in the *Codex Borbonicus*. In fact, the building in which the New Fire is depicted is the largest building in the entire manuscript, which reflects, if not its size, its prestige as a ceremonial center. There has been extensive discussion as to whether this image depicts the building on the top of the mountain or one of the chief temples in Tenochtitlan or Colhuacan to which the New Fire was brought before being distributed throughout the empire.[29] Whether it is *the* building on the mountain or not, the physical structure gives us a sense of the cosmo-magical meaning of the grand drama taking place. Christopher Couch, in his study of the manuscript, *The Festival Cycle of the Aztec Codex Borbonicus,* writes,

> The temple rests on a low platform of four steps. The jambs and lintel are painted black with a Maltese cross design left white in the center of each. The same design is seen on a building in the Codex Mendoza which appears as the name glyph for an official, glossed "itlilancalqui." Seler and Paso y Troncoso identify the building as a *tlillan* or Tlillancalco, "place of or house of darkness."[30]

In the middle of the temple is a huge blue brazier in which the new fire is roaring.

In the *Codex Borbonicus*, there is pictorial evidence that this temple is the one on the mountain in the form of the nearby place glyph for Huixachtlan, "place in which abounds the *huisache* tree" (a kind of mimosa). But the place glyph has an important difference that refers to the sacred power of the objects involved. The usual image of the tree on the hill has been replaced with a *mamalhuaztli*, a fire drill used to ignite fires. The image consists of two parts, the horizontal stick called *teo-cuahuitl*, or "divine wood," and the vertical pole of strong wood that works to start the fire. The place sign is associated with the sacred event of the New Fire Ceremony.

Assembled in the ceremonial center, the group of priests and lords, sharing a heightened sense of expectation and fear, seek another procession—the procession of the stars through the meridian.[31] Sahagún reports the crucial moment of observation:

> They reached the summit at mid-night, or almost, where stood a great pyramid built for that ceremony. Having reached there, they looked at the Pleiades to see if they were at the zenith, and if they were not, they waited until they were. And when they saw that they (the Pleiades) had

now passed the zenith, they knew that the movements of the heavens had not ceased and that the end of the world was not then, but that they would have another 52 years, assured that the world would not come to an end.[32]

Once the procession of stars is recognized, the heart sacrifice is carried out, the new fire is lit, "and all his body was consumed in the fire," amid universal rejoicing and bleeding. Multitudes of people were gathered on the mountains around the Basin of Mexico (Texcoco, Xochimilco, and Quauhtitlan), "waiting to see the new fire, which was a signal that the world would continue. And when the priest made the fire, with great ceremony, upon the pyramid on the mountain, then it was seen from all the surrounding mountains. Those who were there watching then raised a cry which rose to the heavens with joy that the world was not ending."[33]

In the imagery of the *Codex Borbonicus*, this central action takes a slightly different form. We see four elaborately arrayed fire priests who have walked in a procession to the temple placing four bundles of tied wood into the fire. These bundles of wood, which are to be burned up in preparation for the birth of the new cycle, represent the four groups of thirteen years, or the fifty-two-year cycle. Along the side, seven deity impersonators, each carrying tied bundles of wood, walk in procession toward the temple opening. Then, in what I see as the most meaningful social and symbolic gesture, priests take the New Fire down the Hill and "before doing anything else" take it back along the causeway into the heart of the city to Huitzilopochtli's shrine at the Templo Mayor. Following this symbolic communication to the Sun and War god, a communication that gives his temple new light and new life, priests and runners dispense the fire through the city from temple to temple, school to school, to "each *calpulli*," as people hurl themselves on the fire to blister themselves with its sacred power. Then runners who have "come from all directions," not just the four cardinal directions, to Templo Mayor take the fire back to the towns and cities of the periphery. It is as though the fire is creating or following a circuit of energy that results at the end of the ceremony in the saturation of social and geographical space with the New Fire. This filling with fire is accomplished in a series of relay marathons where runners are set up and waiting to carry it to all the villages, towns, temples, and neighborhoods in the empire. In Motolinía, we are told that the fire was taken back to the temples only "after asking permission from the great chief of Mexico."[34]

The ceremony does not end here. For just as we have seen a series of ritual actions and places symbolizing the end of cosmic and social order (the breaking of hearthstones, the destruction of god statues, the sweeping of houses, the end of sleep, the extinction of fires, the burning of years, the temple or "house of darkness"), we now see a series of actions symbolizing the renewal of cosmic and social order.

> Then, at this time, all renewed their household goods, the men's array, and the women's array, the mats—the mats of large, fat reeds—and the seats. All was new which was spread about, as well as the heart stones and the pestles. Also, at this time (the men) were newly dressed and wrapped in capes. A woman (such as she) dressed newly in their skirts and shifts.[35]

Amid rejoicing and emotional relief the people cried out as though an apocalypse had been averted, "For thus it is ended: thus sickness and famine have left us." Birds were decapitated, incense offered to the four directions, amaranth seed cakes covered with honey were eaten just before a short fast. New human sacrifices were carried out, and a quick census was taken as to who had given birth during the critical night of the New Fire. Names with the symbolic titles of Molpilli, Xuihtlalpil, Xiuhtzitzqui, Xiuhtli, Texiuh, Xiuhtlatlac, Xiuhnenetl, and Xiuhcue, carrying the meaning of new time, were given to the newly born. Clearly, the apocalypse of the house of darkness had been avoided and a New Age had begun.

By focusing on the minor details of Moctezuma's role and the movements of the New Fire to and away from the Templo Mayor to the capital and then to the general populace, I see a skillful symmetry reflecting the Aztec commitment to interconnections—the dialectical interrelationships of royal authority, sacred space, and celestial action. By symmetry I mean the orderly arrangement of symbolic component parts around a major axis. This symmetry consists of six elements: (1) the fire, (2) the cosmic mountain (in this ceremony there are two, the Hill of the Star and the Templo Mayor, (3) astronomical events, (4) human sacrifice, (5) sacred kingship, and (6) the circuit of fire throughout the empire. I see the center, or central zone, of this symmetry to be the interplay between the king's flow of authority and the axis of Aztec society, the Templo Mayor and the capital. This interplay constitutes what the University of Chicago scholar of social thought Edward Shils calls a "central zone," by which he means "the point or points in a society where its leading ideas come together with its leading institutions to create an arena in which events that most vitally affect its members' lives take place."[36] What is taking place in the New Fire Ceremony is the integration of one of the leading ideas (Moctezuma is *tlatoani,* ruler, of the world) with the leading institutions (symbolized by human sacrifice), and the Templo Mayor (the first home of the new fire) with the cosmic renewal integrated by an astronomical event. And stargazing is the practice that ties these elements together. But what is impressive to me is that whether the temple in the *Codex Borbonicus* is Mexica or not, it is *the capital city that is first lit up completely like a sun on earth or a heaven on earth.*[37] As we have seen in other rituals, the capital city is the axis of the ceremonial landscape and it serves here as the centripetal and centrifugal center to which and from which the New Fire is distributed.

THE FIRE GOD AT THE CENTER OF THE UNIVERSE

In this grand ceremony, it is fire that remakes the capital into a central zone. The New Fire inhabits the central zone of houses, temples, schools, and the horizontal *and* vertical center of the entire cosmos. As one early commentator remarked about native beliefs, "They also believe the same of the rivers, lakes and springs, since to all they offer wax and incense, and what they most venerate and almost all hold to be a god, is fire."[38] Fire seems to have been the oldest, or one of the oldest, gods of center place in Mesoamerican cosmology. As a prodigious sign of this centrality, the fire god had one of the most extensive series of names, which includes Xiuhtecuhtli (Lord of the Fire), Huehueteotl (Aged God), Ixcozauhqui (He Whose Face Is Yellow), Nahui Acatl (Four Cane, which is one of his calendrical names), Nauhyotecuhtli (Lord of the Group of Four), Chicunauhyotecuhtli (Lord of the Group of Nine), Xipil (Noble of the Fire), Tocenta (Our Single Father), Huehue Ilama (Ancient Man, Ancient Woman), and Teyacancatzin Totecuyo (Our Lord the Venerable One Who Guides the Rest). Even though this list is incomplete, we can see this god as lord or center of the sacred number (groups) four (the cosmic directions) and nine (the nine levels of the underworld), lord of fire, the unique parent who is male and female, and the guide of the gods. The Lord of the Fire had this prestige in every home where he dwelt on or near the hearthstones (including the ones thrown out at the end of the fifty-two-year cycle). The god had the powers of fire to transform through cooking, and he was the central zone of domestic arts and nurturance as he assisted in the growth of children,[39] changed water into steam, limestone into lime, cold into heat, raw food into cooked food, and on the grand cosmic level, his power as fire was changed into the celestial sun!

In his remarkable "The Masked God of Fire," which is a methodological tour de force of iconographic analysis,[40] Alfredo López Austin explores the cosmological connection between fire and the three general regions of the universe, the upperworld (Ilhuicatl), the earthly level (Tlalticpac), and the underworld (Mictlan). He notes that the fire god was believed to dwell in all three regions of the world connecting them at the center, the *axis mundi*, of the domestic and divine hearth. "His palace is central; it is on the *axis mundi*."[41] One symbol of this connectedness through fire is the fire drill, the shaft and divine wood of the symbol we saw in the *Codex Borbonicus*. Through the use of the fire drill, the fire descends from the sky to the earthly center and permeates the earthly landscape through the sun's travels and ritual actions, which spread him through society. In my view, this is the chief purpose of the New Fire Ceremony; to connect the celestial regimes of the Pleiades with the earthly regime of the city through a circuit of spreading fire that leads back to the central shrine and outward through the world to the horizon.

López Austin's comments on the relationship of fire to the underworld may also have a bearing on the symbolism of darkness and light that is acted out in the New Fire Ceremony. Xiuhtecuhtli, in his form as Lord of the Group of Nine, lived in the underworld and participated in the cycle of the journey to Mictlan. Xiuhtecuhtli participated in the rebirth of certain divinities and was symbolically present in a number of ceremonies involving the journey to the underworld and rebirth. In more than one case we have images of the god of fire

> represented in Mictlan, as dead, in invigorating repose, and in a position which does not differ from that which he has in the upper levels; it agrees with the functions of dominion which he may exercise in the lower world, where not only does he gain strength, but also offers the power of his flames, of his transforming force, to the beings who will return again to the surface.[42]

In this instance, the fire god is the center of regeneration, lying in wait in the underworld. This journey to the underworld, which was also a house of darkness, may be what is symbolized in the period of darkness, the extinguishing of fire (which Durán says lasts four days), the breaking of hearthstones, which could be an act of insult to the god or the end of his existence in the previous calendar round.[43]

LOCATIVE ARRANGEMENTS

The symmetry of the New Fire Ceremony is related to what Jonathan Z. Smith, in his book *Map Is Not Territory: Essays in the History of Religions*, calls a locative view of the world, which consists of "a map of the world that guarantees meaning and value through structures of conjunction and conformity."[44] This locative view, which has been discerned in the seven traditional societies of primary urban generation in which everything has value and even sacrality when it is in its place, is an imperial view of the world designed to ensure social and symbolic control on the part of the king and the capital. It is informed by a cosmological conviction consisting of five facets that dominated human society in China, Mesopotamia, Egypt, the Indus Valley, Mesoamerican, and Peru for over two thousand years: (1) there is a cosmic order that permeates every level of reality; (2) this cosmic order is the divine society of the gods; (3) the structure and dynamics of this society can be discerned in the movement and patterned juxtaposition of the heavenly bodies; (4) human society should be a microcosm of the divine society; and (5) the chief responsibility of priests and kings is to attune human order to the divine order. In the New Fire Ceremony, at least in 1507 in Tenochtitlan, Moctezuma II is carrying out his chief responsibility by attuning human order to the divine order through the discernment of an astronomical event and the communication of his authority by fire in a sequential process.

There are numerous illustrations of the locative emphasis of the Aztec religion, including many that link astronomical events and processes to ritual offerings, dances, and sacrifices carried out in the city and its ceremonial centers. Consider these two narrative fragments relating the precise time of day to dances and other bodily movements, decorations, roles, and the relationship of ritual to luxury and gender relations. In the festival known as Huey Tozoztli, or Great Vigil, in which children and women were sacrificed in the service of agricultural regeneration (this is discussed in more detail in chapter 7), we witness a ritual micromanagement of human action,

This (feast of) Uey Tozoztli was thus celebrated: to begin with, for four days there was fasting in each person's home. (There) the young men set up the sedges, covered with blood, bloodied, sprinkled with blood, everywhere (in the houses).

They arranged them all in rows in each one's house. They offered the sedges, erected them, set them up carefully before their gods. They injured the (white) bases, they bruised them, they cut the bases; there they rubbed in the blood . . .

And where there were riches, where there was prosperity, in the houses of the lords, the leaders, the constables, the merchants, (the youths) laid out a bed of fir branches for the sedge. There were balls of grass with designs with the edges interlaced. In the middle of these they placed maguey thorns; these they set (on the balls of grass). They also were bloodied, sprinkled with blood. It was at eventide, when still a little sun (shone), when the sun had not yet entered this house, that they made their offerings.[45]

I am impressed with the locative terms that order this sacrificial ceremony: "four days," "each person's home," "blood everywhere," "set them up carefully," the sedges are "erected" and "set up carefully," the injury to the maguey plant, and the sedge, which is exactly located at "the bases." The emphasis is on the "arrangements of them all in rows" and on "edges" and in the "middle" of the ritual presentation. It is important that the narrators relate Aztec *social arrangements,* "riches," "prosperity," and "houses of the lords" to the ritual ordering of the offerings. It is also clear that a key, time-factored event integrates these different parts of Mexica life. They must take place "at eventide, when still a little sun (shone), when the sun had not yet entered this house."

Another expression of the locative world view appears in the feast of Tlaxochimaco, (in fact, all the festivals had this locative emphasis) in honor of the Aztec god of war Huitzilopochtli where conformity to a ritual order is required. In the courtyard of his temple, "women danced . . . not one's daughters (but) the courtesans, the pleasure girls. They went, each one, between (pairs of men); they each went grasped in their hands; they were grasped about the waist. They were all in line; they went all in line; they went winding to and fro. Nowhere did the line break; nowhere were hands loosed. They went in order."[46] Again, the sustained locational emphasis with the women, "each one," "between (pairs of men)," "grasped," and "all in line . . . all in

line . . . nowhere did the line break . . . order." This commitment to
fit and position extends to the presentation of music as the drummers
are confined to their own bailiwick, "the singers, those who sang for
them, those who beat the drums for them, who beat the ground
drums for them, were quite apart, quite to one side. They were against
a building, against a round altar (or pyramid). And the altar was completely round, circular like a spindle whorl. Against it, by it, stood the
musicians."[47] This is followed by a series of stage directions about how
the dancers, often prone to break the confines of "place," are to re-
frain from any break in the symmetry and keep order. The locative
view of the world depends on *negative* instructions as well as positive
orders.

> And as they danced, they did not keep leaping nor did they make great
> movements; they did not go making dance gestures; they did not go
> throwing themselves continually about; they did not go dancing with
> arm movements, they did not continually bend their bodies, they did not
> continually go whirling themselves, they did not keep going from side to
> side, they did not keep turning their backs.
>
> It was quite quietly, quite calmly, quite evenly that they went going,
> that they went dancing. Very much as a serpent goeth, as the serpent
> lieth, was the dance. None disturbed, none intruded, none encircled.
> None broke in.[48]

The terms "quite quietly, quite calmly" carry the locative view
into the realm of sound and dignity that, in the next passage, extends
to another distinction in the social order, "And those who embraced
the women were only the great, brave warriors. But those who were
only masters of the youths did not embrace them." All this order and
conjunction of music, position, body contact, posture, and silence
must take place at a certain time, at a specific astronomical moment.
"And where there was an end to the dancing, there was only a little
sun; already the sun was about to set. There was dispersion, there was
going on the part of each one."[49]

In these two ceremonies we witness the Aztec commitment to the
symmetry between celestial moments located strategically in the narrative and a series of ritual actions in the service of regenerative ceremonial life. Though they are mentioned almost in passing, it is clear
that precise celestial moments, the moment just before sunset, mark
the correct time for these ritual actions.

Perhaps the best illustration of the locative emphasis of Aztec religion, to be discussed in detail in chapter 4, appears in the detailed description of the human body chosen to impersonate the king's patron deity, Tezcatlipoca, Lord of the Smoking Mirror. Tezcatlipoca, known alternately as "He Who Created and Brought Down All Things" and "The Enemy from Both Sides," was, along with Huitzilopochtli, one of the supreme manifestations of the Aztec high god. As the patron of Aztec kings, he created, inspired, guided, and, according to the text, could turn and kill one of them if they governed badly. Most Aztec gods had human impersonators, usually captive warriors or slaves who were ritually costumed and walked in a procession through the streets, plazas, and temples during the festivals of the Aztec calendar. These living, moving cult images symbolized numinous impersonal forces and, according to the figures in the pictorial screenfolds, some were so lavishly dressed that their human forms were often obscured to the point of being invisible. Consider this short description of the physical microcosm of the "impersonator without defects" hidden beneath Tezcatlipoca's costume during the fertility and war festival of Toxcatl:

> He was like something smoothed, like a tomato, like a pebble, as if sculpture in wood, he was not curly haired, curly headed; . . . He was not round of forehead; he had not pimples on his forehead; . . . he did not have a baglike forehead. He was not long-headed; the back of his head was not pointed; his head was not like a carrying net; his head was not bumpy, . . . he was not of swollen eyelids; . . . He was not thick lipped, he was not big lipped, . . . he was not a stutterer, not ring-tongued, he did not speak a barbarous language . . . he was not of hatchet shaped navel, he was not of wrinkled stomach, . . . he was not of flabby thighs.[50]

He also had an astronomical appellation, for he was referred to, in his exceeding height, as "tree-shaker, star gatherer"! This prescription of correct physical human order—we are told what the *ixiptla isn't*, not what he *is*—lived in honor, luxury, and ritual esteem for one year prior to his sacrifice during the festival of Toxcatl. At the appropriate time during his tenure of office, the king Moctezuma came forward and "repeatedly adorned him, he gave him gifts, he arrayed him, he arrayed him with great pomp. He had all costly things placed on him, for verily he took him to be his beloved god."[51] In this festival, the king adorns the image of perfect order to renew his own legitimate authority.

NEW DIRECTIONS AND A GRAND DESIGN

In my own embryonic study of archaeoastronomy, and in particular with Johanna Broda, Edward Calnek, and Anthony Aveni, I have tried to develop an approach for understanding how astronomy, sacred space, and kingship interrelate. Contributing to this approach, in which alignments are viewed as integral but subordinate to larger symmetries, is the view put forth by Johanna Broda in her studies of Mesoamerican cosmovision. Broda's detailed analysis of astronomy and mountain cults in the Valley of Mexico shows that "we find here an extreme complexity in the relations among settlements, natural features, alignments, interactions and symbolic forms—'a grand design' derived from an ancient tradition."[52] Central to the grand design were the mountains and ancient mountain cults and the capacity of pre-Hispanic peoples to practice their own, precise brand of observational science! In a series of publications, Broda has illuminated the dialectical relations between the "exact observation of nature, on the one hand, and myth, magic and ritual on the other." Central to both hands, which helped the Mexica grasp time and its shapes—that is, the observation of nature hand and the magic hand—was astronomical observation, which became vital to the sense of the whole, the cosmic order in Aztec society.[53]

By relating archaeoastronomy to the study of ritual space in my research, I discovered a number of new ideas that enlarged my perspective on Mesoamerican religions. The first had to do with the impact that astronomical events *on the horizon* had on the ceremonial order of Tenochtitlan. Celestial archetypes and the Aztec sky manifest their order largely through horizontality—or horizon astronomy. While the Aztec conception of the sky includes the apprehension of the sky as "up there," "on high," and "everywhere," in fact, it is the celestial events on or near the horizon that play the fundamental roles in the spatial organization of capitals and the complex cycles of ritual activity. I find that this point alters in an important way one of the fundamental impressions in the discipline of the history of religions concerning the significance of the sky. From reviewing, for instance, the marvelous chapter on the sacredness of the sky in Mircea Eliade's *Patterns in Comparative Religions*, and from an initial study of twenty-four articles published in *History of Religions*[54] since 1961 on the organization of sacred space in comparative religions, one gets the impression that (1) astronomy, or sky watching,[55] had almost no significant role in the construction of celestial archetypes and ceremonial cities, and (2) when it did, it was through the influence of a static vertical sky.[56] Almost everywhere we have the dominant view that mountains are sacred because they are vertical, up high, and therefore are the meeting of earth and sky. But in Mesoamerica, hills, mountains, and temple pyramids are also sacred because they have been aligned with the appearances of stars along the horizon. They are observation points of celestial events along the horizon. I call these events horizon hierophanies and archetypes because they become paradigmatic for the ritual orientation of buildings, highways, calendars, even entire cities, as well as the ritual activity of thousands of people.[57] While this kind of celestial alignment may be well known in astronomical studies, it receives little attention in the discipline of history of religions.

The second idea that emerges from placing archaeoastronomy in contact with the history of religions has resulted in a new sense of how the categories of "center" and "periphery" can be conceived in Aztec studies. Where previously the leading associations with the category of the "center," at least in the research program of the Mesoamerican Archive, have focused on the city, the human body, the Templo Mayor, the body and paraphernalia of the ruler, and leading markets, it is now understood that the construction, maintenance, and renewal of these elements were deeply intertwined with sky watching and its discoveries. The "center," *however conceived,* was often influenced through observations of or direct associations with sky watching and celestial events (not just stories about celestial events). The well-being of the "center" and its future was more often than not influenced by the observable patterns of the heavens. Even when we consider what constitutes a "periphery" in Aztec studies (battlefields, agricultural fields, frontiers, or bodies of water supplying tribute), we are now inclined to also (1) look to the ways in which astronomical events regulated relations with the "center," and (2) find astronomical markers on the edges, or within sight of the ceremonial centers, which functioned as sight lines, calendrical markers, or symbols of celestial events on the horizon.[58]

The third idea that emerges from placing archaeoastronomy in contact with the history of religions runs counter to the impression that a locative view of the world dominated Aztec religion. My reading of the New Fire Ceremony suggests that a seventh facet informed the cosmological conviction of Mesoamerica—the apocalyptic fear that the cosmic order was periodically filled with so much tension, threat, and instability that it could not be rejuvenated. Other evidence in the ethnographic record suggests this as well. In addition to the repeated reference to the fear of the populace and their anxiety concerning cosmic renewal in the New Fire Ceremony, we read in Book 2 of the *Florentine Codex* that each day when the sun rose there was uncertainty about its movement,[59] and the people felt danger. Other celestial events such as comets were omens announcing the death of rulers, the onset of war, or famine. The recent research of Ulrich Köhler on comets and falling stars in the perception of Mesoamerican Indians reveals that the prognostic significance of many astronomical events was decisive, though not always negative. Whether falling stars and meteors were considered cigar butts of certain gods, star excrement, or projectiles sent by stars, they were often associated with a coming disaster.[60] Also, the omens associated with the conquest indicate the apocalyptic element in Aztec astronomy. Likewise, comets were associated with the great famine of 1545, and even the beginning of the Mexican Revolution of 1910. In my view, the most profound example of the instability factor relating myth to astronomy, and horizon astronomy at that, is the tentative account of the unstable Creation of the Fifth Sun.

We remember from chapter 2 that following the collapse of the fourth cosmic era, the gods gathered in the primordial darkness in Teotihuacan to discover "who would take it upon himself to be the sun, to bring the dawn." Following a fifty-two-year period of darkness, Nanauatzin, the Pimply Faced One, musters his courage and throws himself into the sacred fire. Waiting for the sun to rise, the gods fell upon their knees looking desperately in all directions. Then, following the description of ponderous waiting, comes the striking passage "When the sun came to rise, he looked very red. He appeared to wobble from side to side."[61] This is also the cosmological conviction facing mankind in the Aztec world. The primordial sun is the *first* New Fire, swaying from side to side, unable to achieve stability, to find its place, or to initiate a creative moment. Fear of an apocalypse, and not just locative order, is the constant concern of Aztec religion. Even at the mythic level, the level at which cosmological order was achieved, the Fifth Sun, which rose out of a new fire, had a profound difficulty finding its place and orienting the world.

Perhaps the Aztec quest for a locative, even imperial, cosmology is most succinctly stated in an important passage from another very important colonial manuscript, Toribio de Benavente's, or as he was better known, Motolinía's *Historia de los Indios de Nueva España*.[62] Motolinía was one of the priests whose ministry and research in the early decades of the colonial period generated valuable accounts of Mexica ritual. This passage tells about the special architectural circumstances at the Templo Mayor on the occasion of the equinox sunrise. My reading of the passage suggests another example of the sevenfold symmetry discerned in the New Fire Ceremony.

We are told that the fiesta of Tlacaxipeualiztli, the Feast of the Flaying of Men, at which men were flayed (first the boys and then the great men) and their flesh was eaten, took place "when the sun was in the middle of Uchilobos, which was at the equinox, and because it was a little wrong, Moctezuma wished to pull it down and set it straight."[63] The inference here is that Moctezuma was looking east from the Temple of Quetzalcoatl toward the Templo Mayor as the equinox sun rose over Huitzilopochtli's temple. From this perspective, a ruler's eye view, a symmetry is sought between the horizon equinox sun, the orientation of the Templo Mayor, the sacrificial festival, and the king's own authority. There are three aspects of this rare passage that I want to highlight: (1) the actual astronomical alignment of the Templo Mayor, (2) the role of the king in the Festival of the Flaying of Men, and (3) the fact that Moctezuma wanted to tear the temple down and realign it.

When the excavation of the Templo Mayor uncovered seven rebuildings of the basic structure of the temple over a hundred-year period, Anthony Aveni and Sharon Gibbs measured the alignment of the rebuildings with a surveyor's transit and astronomical fix.[64] Their first measurement found the alignment of the building deviating seven degrees and six minutes to the south of a true east-west line. Subsequent measurements of the rebuilding of the temple revealed

> a remarkable similarity of alignment in the seven rebuildings pervading all the structural stages that make up the Templo Mayor. Scarcely a full angular degree of extreme separation in azimuth could be found . . . At first the results appeared to contradict Motolinía's historical statement about the use of the building to register the sun and equinox. But upon further reflection, we realized that if the sun had been observed from ground-level over an elevated horizon one should anticipate an align-

ment to the south of east because as the sun rises it also drifts slightly
southwards, that is to the right as the observer faces east upon ascending
into the sky . . . In fact, using the supposed location of the Temple of
Quetzalcoatl as a hypothetical observing point along with estimates of
the dimension of the temple from a number of sources, we discovered
that the equinox sun observation could be fulfilled by Motolinía's statement *only* if the Templo Mayor were skewed about seven degrees south
of east.[65]

This indicates a self-conscious attempt by Moctezuma and other *tlatoanis* to align the Templo Mayor with the equinox sunrise.

Another example of the Aztec expression of symmetry appears in
the ethno-historical record about the Festival of the Flaying of
Men.[66] The greatest number of victims and the most important prisoners of war were slain at the festival of Xipe, which served as an initiation of warriors and linked warfare to astronomy. And, as before, the
core of the event consisted of the relationship of Moctezuma to his
temple. The hierarchical element is suggested when we read elsewhere in Motolinía that the third day of the festival, the ceremony of
"the Bringing Out of the Skins," took place at the great palace where
the nobles of the major cities danced. For this festival a prestigious
personage, a lord from an enemy city, was flayed and his skin was worn
by Moctezuma, who danced with great gravity." In this case, it is
Moctezuma who has become a deity impersonator. The hierarchical
emphasis of the ritual is repeated when we see that "many people
went to see" the king dancing—"a most marvelous thing" because in
other towns, it was not the lords but other leading men who put on
skins of the flayed victims. And all this, the numbers, the prized warriors, the king dancing with skins of sacrificed victims, impersonat-
ing Xipe Totec, was enacted before the eyes of foreign rulers and nobles who were forced to watch from clandestine and public locations.
The text reads, "And also from cities which were his enemies, from
beyond (the mountains), those with which they were at war, Moctezuma secretly summoned, secretly admitted as his guests. . . . There
was witnessing, there was wonder."[67]

But the most vivid example of imperial authority and kingly
worry appears in the statement that there was a misalignment, like
Thurber's microscope, between the king's vision and the temple's orientation. As in the myth of creation, alignment is difficult to achieve,

and if it cannot be achieved, the king's authority comes into question and the cosmos is in danger. As in the case of European royalty where "a woman is not a duchess 100 yards from a carriage,"[68] Moctezuma is not a king if the temple is out of line. So, in an act of immense responsibility, Moctezuma orders the temple reoriented between the equinox sun and his own perspective.

In this interpretation of a sacred and fearful symmetry in the New Fire Ceremony, I have related several developments in the field of archaeoastronomy to my work as a historian of religions, reflecting on the problems of interdisciplinary scholarship and specifically the symmetries of sacred space in and beyond Tenochtitlan during the New Fire Ceremony. I have argued that Aztec cosmovision, infiltrated by stargazing, was a vigorous interplay between a locative view of the world and its counterpoint, an apocalyptic view of the world. This kind of cosmic duality, expressed in part through a variety of celestial events, was precisely expressed in the tensions, symbols, and ritual actions and movements of the New Fire Ceremony. However, this ceremony resolved the tension for a period of time by favoring the locative, secure, repetitive, creative pattern of the Aztec universe through the luminous motion of saturating the Aztec world with fire spread into and through the capital and then outward and throughout the empire. My view is that the Aztec dynasty believed that its power and authority depended on its capacity to integrate major elements of its world into a cohesive symmetry, a symmetry achieved in a grandiose ceremony of cosmic renewal. It is also likely that astronomy was one of the most effective cosmo-magical systems, which enabled the continuity and renewal of Aztec social and cosmic life.

Perhaps, like Thurber, I am seeing more of my own eye than their symmetry, but I am working, along with an interdisciplinary group of scholars, at adjusting the lens.

CHAPTER 4

The Sacrifice of Tezcatlipoca

To Change Place

> This locative vision of man and the cosmos is revealed in a variety of descriptions of the places in which men may stand. The world is perceived as a bounded world; focusing on the etymological roots, the world is felt to be an *environ*ment, an *ambi*ance. That which is open, that which is boundless is seen as the chaotic, the demonic, the threatening. The desert and the sea are the all but interchangeable concrete symbols of the terrible, chaotic openness. . . . Order is produced by walling, channeling, and confining the waters.
>
> Jonathan Z. Smith, *Map Is Not Territory*

> And the city, will it perhaps here in his absence be mocked? Will it divide? Will it scatter? Truly he came spreading his wings, his tail feather over it. Truly he spread himself over it.
>
> Bernardino de Sahagún, *Florentine Codex*

In a series of sharp, critical essays aimed at shifting the direction of the discipline of the history of religions, Jonathan Z. Smith urges a focus on the category of place rather than sacred space. In his book *To Take Place: Toward Theory in Ritual*, Smith develops his critique of the model of sacred space elaborated by historians of religions and describes his own enterprise as "a matter of theory: the issue of ritual and its relation to place." Smith begins with his favorite quotation from Claude Lévi-Strauss, "All sacred things must have their place," and demands that we choose to concentrate on the refinements of ritual that carry "more of the social and verbal understanding of place than does the more familiar substantive sacred space in writings by so-called phenomenologists or historians of religion. It is this former

In the ceremony of Toxcatl, the most perfect captured male warrior was
sacrificed and beheaded, and his heart was offered to the sun. He had lived as
a god for one year, walking throughout the capital playing flutes, displaying
cultivated arts, and, just a month before his sacrifice, provided with four female
consorts. In this scene, he has ascended the temple steps, breaking his flutes, and
is sacrificed. Note how the sun observes the sacrifice. From the *Florentine
Codex*. (After Paso y Troncoso, courtesy of the University of Utah Press.)

sense of "*place* in relation to the 'microadjustments' of ritual that supplies the focus for these inquiries"[1] (emphasis in the original).

At a certain point in his inquiry, Smith argues that we should discard Mircea Eliade's symbolism of the center found in cities, temples, trees, dwellings, and in certain human beings. Smith's critique of the notion of the *axis mundi* begins in his essay "The Wobbling Pivot," where he asks "whether one can pay such attention to the center without giving equal attention to the periphery," while in a later essay, he declares that Eliade's notion of the "center" is "not a secure pattern to which data may be brought as illustrative: it is a dubious notion" in the study of religion. Smith posits the alternative categories of visions of the world as "locative" and "utopian" places. The locative vision referred to in the opening quote of this chapter emphasizes place and truly being *in place*, while the utopian vision of the world emphasizes the value of being in no place, of transcending boundaries and limits or, in the words of the Aztec speaker in the second quotation that opens this chapter, referring to the crisis of the city when the ruler died, "Will it divide? Will it scatter? Truly he came spreading his wings . . . Truly he spread himself over it."

In fact, all three of these models of spatial ordering illuminate aspects of the Aztec urban order. Some cities were situated around temple precincts that symbolized cosmic mountains and the Flowering Cosmic Tree and were perceived as openings to the celestial and subterranean realms. And space and time, especially time, were measured according to a rigorous, locative model.[2] There are also a few outstanding cases of rulers, such as Moctezuma Ilhuicamina, who challenged traditional, locative conceptions of imperial space and broke through resistant frontiers to remap the Aztec Empire into a utopian scheme. Smith is well aware of the spectrum of social and symbolic places, as his chapter titles in *To Take Place* show. He repositions the category of place, "In Search of Place," "Father Place," "To Put in Place," and "To Take Place."

In my exploration into a number of sacrificial ceremonies, especially Toxcatl, which is the focus of this chapter, another conception of spatial order and transformation that is less fixed and more dynamic and momentary has become apparent to me. Sacred space and ceremonial landscapes in Aztec ceremonies expand and retract, meander and transform, and link and fold into one another in a "metamorphic vision of place" or, to add to Smith's spectrum, the motion and movement and the microadjustments of Aztec rituals suggest the notion "To Change Place." Deity impersonators, pilgrimages, processions, and mock battles alternate, change, and move beyond static conceptions of sacralized space and social place. We find a vision of place in which change and transformation are the sustained pattern. People change places, bodies are completely transfigured, the places are transformed by hierophanies, and the city is regenerated. In my conception of a metamorphic vision of ritual space, circumferences and asymmetrical actions are crucial (patterns that Eliade ignores), and movement, change, and transformation are key (basic facts that Smith avoids). As a means of exploring this metamorphic vision of place, I begin with a description of Toxcatl during which the *teotl ixiptla*, or image of the "true" god Tezcatlipoca, Lord of the Smoking Mirror, was sacrificed during the month of May.

THE CEREMONY OF TOXCATL

In the month of Toxcatl (dry season), the people celebrated a festival for the "god of gods," Tezcatlipoca. One of the final acts was the sacrifice of a captive warrior who was chosen on the basis of his perfect physical features, one "who had no blemishes upon his body." This warrior had been changed into a *teotl ixiptla*, or image of Tezcatlipoca, and received extraordinary care and public attention as he lived for one year in "all luxuries" while being trained in music, singing, speaking, and walking. For a short time prior to his ritual death, the god-image was provided with four wives for sexual pleasure and ritual union. At the end of this year, the Tezcatlipoca *ixiptla* was sacrificed on top of a temple in the ceremonial center of the city of Chalco. His heart was extracted and offered to the sun, he was beheaded, and his skull was placed on the *tzompantli*, or skull rack.

Toxcatl was considered the "most important of all festivals" and, as with a number of sacrificial festivals, was called a "debt payment," or *nextlaoalli*. The god Tezcatlipoca was "given human form" through the ritual technique of choosing the most physically attractive male from among a special group of captive warriors who served as the yearly supply for this ceremony. This group was supervised and maintained by a special corps of guardians. It was imperative that all impersonators of Tezcatlipoca should have a "fair countenance, of good understanding [and should be] slender, reedlike, long and thin, like a stout cane, like a stone column all over." An extensive ritual description of the requirements for the god's "human form" includes the following:

> He was like something smoothed, like a tomato, like a pebble, as if sculptured in wood; he was not curly-haired. . . . he was not rough of forehead . . . he was not long-headed. . . . He was not of swollen eyelids, he was not of enlarged eyelids, he was not swollen-cheeked . . . he was not of downcast face; he was not flat-nosed; he did not have a nose with wide nostrils; he was not concave-nosed . . . he was not thick-lipped, he was not gross-lipped, he was not big-lipped, he was not a stutterer, he did not speak a barbarous language. He was not buck-toothed, he was not large-toothed . . . His teeth were like seashells . . . he was not cup-eyed, he was not round-eyed; he was not tomato-eyed; he was not of pierced eye. . . . He was not long-handed; he was not one-handed; he was not handless; he was not fat-fingered. . . . He was not emaciated; he was not fat; he was not big-bellied; he was not of protruding navel; he was not of hatchet shaped buttocks. . . . For him who was thus, who had no flaw, who had no (bodily) defects, who had no blemish, who had no mark, . . . there was taken the greatest care that he be taught to blow the flute, that he be able to play his whistle; and that at the same time he hold all his flowers and his smoking tube.[3]

The captive who best approximated this negative description of perfection was chosen and carefully trained in several Aztec arts, including music, smoking, and flower holding. But he was not just a stationary, imprisoned paragon of beauty and culture for "very great care was taken that he should be very circumspect in his discourse, that he talk graciously, that he greet people agreeably on the road if he met anyone." This last point is vital for understanding Tezcatlipoca's relation to the ritual landscape, because his image was allowed to go wandering throughout the city for a year with his public entourage. During these promenades he greeted people who considered him "our lord. There was an assigning of lordship; he was importuned; he was sighed for; there was bowing before him."[4]

At an appointed time during his year-long public displays and contact with the populace, Tezcatlipoca was taken before the *tlatoani* (overlord or king) Moctezuma, who ceremonially "repeatedly adorned him; he gave him gifts; he arrayed him; he arrayed him with great pomp. He had all costly things placed on him, for verily he took him to be his beloved god."[5]

Sahagún's informants provide the details of this further transformation into the ruler's god. His head was pasted with eagle down and popcorn flowers; he was arrayed with "the flowery stole." Golden shell pendants were placed on his ears and turquoise mosaic plugs were inserted in the lobes; a shining seashell necklace and white seashell breast ornament were draped on his neck and chest; a snail shell lip pendant was inserted in his lip. Hardly an area of his body escaped transformation. Golden bracelets covered his upper arms while turquoise bracelets covered "almost all his forearm." A net cape of wide mesh with a fringe of brown cotton thread hung about his costly breechcloth, which reached to the calves of his legs. His legs were covered with gold bells above obsidian sandals with ocelot skin ears. This living image of physical, cultural, and imperial splendor presented himself in the pathways of the city once again, where the citizenry beheld the ruler's "beloved god."

Then, during the twenty days prior to the sacrifice, two major transformations took place. The image shed these luscious ornaments and his hair was cut and a tuft of hair was attached to his forehead. Then, a forked heron-feather ornament with a quetzal-feather spray was bound to his warrior's hairpiece. He was given four wives and "for only twenty days he lived lying with the women, that he lived married to them." The symbolism of this ceremonial coupling is meaningful, as each of these wives is also a *teotl ixiptla* representing the goddesses Xochiquetzal, Xilonen, Atlatonan, and Uixtociuatl. The five of them sang and danced in public for five days and distributed food and gifts to people at a series of specific locations, including Tecanman; then at a place where the image of Titlacauan was guarded; then at Tepetzinco in the middle of the lagoon; and on the fourth day at Tepepulco. Following this series of visits and distributions of gifts, the Tezcatlipoca *ixiptla* was taken by boat—with the women consoling him, encouraging him—to the place called Acaquilpan or Caualtepec. After arriving back on land "near Tlalpitzauhcan," the women separated from Tezcatlipoca, who was now followed only by his servants and guardians.

The entourage returned to the mainland and in a surprising maneuver traveled away from the Templo Mayor more than fifteen miles to the ceremonial center of Chalco, south of Tenochtitlan. Abandoned by his entourage, the image proceeded to a small temple called Tlacochcalco, which, according to Sahagún's text, "he ascended by himself, he went up of his own free will, to where he was to die." As he ascended the temple, he broke his flutes and whistles on the steps. Then the scene speeded up as the offering priests seized him, "threw him upon his back on the sacrificial stone: then cut open his breast, he took his heart from him, he also raised it in dedication to the sun."[6] The *ixiptla*'s body was carefully lowered from the temple and his head severed from his body, emptied of its contents, and eventually hung on the skull rack. Then, according to Sahagún's informants, this journey from imprisonment to lavish deification to death on the stone had the meaning: "And this betokened our life on earth. For he who rejoiced, who possessed riches, who sought, who esteemed our lord's sweetness, his fragrance—richness, prosperity—thus ended in great misery. Indeed it was said: 'No one on earth went exhausting happiness, riches, wealth.' "

THE CEREMONIAL LANDSCAPE

The ceremonial life of Aztec cities was as much a theater of the human physique as it was a form of rhetoric and ideology. To put the matter differently, Aztec sacrificial rites were exuberant forms of cosmo-magical rhetoric expressed through imagery about the human body as it moved through, changed, and mapped out a ceremonial landscape that was concentrated and dispersed, local and imperial, depending on the particular festival. The relationship of the human body to the cosmos in Nahuatl culture has been illuminated by Alfredo López Austin in *The Human Body and Ideology,* in which he writes,

> There is a whole complex of ideas by which the universe was conceived as a projection of the human body and inversely explained human physiology in relation to the general processes of the cosmos. For this reason a knowledge of the concepts about the human organism is indispensable to anyone who wishes to penetrate the complicated cosmological thought of the Mesoamericans.[7]

In a sense, López Austin's work challenges Mesoamerican specialists and historians of religions to explore together the fuller relations of the ritual use of the human body to the larger ceremonial order of Aztec religion; for Aztec ritual moved and transformed human experience through colorful, florid, visual displays of images of highly energized relationships between temples and mountains, between social groups, between distinct levels of social status, and between humans and their gods. While static and non-human images played important roles in linking up these elements of society, it was the living human images of deities, power hierarchies, and nature's forces moving through the landscape that played a central role in the Aztec theater. The decoration, movement, and changes of the human body and its most potent parts, including the head, heart, hair, and blood, constituted a significant portion of the nexus of ceremonial life. And from a slightly different point of view, the eyes were the most important organ. Seeing and movement through the ceremonial landscape were the crucial actions by which to know the cosmos and its interrelated parts.

There is no doubt that all the senses were alert and tuned to the ritual expressions in Tenochtitlan's great ceremonial landscape. The songs were heard, the beat was pounded with feet and interpreted with muscular movements, the blood was smelled, and the gods were touched, and sometimes eaten. As Lawrence Sullivan has shown in his study of South American performances, "synesthesia," or the unity of the senses, was the avenue through which knowledge about the cosmos or unity of the world was communicated. In writing about how these unities are learned, Sullivan contends that what sets performance apart from brute behavior is, in part, a "quality of knowledge" experience in ritual action. The atmosphere necessary for acquiring this quality of knowledge is the experience of synesthesia,

> usually defined as a phenomenon in which one type of stimulation evokes the sensation of another. For example, the research of Marlene Dobkin de Ríos proves the ways in which the hearing of sound, under the influence of sacred plants[,]results in the visualization of colors. Synesthesia translates from the new Latin into quasi-down-home as "unity of the senses" . . . the point is that performance displays the symbolic expression of synesthesia as it is imagined in a culture. In so doing, it renders perceptible a symbolism of the unity of the senses. The symbolic experience of the unity of the senses enables a culture to entertain itself with the idea of the unity of meaning.[8]

Sullivan's approach to synesthesia through a focus on ritual sound offers a valuable lead for new insights into the understanding of Mesoamerican ritual power. But in Aztec ceremonial life, as demonstrated in the ceremony of Toxcatl, synesthesia, or the perception and understanding of unities, was triggered as much by visual experiences as by hearing the gods. The senses were integrated, and the world became meaningful in large part through *seeing* the still and moving images that marked and linked up the wide-ranging ceremonial landscape in and around the capital. People came to Tenochtitlan and moved through its ritual topography in part to see the processions, mock battles, and human sacrifices; to see the images of gods and deity impersonators; to gaze at the sacred places where they were concentrated; to see humans changed into gods; and to see other human beings seeing the divine in ceremony and visions.

I now want to consider, through a focus on one major ceremonial performance, how the human body as both actor and observer combined to organize the senses so that the culture could entertain itself with the idea of unity of meaning and a view of hierarchical differences. On one side of this ceremonial performance we have the human body encapsulating a vibrating, divine force and adorned with sacred images moving, changing, and linking up a ritual landscape. On the other side, we have the participants and observers seeing a cosmology and social world come to life through the movements and changes of a divine image. My intention is to build on Sullivan's approach by following Rhys Isaac's view of a cultural landscape as a terrain or living space that has been subjected to the

> requirements of a conscious and unconscious design . . . A society necessarily leaves marks of use upon the terrain it occupies. These marks are meaningful signs not only of the particular relations of a people to the environment but also of the distribution of control and access to essential resources. Incised upon a society's living space appears a text for the inhabitants—which he who runs may read—of social relations within the world.[9]

I will explore the design that the Aztec placed on their living space and develop a portrait of a ceremonial landscape by using two elements of Isaac's description: (1) the marks and meaningful signs on the landscape, consisting of the temples, neighborhoods, and palaces

that were visited and linked into a ceremonial whole by the movement in the ceremony—these marks are largely transformations created by humans; and (2) "he who runs," or in Tezcatlipoca's case, he
who walked in a procession—that is, the images and series of transformations that the Tezcatlipoca *ixiptla* underwent. In this way, we
will see both a spatial landscape and a landscape of social relations
symbolized in the transformations in the mode of being of Tezcatlipoca's *ixiptla*. This combination will help provide a perspective
through which to view the complicated Aztec attempt at a unity of
meaning as well as the expression of the force of the social hierarchy
with its uneven access to power and privilege. The ceremony of Toxcatl reflects neither an *axis mundi* nor a locative vision of place, but
rather a vision of place organized by powerful transformations and
metamorphoses, a vision of place in which the terrain of the sacred is
not concentrated, limited, or restricted to one or several locations. In
a manner reminiscent of the paths marked by meandering footprints
in the codices, Tezcatlipoca's movements alter our line of vision and
mingle places in striking combinations. This metamorphic vision of
place is best represented in the transformations that Tezcatlipoca's *ixiptla* underwent. He was a capricious god who changed places and
changed forms.[10]

    This ceremonial landscape was connected by the physical move-
ment and contact of people traveling through the land. As the texts
describing Atl Caualo and Toxcatl show, this landscape consisted of
particular places in the lakes and in the mountains as well as the social
markers of roads, temples, and neighborhoods. The ritual cycle ensured that there was a constant, organic flow from the center of the *al-
tepeme* (city-states), through the *calpultin* (corporate groups), and out
into the natural landscape. These paths often led back into the ceremonial centers of local communities.

    A cursory review of just four of the yearly ceremonies reveals both
a tendency to saturate space beyond the ceremonial center and a tendency to reconcentrate people, goods, and symbols within the *axis
mundi*. In the year-opening ceremony of Atl Caualo, the participants
visited seven distant and distinct shrines on surrounding hillsides
where children were left for sacrifice. The ritual covered over 120 kilometers in a variety of directions. The subsequent ceremony of Tlacaxipeualiztli covered a ritual map that was not as wide-ranging but

was meant symbolically to saturate the whole ceremonial world: "The captor went everywhere. He went everyplace, he omitted no place, nowhere did he forget in the calmeca, in the calpulcos. On the lips of the stone images, on each one, he placed the blood of the captive."[11] In the ceremony of Uey Tocoztli, the action crossed the various *calpultin* and *calmecac* of the city and spread to the fields and various ceremonial structures in different locations. And in the ceremony of Etzalcualiztli, the participants visited different locations in the lake (Temilco, Tepexicoztoc) where special reeds were gathered, then moved to the ruler's palace in the ceremonial center, outward again to local schools, then out to Tetamacolco and Totecco at the water's edge, then out into the lake to Pantitlan, and finally back to Tetamacolco. This spatial breadth is also reflected in the ceremony of Tepeilhuitl during which the women who were sacrificed "were representative of the mountains (imixiptlaoan tetepe) . . . Tepexoch, . . . Matlalcueye, . . . Xochtecatl, . . . Mayahuel, representation of the maguey and Milnauatl."[12]

We are fortunate to see, as described in the previous chapter, a map of the metamorphosis of ceremonial place in the New Fire ceremony held on the occasion of the ending of the fifty-two-year calendar cycle. This ceremony, also called the Binding of the Years, began in the capital from which processions left, in public view, from the Cerro de la Estrella over twenty kilometers south of the main ceremonial center. Following an all-day procession of priests, deity impersonators, musicians, and warriors, the entourage arrived in the darkness at the summit of this ceremonial mountain where, following ceremonial preparations, the "new fire" was started in the chest of a sacrificed warrior. This fire was taken down the mountain, retracing the route of the procession into the center of the capital, and placed in the holder of the statue of the god Huitzilopochtli. Then, it was taken to all the communities in the empire where it ignited the new fires (or new time period) locally. This fiery display ignited the imperial landscape as well as the new time period.

This dynamic pattern challenges the static conception of sacred spaces and the direct-line map of pilgrimages (which appear in our books) by emphasizing the strenuous and powerful physical demands that place pilgrims and celebrants in a wide-ranging, heterogeographical territory. In the New Fire ceremony, all the senses were challenged—through walking, climbing, singing, censing——but most important were the eyes; the fire was seen in the darkness as symbolizing a new age.

TEZCATLIPOCA: THE LORD OF EVERYWHERE

The clearest expression of the pattern of the metamorphosis of place is in the cult, symbolism, and ceremony of Tezcatlipoca. In Sahagún's Book 1, titled "The Gods," Tezcatlipoca is called "a true god, whose abode was everywhere—in the land of the dead, on earth, and in heaven." Tezcatlipoca's omnipresence is elaborated in the eleven prayers dedicated to him found in Book 6 of the *Florentine Codex*. Thelma Sullivan, the distinguished Nahuatl scholar, describes Tezcatlipoca this way:

> The nature and powers of Tezcatlipoca are nowhere more sharply etched than in these texts. There are, first of all, the names by which he is invoked: Tloque Nahuaque, literally "Lord of the Near, Lord of the Close," figuratively the supreme lord, the lord who is everywhere, in everything, upon whom all depend. Other names are: Yohualli Ehecatl "Nights, Winds," that is, invisible and impalpable; Moyocoyatzin, "Capricious One"; Monenequi, "Tyrannical One"; Titlacahuan, "Our Master" (literally, "we are his slaves"); Teimatini, "Knower of People"; Techichihuani, "Adorner of People"; Yaotl, "The Enemy"; Necoc Yaotl, "The Enemy on Both Sides"; Moquequeloa, "The Mocker"; Ipalnemoani, "Giver of Life" (literally, "by virtue of whom one lives"); and Teyocoyani, "Creator of Man." They bespeak awesome and frightening powers, an arbitrariness against which man is powerless.[13]

While this series of names speaks to a variety of powers, my eyes are drawn to the spatial reach of Tezcatlipoca, who is near and close, takes the form of the wind, is the enemy on both sides, and knows people wherever they are. In a sense, there is no escaping Tezcatlipoca.

The omnipresence of Tezcatlipoca is also expressed in his ritual mirror, which enabled the god or his priest to "see all that took place in the world." His vision spread out to penetrate everywhere; but this ability was anchored in a specific spot—namely, the mirror called Itlachiayaque (place from which he watches).[14] And from this place his vision could not only stretch into places far away but also penetrate into the interior of hidden things.[15] Consider this prayer from Book 6 of the *Florentine Codex*:

> O master, O our lord, O lord of the near, of the nigh, O night, O wind:
> thou seest, thou knowest the things within the trees, the rocks. And be-
> hold now, it is true that thou knowest of things within us; thou hearest us
> from within. Thou hearest, thou knowest that which is within us: what
> we say, what we think; our minds, our hearts. It is as if smoke, mist arose
> before thee.[16]

In a sense, we see that the god's knowledge of humans and nature
is acquired through a partial synesthesia. First, he sees the things
within the trees, and then he hears the things within the human mind
and heart. He becomes present within the cosmic pillars and the
tonalli and the *teyolia* of the human body.[17] This saturation of space is
transformed into the power to create a sense of direction in space
through the playing of Tezcatlipoca's flute. Ten days before the festival, the image plays the flute "in all four directions so all would perform the rite of eating the earth and of begging the gods for things
they coveted." In this preparatory ritual, sound creates a sense of space
and its cosmic organization. The sound of the flute, as with the word,
depends on the exhalation of the breath or, in Nahua thought, the
soul. This was understood as the diffusion into the world of divine influence. The centrifugal quality of the god's vision and sound is extended to the space and character of warfare and of other gods who
dwell both near and far from the human community.

> On hearing the flute that day, brave and courageous men, all the old sol-
> diers implored the gods, in rare anguish and devotion to be given victo-
> ries against their enemies and strengthened to bring back many captive
> from war; these men prayed to God of all Created Things, to Lord by
> Whom We Live, to Sun, to Quetzalcoatl, to Tezcatlipoca, to Huitzilo-
> pochtli, to Cihuacoatl. All the principal divinities adored by the natives.[18]

In this evocation by warriors, the pattern of center/periphery is explicit. The flute of Tezcatlipoca prepares them to go out of the city to
war and to bring back to the city captives. The flute also stimulated
them to ask for divine help from gods who are spatially near, Cihuacoatl, associated with the earth, and those who are spatially far away,
the sun and divine forces that are everywhere, the God of All Created Things.

The clearest display of the metamorphosis of place is in the route,
or ritual randomness, of Tezcatlipoca's wandering during the year. As

in most festivals, the action began in or near the walled ceremonial center when Tezcatlipoca's image was chosen from a special collection of secluded enemy warriors. Following special training to become a living image of the god, Tezcatlipoca was given the limited freedom (with guards and retainers) to walk throughout the city. His handsome form, idealized further by training and lavish ornaments, displayed the beauty and majesty of this god before thousands whose daily work and movements were interrupted by the entourage. We can imagine the ostentatious impression this retinue made with the *ixiptla* at the center—stopping all traffic and drawing all eyes upon it as the group followed a patterned and random series of routes.

The spreading presence of Tezcatlipoca was heralded, according to Diego Durán's account, by the ritual censing of all homes. At the start of the month of Toxcatl, all homes in the community were entered by a priest who perfumed them with incense "from the threshold . . . to the last corner," including each object in the house, announcing the onset of the time and atmosphere of Tezcatlipoca. Having permeated domestic space and public neighborhoods with sound, smoke, and the living image of the god, Tezcatlipoca proceeded to the palace of the *tlatoani* Moctezuma. This movement crossed not only geographical, domestic, and public space but also hierarchical space as the god's image joined with the office and person of kingship. In the adornment ceremony, the *teotl ixiptla* was transformed into the ruler's version of the god.

Toward the end of the year-long ceremony, Tezcatlipoca visited four designated ceremonial locations associated with the four directions his flute sounded out, as though to transform the apparently random sense of space into an ordered integration of ritual precincts. Then the ceremony moved off land and out into the lake, reflecting the "everywhere" conception of the god of gods. He is present not only on the land but also in the waters that nurture and threaten it. When the ceremonial entourage returned to land, it headed in the direction of Chalco to the south.

According to the historian Chimalpahin, Chalco was organized into four communities oriented in cardinal directions. Tlacochcalco was the main center of the Chalcan kingdom and there the image ascended the temple, moving upward in space, closer to the celestial forces, and was sacrificed. Yet the movement of this illustrious body did not cease at the sacrifice. Not only was the body carried down the steps, but, more important, the head was severed, emptied of its contents, and carried to the skull rack where Tezcatlipoca's gaze met the eyes of countless onlookers. In spatial terms, the *teotl ixiptla* saturated space with Tezcatlipoca's music, mirror, and living image before returning to a ceremonial center to undergo his final transformation.

LIVING IMAGES OF TRANSFORMATION

Some of the most potent vehicles for the communication of religious meaning and social hierarchy are the images, icons, and sacred objects utilized in ritual communities and ceremonies. Scholarship has focused on a rich spectrum of imagery, including sculpture, costume, masks, wall paintings, sand paintings, pottery, amulets, and architecture. For example, some of the most extensive entries in the recent *Encyclopedia of Religion* are the fourteen articles on iconography, defined as a "program in art history that exposes the different meaning of images vis à vis the beholder." This intense focus is as it should be because imagery, perceived through visual experiences, (in large part) has been determined to be "an essential instrument in the development of human consciousness."

This emphasis on the beholder's experience and the link between image and consciousness relates to what I call the experience of "ortho-visus," that is, seeing divine images in dramatic appearances according to an authoritative norm. The ceremony of Toxcatl suggests that ortho-visus, in this case seeing how Tezcatlipoca's images and powers saturate the world, is a potent trigger in the experience of synesthesia. The role of seeing the divine through images in the world is crucial to truly knowing the divine. Moses saw the burning bush, the disciples saw the resurrected Jesus, Black Elk saw the rainbow teepee, the Hindu worshiper sees Kali. This experience of seeing the divine takes a powerful reversal in the case of Tezcatlipoca's statue in Tenochtitlan, which, according to Doris Heyden's research, had obsidian mirrors for eyes. Tezcatlipoca, remember, is "The Knower of People" and with his obsidian mirror eyes, which reflect the image of ritualists who look into them, communicates that the divine sees you, from within your own face. But most studies of imagery and iconography, if the *Encyclopedia of Religion* is representative, focus on still, immobile, non-human images of the divine. The beholder sees the divine image solidly in place or on display. An outstanding example of this approach is found in Diana Eck's study *Banaras: City of Light*, in which she shows how pilgrims go to the sacred capital for *darshana*, defined in popular terms as "not sight seeing but sacred sight seeing" or beholding the divine and being in its presence. Eck's study includes Mark Twain's observation that the collection of divine images embodying Hindu gods were a "wild mob of nightmares." The Aztec materials highlight the visual power of their rituals—the performative display of forces, meanings, directions, ancestors, gods, kings, warriors, and mythologies. It is crucial to emphasize that in the cosmo-magical world of the Aztecs, these images often move and are alive with divine force, participate in the ritual as much as humans do, and also (in various ways) see, hear, speak, taste, and touch the social world. In what follows, I give attention to the powers of the visual experience to trigger *and* organize the synesthesia of ritual.

As a means of approaching what I believe to be special in Aztec religion, namely, the major role played by living, human, perishable images of deities, I will draw a picture of a distant but relevant cultural pattern of seeing the divine. Specifically, let us turn briefly to a Catholic pattern of sacred sight seeing as described in the chapter "The Palace of the Virgin" in Otto von Simson's *The Gothic Cathedral*. We find here a classic example of how seeing the divine in a material image causes a metamorphosis in the community that views it.

On the night of June 10, 1194, a huge fire destroyed a large part of the town of Chartres, including the entire cathedral except for the west façade. The main relic of the cathedral, the tunic that the Virgin Mary was said to have worn on the night of Christ's birth, which for centuries had drawn pilgrims from all parts of Europe, was also believed destroyed. This devastation, according to Simson,

> kindled the deepest human emotion. The historian has every reason to take such emotions seriously. They provide the impulse without which great collective efforts are impossible and unintelligible. In Chartres, the grief over the destruction of the ancient shrine prompted, soon after the calamity had occurred, the resolution to rebuild it more splendidly than it had ever been before. The general mood during those days can perhaps alone explain the almost incredible effort that produced within the brief span of one generation the cathedral that we admire today as the loftiest example of medieval art.[19]

The townspeople, according to a number of records of the day, felt that the disaster indicated that the Virgin had abandoned her shrine and fled in a moment of divine wrath. But in response to the deep mood of despair, the church leaders dedicated three years of revenues to rebuild the church. Then, on the feast day chosen to inaugurate the rebuilding, a miraculous event occurred:

> Before this crowd . . . the cardinal of Pisa repeated his plea with an eloquence that brought tears to the eyes of his audience. And, by what seemed to be a happy coincidence, at the very moment the bishop and chapter appeared carrying in solemn procession the Sacred Tunic, which contrary to general belief had, safe in the cathedral crypt, survived the conflagration undamaged. The wonderful occurrence caused an incredible impression. Everyone pledged the possessions he had salvaged to the reconstruction of the sanctuary. The medieval temper, as we can often observe, was given to sudden changes from despair to joy. In Chartres it was now suddenly believed that the Virgin herself had permitted the destruction of the old basilica because she wanted a new and more beautiful church to be built in her honor.[20]

There are a number of rich meanings in this orchestrated miracle of the Virgin's reappearance, but I will emphasize only one: It is the seeing of the divine image returning and traveling through the human community that brings about a radical emotional change, as well as generous financial offerings. We have a synesthesia of the senses and the pocketbook! But even here, as in Eck's work, the emphasis is on inanimate objects filled with the divine. In Aztec religion, the divine presence in terrestrial objects takes place most significantly in human beings called *teteo imixiptlahuan* (human images of the gods). Many ceremonies involved human beings in whom the gods became encapsulated. López Austin sums up this view of how the human body is filled with the nature of divinities when he writes of deity impersonators as

> *teteo imixiptlahuan*, . . . men possessed by the gods, who, as such, died in a rite of renewal. The idea of a calendric cycle, of a periodic returning, in which the power of a god was born, grew, decreased, and concluded made it necessary in a rite linking the time of man to mythical time that a god would die so his force might be reborn with new power. It was not men who died, but gods—gods within a corporeal covering that made

possible their ritual death on earth. If the gods did not die, their force would diminish in a progressively aging process. Men destined for sacrifice were temporarily converted into receptacles of divine fire, they were treated as gods, and they were made to live as the deity lived in legend. Their existence in the role of ixiptlatin, or "images," could last from a few days up to four years.[21]

There is much still to be understood about the significance of *teteo ixiptla*.[22] Some were chosen on the basis of mimesis, or striking physical similarities with the gods. For example, children were *ixiptla* of Tlaloc because they appeared to be little *tlaloque* with similar round faces, round eyes, and small bodies. These children, indeed all images of the divine, were considered vessels. The terms for god-image were *teixiptla* and *toptli*. *Teixiptla* derived from *xip*, meaning "skin, rind, or covering." *Toptli* means "covering or wrapping." In a sense, gods fill up the human and natural images (rocks, trees, plants) that are thought to resemble them.[23]

The narratives of Aztec ceremonies show us a rich series of images, flowing, jerking, moving, and immobilized in the landscape. In fact, Aztec ceremonies and the city itself were landscapes "made of images." The seminal image in the ceremony of Toxcatl was the *ixiptla* of Tezcatlipoca. In order to appreciate the power of this living image who linked up the ceremonial landscape, I will discuss two of the "scenes" of Tezcatlipoca's appearances: (1) the static ceremonial stage consisting of his temple and stone *ixiptla*; and (2) the series of transformations that the human image of the deity underwent.

THE CEREMONIAL STAGE

References to Toxcatl emphasize that it contains the "most splendid ceremonies," which carried colorful, lavish images throughout the city. The stationary focus of this splendid ceremony was Tezcatlipoca's temple, "constructed with such a profusion of figures, sculpture and work in stucco that it gave pleasure from any point of view. . . . Within its walled enclosure were many chambers, some occupied by the dignitaries of the temple, since there existed a hierarchy. These temples can be compared to cathedrals, especially the temples of the greatest gods."[24]

This hierarchy of temple space was paralleled by a hierarchy of costume, although commoners and lords alike displayed themselves

in lavish, even ostentatious dress. "All crowned themselves with headdresses or miters made up of small painted wreathes, beautifully
adorned like latticework." And children became living images of
Tezcatlipoca when the priests "took the infants, dressed them in the
garb and insignia of the idol, smearing them with divine pitch and
feathering their heads with the plumes of quail or turkey."[25] Durán
notes that the children were "offered" to Tezcatlipoca, meaning that
their lives were dedicated to his service. At the upper end of the hierarchy, the "lords or chieftains" displayed their superior position by
hanging "little figures of gold or stones or many other finely worked
things" on their headdresses. But the most lavish costumes were given
to the god.

During the month of May, "the lords came to the temple carrying
a new attire and gave it to priests so the idol could be clad in it." The
stone image of Tezcatlipoca was dressed in jewels, bracelets, and
feathers stored in boxes "more reverently than we put away sacerdotal
vestments . . . so carefully stored that they served no other purpose
than that of being adored as if they had been the god himself."[26]
However, this image was not normally seen by the common eye. Tezcatlipoca was hidden away from sight in a lavishly decorated inner
room, "hung with splendidly worked cloth in the Indian manner, in
different colors and designs, all covered with feathers so favored by
these people in their decorations and garments."[27] The inner chamber
with an altar and Tezcatlipoca's image was hidden by a "veil or with a
finely worked door covering" and in this way was kept closed off and
dark, and the idol hidden. No one dared enter this place, with the sole
exception of priests appointed to serve the cult of the god." The altar
was a gorgeous sight, "as tall as a man . . . covered with the most elegant, most finely wrought richest mantles ever woven or embroidered." Then, at the right moment, after "special ornaments were
added, such as featherwork, bracelets, sunshades—all the best that
could be given to him"—the veil was lifted in a hierophanic drama
"so that Tezcatlipoca could be seen by all."[28]

TEZCATLIPOCA'S TRANSFORMATIONS

What is very important for an understanding of the "sense of unity"
encapsulated in this ceremony is the series of changes that the *teotl ixiptla* underwent. As he changed places, he linked up the marks and lo-

cations of the spatial landscape. As he changed his identity, he re-vealed a powerful spectrum in Aztec experience. In other words, the image of Tezcatlipoca was alive, not only in the sense that a human being was the public image, but also in the changes he underwent at different stages of the year-long ceremony. The ideal person who started the ceremony was changed into the cultural paragon of Aztec society. Although it is nowhere stated as such, the impersonator was akin to a human "flower and song," an excellent aesthetic form on the earth, manifesting divine powers in a human body, costume, and arts. After parading before the populace, he was changed into the ruler's god, the lord of the palace, and then again paraded before the eyes of the people who were humbled in his presence. Then, in a remarkable reversal, he is stripped of his divine adornments, both the ones be-stowed by Moctezuma and the human ornaments in the form of women who were *ixiptlatin* of goddesses. Another transformation is signaled when he breaks his whistles and flutes on the steps, for he has returned to the image of the warrior, akin to the battlefield status he held before his capture.

Studies of iconography and image do not afford us much help in understanding this series of transformations. Rather, it is in the genre of theatrical studies that we can directly approach the meaning of these changes. Richard Schechner, studying transportation and trans-formation in theatrical performances, discusses the diversity of per-formances and the processual structure in which images reject, re-place, erase, and superimpose themselves on other images during the history of a theatrical form.[29] But even within a single performance, there are two general types of changes that the images undergo. First, there are transportation performances in which a performer is "taken somewhere"—that is, "goes to another time/space reference, per-sonality reference, geographical reference—but in the end returns to where he started, namely, the "ordinary world." Second, there are transformation performances in which a performer's social and sym-bolic identity is permanently changed, as in an initiation rite. In the end, there is no return to the previous identity for when one "cools down," one is in a new place, location, relationship with the cosmos.

Schechner's categories are helpful, but they must be adapted in or-der to clarify the changes in Tezcatlipoca's impersonator. As the ritual of Toxcatl shows, the performers underwent a series of transformations that led to an ultimate transformation of the Tezcatlipoca *ixiptla*. This emphasis on a real, final transformation is important because the radical nature of Aztec human sacrifice in general and Toxcatl in particular represents a most convincing example of what historians of religions call a "change in the mode of being." And more important, Toxcatl as a whole presents, through this series of transformations in the human image, an image of the whole society, or at least an image of the whole male society, acting out its idea of perfection ("the perfect embodiment of a quality"). This image of perfection consists of a series of metamorphoses moving through the scheme: warrior = perfect body = cultural paragon = sexual potency = king's god = seasoned warrior = sacrificed deity.

AN ULTIMATE TRANSFORMATION

It is in the rapid series of movements that demarcate the actual sacrifice that the meaning of the year-long ceremony can be found. As in the case of most human sacrifices, the act of killing occupies a very small portion of the ceremony and its description. There are three outstanding moments in the ceremonial killing of Tezcatlipoca: (1) the ascent of the temple, (2) the offering of the body parts, and (3) the Aztec comment on the significance of the sacrifice.

We are told that the *teotl ixiptla* "went up of his own free will, to where he was to die"[30] and that on each of the steps, "he shattered one of the flutes that he had played as he had walked, all during the year."[31] This ascent toward his death is marked by astonishing self-control and a commitment that is hard to believe. In fact, we know from descriptions of other sacrifices that the captives sometimes attempted to run away or swooned and fainted on the steps of the pyramid. (In some sacrifices of young women there were elaborate efforts to distract and fool the victims about their impending death; those divine images were in fact not perfect victims going along of their "own free will.") But the implication, at least by Sahagún's informants, is that this individual was the perfect "god within a corporeal covering," ascending the temple without aid or coercion. The point is that Toxcatl was designed to display the perfect sacrifice of the perfect *ixiptla*, who was the perfect physical image of an enemy warrior who had been enculturated into Aztec ceremonial style.

The ideal sacrifice is accomplished in a remarkably simple description of the actual killing. Diego Durán reports that "four of the sacrificers seized the victim by the feet and the hands while the priest opened his chest and extracted his heart, raising it with his hands as high as he could, offering its steam to the sun."[32] Then, a special distinction is expressed in Sahagún's report, "For in this manner were all (these) captives slain. But his body they did not roll down, rather they lowered it. Four men carried it. And the severed head they strung on the skull rack."[33] While other victims were killed in this same manner, Tezcatlipoca's impersonator's body was exceptional in that it was not rolled down the stairs as was often done in other sacrifices. Rather, he was carried carefully away to where his head was severed and then displayed on the skull rack as a visual image of human destiny.

My argument that this sacrifice was meant to be the perfect sacrifice becomes enlarged. The entire ceremony is the image of the perfect life and ideal death of the elite warrior in the Aztec world, a contention reflected in the short paragraph within Sahagún's text, which constitutes a rare Aztec interpretation of their ritual: "And this betokened our life on earth. For he who rejoiced, who possessed riches, who sought, who esteemed our lord's sweetness, his fragrance—richness, prosperity—thus ended in great misery. Indeed it was said: 'No one on earth went exhausting happiness, riches, wealth.'"[34] This remarkable commentary represents in miniature a revered linguistic form in Aztec culture, namely, the *huehuetlatolli*, or "rhetorical orations of the elders." This complex linguistic form has many characteristics, but the relevant one is the commitment to formal, even lavish expressions of "oughtness" in conduct and social relationships. The *huehuetlatolli* were rhetorical orations delivered on ceremonial occasions telling how life should be lived, acted out, and gestured from generation to generation. Often these ideals were expressed using the dual form of speech *in xochitl, in cuicatl*, flower and song. In this Aztec interpretation we see the expression of a profound duality: "This is how one must live; this is how one who lives in this fashion must die." We are told that it is acceptable and even desirable to live in riches, esteeming Tezcatlipoca and his sweetness, his fragrance, his wealth. But it is also the cosmic law that a person, especially the warrior who becomes Tezcatlipoca, must undergo an elaborate initiatory elevation and humiliation, must die a perfect death, and be displayed on the skull rack. In fact, it appears that Tezcatlipoca becomes the model for all humans as "no one on earth went exhausting happiness, riches, wealth."

A HIERARCHY OF MEANING

In this performance and ceremonial landscape, the Aztecs were showing that Tezcatlipoca's perfect life and ideal death represents, through synesthesia, their way of entertaining themselves with one unity of meaning in their world, that Tezcatlipoca occupies all places always; humans occupy Tezcatlipoca's place on earth for a year at a time. The Aztec community learns and relearns this message each year. Yet we cannot ignore what has been everywhere present in some form, namely, the pervasive message of social and symbolic hierarchy and the concomitant meaning that access to the message of Tezcatlipoca's power, riches, and sweetness is not the same for all. We are faced with a performance that illustrates Stanley Tambiah's contention that synesthesia reveals both ontology and hierarchy, a oneness of meaning and a symbolism of ranking and differential access to happiness, riches, wealth—a juxtaposition emphatically performed in urban society. This combination of ontology and hierarchy is made clearer when we follow the clue of this *huehuetlatolli* fragment from Book 2 of Sahagún to the extensive prayer dedicated to Tezcatlipoca spoken by a priest on behalf of the commoners in Book 6.

The prayer begins with a lavish pouring forth of formal addresses to the god, followed by a portrayal of the condition of how

> the common folk endure suffering, endure fatigue, live in want on earth. Poverty, misery, uselessness prevail. They escape nowhere; indeed they are in dire need as they go seeking sustenance, going through all the forest, all the desert. And here, in truth they glory in their thin intestines; their viscera go stuck to their sides; go rumbling. Verily they go skin and bones, like a skeleton.[35]

This pathetic image of poverty takes on a spatial image as "they become all thin. They continue all to run about. They go about weeping, sighing. Truth they go about in great affliction. The entire day, the entire night they are ranged about the fire."[36] The priest who speaks this prayer then asks compassion of Tezcatlipoca for the common folk in this fashion:

Show mercy, have compassion for thy common folk. May thou honor them . . . with a little of thy freshness, thy tenderness, thy sweetness . . . for in truth they struggle for it. May they a little through thy grace raise their head. May they through thy grace know repose for a little time. Through thy grace may the common folk have what is necessary for their bones, their bodies. May they for a little time keep it for thee. Perhaps it will be taken, removed and hidden, concealed. That which was only for a little time, even as the flower which one hath smelled, hath marveled at.[37]

What is outstanding in this parallel statement of the sacrificial gloss discussed previously is that misery in life for the common people is to be relived with a "little" riches, which "for a little time" will give some happiness and provide limited access to the sweetness of Tezcatlipoca. The hierarchy of access is further expressed in the priest's promise to Tezcatlipoca that if the commoners try to act above their social place, they will suffer terribly.

If perhaps the people I now present before thee should become arrogant, these very same will discover, will earn as their reward, their merit, torment, pain, misery and blindness, paralysis. They will not be esteemed, will not be glorified; and they will be incapable on earth. Truly this thou wilt have in store for them. And that is also the time when they will sob, they will be terrified.[38]

The problem of unity/hierarchy deserves further investigation. The text and its interpretations suggest a redirecting of terms toward an expansion of categories to join a *hierarchy of meaning* to a *unity of meaning* when exploring synesthesias in urbanized societies. For while Tezcatlipoca may have been the Lord of Everyplace, it appears that in the spirit of his metamorphic powers, people did not have the same access to his powers in every social, geographical, or sacred place.

It is appropriate to recall the thematic context for these essays, namely, the nature and character of ceremonial centers in Mesoamerican traditions. In the past, I have focused on the spatial order and symbolic alignments of Aztec urbanism with its dynamic hierarchical tensions between centers and peripheries. Now, I am striving to combine that focus with new research into the ceremonial landscapes organized and imprinted by performance. My discussion here has attempted a rethinking of the theme of the ceremonial center by focusing on the exceptional festival of Toxcatl. While it seems correct to view the ceremonial landscape of the Mexicas as defined by both sacred spaces and locative places, the landscape of Tezcatlipoca, incompletely described here, with its prodigious, moving displays of a god's image among humankind, seems as much inhabited by shape-shifters, mosaics, magic, and metamorphosis as by *axis mundis* and bailiwicks. A broad study of the sources indicates that not just ritual but most of Mexica social life can be viewed as performances of transformations that communicate an urbanized, hierarchical way of life. These public performances mirrored and gave life to the ceremonial landscape and helped the world breathe with meaning.

This tie among the ceremonial city, metamorphosis, and hierarchy is reflected in the passage describing the crisis felt by the community on the death of a *tlatoani*. The priest, speaking of the lost ruler, prayed to Tezcatlipoca, "And the city, will it perhaps here in his absence be mocked? Will it divide? Will it scatter? Truly he came spreading his wings, his tail feather over it; truly he spread himself over it."[39]

CHAPTER 5

Give Me Some Skin

The Charisma of the Aztec Warrior

> Of the possible methods of subjugation, absorption is—theoretically at
> least—to be preferred over destruction and dispersal, not least because it
> implies an augmentation of the conqueror's own power through incor-
> poration of that of his enemy, an outcome not necessarily achieved by
> the alternative method.
>
> Paul Wheatley, *Melaka: The Transformation of a*
> *Malay Capital, c. 1400–1980*

TLACAXIPEUALIZTLI—FEAST OF THE FLAYING OF MEN[1]
In the month of Tlacaxipeualiztli (the Flaying of Men), the people
celebrated a festival in honor of Xipe Totec, Our Lord the Flayed
One.[2] One of the central acts was the sacrificing and flaying of captive
warriors and slaves who were led through an elaborate series of rituals
in the *calpultin*, or communities, and main ceremonial center of Tenochtitlan. Prior to the actual sacrifice and flaying, the warriors were
transformed into sacrificial images. In one account, slaves and captive
warriors were bathed, purified, and dressed as a *teotl ixiptla*, the living
image of the god Xipe Totec, forty days before the feast day and displayed in public in each of the city's barrios.[3] The captive warriors
were taken to Xipe Totec's temple and "put to the test" when *yopi* tortillas, representing their hearts, were torn from them. Then they were
displayed four times before the people, adorned as sacrificial victims,
and accompanied by their captors, who were also ritually adorned to
designate their honor. At the height of this festival, the victims were
given new names, forced to dance with their captors, and eventually
sacrificed either at the top of Xipe's temple or on the gladiatorial
stone. Their hearts were "torn from them," and their blood poured
into a *cuauhxicalli*, a ceremonial bowl or "the eagle vessel." Their bod-

Xipe Totec, "Our Lord the Flayed One," is shown in procession wearing the
flayed skin of an enemy warrior. Note how the arms and legs of the *teotl ixiptla*,
the living god image, is covered by the skin of the sacrificial victim. (From the
Codex Borgia. After Laurette Séjourné, *El pensamiento náhuatl cifrado por los
calendarios* [Mexico, 1981], courtesy of Siglo Veintiuno Editores, S.A.)

ies were dismembered and divided up so that several parts could be
ceremonially eaten. Before being dismembered, the sacrificed captives were flayed and their skins worn by individuals who moved
through the neighborhoods of the city and fought intense mock battles in the streets or collected gifts from the homes of citizens.

At first glance, this short description indicates the central role the
transformation of the human body played in the ritual theater of

Aztec religion. A more sustained view shows the importance of social and symbolic movements and the redistribution of the charisma of the warrior throughout the ceremonial landscape of Aztec Mexico. We will also see how this feast of the flaying of men transforms the city into the perfect battlefield where "no one fears to die in war."

This spectacular festival was a *nextlaoaliztli,* or debt payment, that covered the entire second month of the calendar cycle during which "all the captives died, all those taken, all who were made captive, the men, the women, all the children." On the day before their ritual deaths, the captives were transformed into *xipeme* or *tototecti,* meaning skinned ones or the "dead in honor of Totec," through dancing, an all-night vigil, and the cutting of hair from the crowns of their heads by their captors. The next day, offering priests seized them by the hair on the tops of their heads and forced them to climb the pyramid to the temple of Huitzilopochtli. Some captives resisted or fainted, but some "did not act like a woman; he became strong like a man, he bore himself like a man, he went speaking like a man, he went exerting himself, he went strong of heart, he went shouting . . . he went exalting his city . . . 'Already here I go: You will speak of me there in my home land.' "[4]

The captive who reflected this political sense of landscape was stretched out on the sacrificial stone by six offering priests who extracted his heart, called "precious eagle-cactus fruit," and offered it to the sun (the text says it "nourished" the sun) before it was placed in the eagle vessel. The slain captive was now called eagle man and his body was rolled "breaking to pieces, they came head over heels . . . they reached the terrace at the base of the pyramid."

This fragmented body was carried by *calpulli* elders to the local temple where the captor had previously vowed to bring a captive. Then the body was taken to the captor's house "in order to eat him," and it was cut to pieces and distributed, with one thigh going to the palace for Moctezuma and one piece of flesh eaten by the blood relatives of the captor in a bowl of dried maize stew. Then the captor was decorated with bird down, covered with chalk, and given gifts and was given the names of "sun," "chalk," and "feather" because he "had not died there in war, or else because he would yet go to die, would go to pay the debt [in war or by sacrifice]." This means that he was declared a potential sacrificial victim.

On the second day of the main festival, the "striping" (painting of red longitudinal lines on the body) of more captives took place following an all-night vigil during which hair was taken from the crowns of their heads. This hair was guarded by the captor as potent pieces of "eagle men" whose destiny after the sacrifice was to dwell "in the presence of the sun." It was said that "the eagle man is taken upward" in honor, as opposed to the fate of dwelling in the "place of the dead," that is, the underworld, for he had taken the power of an eagle man, "he who died in war went . . . sat resting in the presence of the sun." The vertical symbolism is emphasized repeatedly. This hair would guarantee honor, flowers, tobacco, and capes, and "his valor would not in vain perish: it was as if he took renown from the captive" (*contleiocujliaia* = glory, fame, grandeur). The captor was taken to the temple of Tecanman and adorned with white turkey down.

The captives and the *tototecti*, or "dead in honor of Totec," were displayed in different places in the city, arranged in rows upon white earth or grass. *Young Aztec warriors could also assume the role of* xipeme *by putting on the skins of sacrificed warriors.* They traveled from door to door collecting food for themselves and for the owners of the skins, that is, the captors. These movements through the neighborhoods were considered provocative displays, and they often resulted in boisterous, unruly mock battles between the *xipeme* and young Aztec warriors. The young warriors snatched at the navels of the *xipeme,* trying to get a piece of skin, in order to "bring out their rage, their anger."[5] The *xipeme* chased them through the ceremonial area, beating warriors with rattle sticks and arousing anger. This group was followed by an image of Xipe and the priestly figure Youhallan, or Night Drinker, who menaced the warriors, occasionally capturing them and ransoming them at a temple for turkey hens or mantles.

Then the gladiatorial sacrifice began with "the entire city" present at the spectacle to see the captives and their captors walk in procession to the gladiatorial stone following eagle and ocelot warriors who danced, pranced, and displayed shields and obsidian-bladed clubs raised in dedication to the sun.[6] Sahagún presents a detailed choreography of this dance/procession to the top of the temple of Yopitli. This boisterous display of great warriors gave way to a high moment when they descended the temple, dancing with a group of *teotl ixiptlas*, or images of gods.

Thereupon came forth, arrived, were ranged in order all the impersonators, the proxies of all the gods. They were called the lieutenants, the delegates, the impersonators. In just the same way they went. They went in order: they went together. Thus they came down: they started from there at Yopico, from the very top of the Temple of Yopitli. And when they had come to arrive down below, on the ground, on the earth, they encircled the round stone of gladiatorial sacrifice. When they had encircled it, they seated themselves. [7]

All were led by the Youallauan, the principal priest, at whose hands "would be hacked open all the eagle men."

Other people, strangers to the city, were also present. Foreign rulers and nobles "from cities which were his enemies from beyond (the mountains) . . . those with which there was war, Moctezuma secretly summoned" to the ceremony and placed behind an arbor of flowers and branches so they would not be seen by the citizens of Tenochtitlan.

Amid the sounds from conch shells, singing, and whistling the sacrifice began when the captor seized the captive by the hair, led him to the sacrificial stone where he raised *pulque* four times and drank it with a long hollow cane. A quail was beheaded for the captive and cast away. The captive was made to drink *pulque* and forced up on the round stone where a priest dressed in bear skin, the "Old Bear," tied him with the "sustenance rope" to the center of the stone. Given a war club decked with feathers, the captive was attacked by a dancing jaguar warrior armed with a war club filled with obsidian blades. The text reads,

Then they fought each other, they kept menacing each other; they threatened each other. They looked at each other well (to see) where they would smite each other, would cut each other in a dangerous place, perchance in the calf of the leg, or in the thigh, or on the head, or in the middle.

If the captive was valiant and courageous and managed to defeat four seasoned warriors, then the "left handed one" finished off the captive, "he faltered, he fainted, he fell on the surface, he threw himself down as if dead, he wished that breath might end, that he might endure it, that he might perish, that he might cast off the burden of death." [8]

Then the Night Drinker, in the image of Totec, sacrificed the captive, extracting his heart, saying, "Thus he giveth the sun to drink." These words followed the action of an offering priest who set a hollow eagle cane in the captive's breast cavity. This gesture, the submerging of the hollow cane in the blood and the raising of the blood toward the sun, meant that the sun was nourished.[9] According to Diego Durán's account, the lords of foreign provinces and cities dispersed full of "*temor y espanto*," dread and fear.

Then, in a gesture of inclusiveness, the captor, dressed with his warrior's insignia, takes the eagle bowl filled with the captive's blood to "every place . . . nowhere did he forget in the calmecas, in the calpulcos. On the lips of the stone images, . . . he placed the blood." After visiting the neighborhoods and schools, the captor left his insignia at the palace.

The body was taken to the *calpulco* where it was flayed and then taken to the captor's home, where it was cut up for a ritual meal, and those who ate "would be considered gods."[10] One thigh bone was sent to Moctezuma as a gift, while the other thigh was kept by the captor as a trophy and put up on a pole in the captor's house twenty days later.

At this point in the drama, a revealing ritual relationship is acknowledged when the captor, who cannot eat any part of his captive, says, "Shall I perchance eat my very self?" For when he had captured the enemy, he had said, "He is as my beloved son," with the captive answering, "He is my beloved father."

Then the captor lent the skin to his assistants, who, wearing the skins, begged for gifts for twenty days, after which the gifts were divided among them. In this ritual, called Neteotoquiliztli, which according to Durán meant "the impersonation of a god," some warriors added an extra layer of their insignias to the image of Xipe as it paraded in the streets. This begging ritual involved skirmishes, mock battles, and visits to family homes where the common people gave ears of maize and nobles offered clothes, feathers, and jewels. According to Durán, women would bring children out to the *xipeme,* who took them into their arms, spoke special words, circled the courtyard of the house four times, and returned the children to their mothers, who then gave gifts to these living images of Xipe.[11] The heads of the captives were also carried during the dances and it was said that "they dance with the severed heads." The visitors from cities with whom the Aztecs were at war dispersed as dancing, feasting, and adorning continued on late into the night near the great palace.

On the third day, the scene began at the "great palace" with more lavish displays as Moctezuma danced into the ceremonial center, leading the rulers from Texcoco and Tepaneca. According to Motolinía, these rulers wore the skins of the most important flayed victims. After a long, eloquent speech, Moctezuma distributed presents of cloaks and food to the warriors for their accomplishments. A description of the ceremonial dance goes,

> Then the offering priests . . . adorned themselves, they danced in quite mixed things, quite various arrays; butterfly nets, fish banners, clusters of ears of maize, coyote heads made of a paste of amaranth seeds, S-shaped tortillas, thick rolls covered with a dough of amaranth seeds which they covered on top with toasted maize, and red amaranth (only it was red feathers) and maize stalks with ears of green or tender maize.[12]

Toward the end of the month, flowers were offered:

> . . . all the various flowers which for the first time blossomed, the flowers which came (out) first, the flowers which came (out) ahead, were then given as offerings. No one first smelled them unless he would first make an offering, would give them as gifts, would lay them out as offerings . . . which spread out blossoming, spread out bursting, spread out popping into bloom-the flowers of spring.[13]

Then they ate tamales of wild amaranth seeds. And the people of the *calpulli* of Coatlan made offerings to Coatlicue, "they placed trust in her; she was their hope, they depended upon her."[14]

On the twentieth day, the captor gave a banquet for kin and friends. The captors and the men wearing skins went dancing, jumping, stinking, and wearing the skins through the streets to Xipe's temple where the dried, crackling, disintegrating human skins were placed in a basket and buried in a cave at its base. The *xipeme* bathed themselves and returned to the captor's courtyard where the captor took a thigh bone and planted "a pole of the flaying of men signifying that he had flayed a captive." At the top of the pole was a "sleeveless knotted cord jacket and small spray of heron feathers. He wrapped the thigh bone in paper and gave it a mask and this was called 'the god-captive.'" The captor held a feast for his friends and kin, and there was intoxication of the old men and women while a man dressed in the captor's insignia offered white *pulque* in four places, singing often until the month came to an end. The text reads, "Here they finished when he had done similarly in all places. It was done in no more than one day. But song did not end in the song house until they went ending when it was the feast of Uey tocoztli."

A METAMORPHIC VISION OF PLACE

Aztec religion was as much a fantastic display of sound, sense, body, and fury as it was a political statement. To put the matter differently, the ceremonies of Tenochtitlan were political dramas that displayed the supernatural substance of the human (often while dying), the social body congealing and erupting, and the state linked by the ritual movements through a ceremonial landscape that was concentrated and dispersed, local and imperial, depending on the particular ceremony. Together these performances and ritual territories communicated parts of a cognitive system that could only be known through experience and direct encounters with gods and other human beings. In the previous chapter, I explored some ritual dimensions of what I call the "metamorphic vision of place," which I believe animated much of Aztec religion. This notion was developed from a close reading of the dynamic movements between royal centers (temple and palace) and common thoroughfares (streets, neighborhoods, towns) that the deity impersonator for the great god Tezcatlipoca made during the ceremony of Toxcatl. The Aztec city was ritually mapped as an *axis mundi*, a sensitive grid, and a labyrinth.

This conception of a metamorphic place can be expanded in a new direction and in a way that complicates the model when reflecting on the Feast of the Flaying of Men. In general, Tlacaxipeualiztli shows that the metamorphosis of geographical, ritual, and social place is accompanied by a metamorphosis of power, the cosmomagical power the Aztecs believed permeated their material world and, especially, their bodies. This expansion of the model comes from the close associations between warfare, spaces of war, ritual, and places of ritual warfare. While some scholars of Aztec warfare labor to see religious symbolism and cosmology as "ex post facto rationalizations for warfare—ideological overlays to justify actions they were determined to take" and that "religion and ideology were manipulated in the service of the state,"[15] the record shows a more complex, intertwined, reciprocal relationship between war, empire, and religion. In my view, neither the battlefield nor the temple, neither politics nor religious ideology are independent, or ex post facto, of the other in the social world of the Aztec, but are in fact intertwined and interdependent.[16] Sixteenth-century descriptions of sacrificial ceremonies dedicated to warfare suggest that the Aztec capital of Tenochtitlan was ritually transformed for designated periods of time into a ceremonial battlefield where the true power of the empire was publicly perceived and rejuvenated. As we shall see, what was supremely at stake was, referring to Wheatley's formulation, a method of subjugation that was both "absorption" and "destruction and dispersal" within the sacrificially sacralized confines of the Aztec ceremonial city. Conforming to a cosmo-magical theory of sacrifice as debt payment to the hungry gods and the re-creation of divine energy, Aztec kings and priests performed rituals on enemy warriors that *absorbed their souls* into the capital, various temples, and neighborhoods through their bodily destruction and redistribution. Their blood was fed, that is, absorbed, by the statues of the gods and the sun, and their bodies, or limited parts of them, were eaten by participating citizens. In this ritual manner, the battlefield and the temple were intertwined, but primarily in the service of subjugating the former to the latter. The metamorphosis of place and power, city and battlefield, follows three important patterns.

First, the ceremonial landscape of Tlacaxipeualiztli is concentrated in the ceremonial centers and neighborhoods of Tenochtitlan. The capital is transformed into a militant ceremonial center. While in the first month of the year, Atl Caualo, the ceremonial landscape breaks out beyond the limits of the city and involves a number of mountaintop terrains and locations, covering over one hundred kilometers,[17] a quick map of the ritual dedicated to Xipe moves in the opposite direction, from outside to inside the city. The ceremonial landscape shifts from the battlefield to the island settlement and into the barrios and various *calpultin*, gaining clearer focus at the Templo Mayor and the gladiatorial stone, then spreading through streets and into homes, and back to the main ceremonial area. In this pattern, the city not only becomes a ceremonial center, it becomes a symbolic ceremonial battlefield, a cognitive map of violent cosmic and social renewal.

Second, people not only change places, they change skins and exchange "the appearance" of skins for valued objects in a number of
different places. The skins of sacrificed warriors have *careers,* that is,
they progress along a course. These careers are motivated by the Aztec
need for charisma—living, pulsating gifts of gods. These changes and
exchanges of charisma are accompanied with blessings of homes, battles in the streets, ransoms, and a hoped-for change of vision. These
skins are not just animal skins, although animal skins are used, but human skins that move around the city, embodying and dispensing charisma that is seen by all as they deteriorate and perish before the eyes.

Third, the shape and movement of some of the ritual objects and
places reveal a pattern of "pivoting the sacred." The Aztec ritual periodically relocates the center of action and therefore sacrality to a
number of different locations, resulting in controlled and random
contacts with charismatic energy and prestige. This notion of pivoting the sacred is reminiscent, on the one hand, of Paul Wheatley's focus on the pivot of the four quarters in traditional urban societies.[18]
Wheatley revealed the prominence and prestige of the quintessential
and monumental ceremonial centers and their capacity to integrate
highly structured ecological complexes in seven areas of primary urban generation. At the center of these "centroids" are cosmo-magic
circles that concentrated and clarified the worldview and the living
experience of the populace. On the other hand, the Aztec practice of
pivoting the sacred is reminiscent of Hubert and Mauss's conception
of the magic circle in the scheme of Hindu sacrifice. At the center of
the ritual space were magic circles, consecrated areas, usually temples
and altars (but also fires, holes, or poles), that functioned as "the turf
that the gods to whom sacrifice is addressed come and sit; there, invisible yet present, they attend the ceremony."[19] As we shall see, the
gods did indeed descend in bodily form during Aztec rituals and occupy the turf of moving pivots of sacrality. In what follows, I discuss
all three patterns: the city as a ceremonial battlefield, the career of
charismatic skins, and the pivoting of the sacred throughout the ceremonial landscape.[20]

THE CEREMONIAL LANDSCAPE

During this second month, the entire city, or at least many of the barrios, became part of the ceremony when the captured warriors were

brought back from war and incorporated into the city. They were distributed to the different barrios of their captors with the noblest captives taken to the nobles' communities. Diego Durán tells how men
dressed as the god Xipe were displayed in every barrio of the city.

> Once he had been purified, they honored and glorified him during forty
> days, exhibiting him in public as if he had been the god himself. The
> same was done in each ward, and these wards were like our parishes. Thus
> they had the name and avocation of the idol who made his home there;
> this was the church of the ward. . . . Thus if twenty wards existed, twenty
> men went about impersonating this god of the entire land. Each ward
> honored and revered this man who personified the deity, just as in the
> main temple.[21]

This pattern of adornment, transformation into the images of gods,
and visual incorporation into the city was repeated when the captive
warriors were "displayed four times before the people" adorned as
sacrificial victims, accompanied by their captors who were also ritually adorned to designate their honor. After these displays throughout
the city, the victims were paraded to the main ceremonial center of
the city and forced to dance in public with their captors. They traced
the path of the enemy warriors in myths, who attempted to conquer
the capital and arrived at the sacred heart of the settlement.[22]

While there is this initial *incorporation* of enemy warriors and the
images of the gods into the community, there are also moments when
a spatial awareness of center and periphery is expressed.[23] For instance, the warrior who was sacrificed on the towering Coatepec,
Serpent Mountain, cried out, if he was able, to his distant homeland.
Sahagún tells us, "he went extolling, he went exalting his city . . . he
went with firm heart: he went saying 'Already here I go: you will
speak of me there in my home land.' "[24] As mentioned earlier in the
description of the festival, the rulers from other cities, friend and foe
alike, came from "beyond the mountains" and were forced to see,
hear, and smell the central space and action of sacrifice before returning home to tell the story. The center of the world for the sacrificed warrior (and foreign rulers) is displaced during this month to the
Aztec capital, but his final words relocate him back in his homeland.

The transformation of the city into a ceremonial battlefield is
elaborated during the various public sacrifices, which take place at

two different locations, and one is, in fact, a magic circle. The initial sacrifices take place at the Great Temple of Tenochtitlan on the side of the temple dedicated to the war god Huitzilopochtli. While this sacred precinct is not shaped like a circle, it is a place of concentrated, circumscribed sacrality, the image of the cosmic mountain where primordial sacrifices were carried out in the mythic era. It is interesting that the description of the victim's body crashing down the steps after death, "rolled them over; they bounced them down. They came breaking to pieces . . . Thus they reached the terrace at the base of the pyramid," is reminiscent of the battle and sacrifice in the myth of Coyolxauhqui at Serpent Mountain. After attacking the shrine on top of the mountain, Coyolxauhqui was defeated, sacrificed, and dismembered. The text of her demise reads, "The body of Coyolxauhqui rolled down the slope, it fell apart in pieces, her hands, her legs, her torso fell in different places."[25] It is significant in light of our concern for the "magic circle" that her image is carved on a huge circular stone that was placed at the bottom of the stairs down which fell the bodies of sacrificial victims during the height of the Aztec empire.

The second place of sacrifice during the Flaying of Men, the *temalacatl*, or round gladiatorial stone, incorporates the battlefield into the city even more vividly. And in a description that is hauntingly like Marcel Mauss's language of the occupation of the gods at the sacred shrine, "the impersonators, the proxies of all the gods . . . came down: . . . from the very top of the Temple of Yopitli" in order to witness the ritual combat. In Mauss's terms, they do indeed come and sit on the turf of sacrifice. "And when they had come to arrive down below, on the ground, on the earth, they encircled the round stone of gladiatorial sacrifice. When they had encircled it, they seated themselves. They were in order upon large backed seats called roseate spoonbill feather seats."[26] Then amid the cacophony of musical instruments and the whistling with "fingers placed in the mouth, and there was singing," the captors seized a captive and took him to the round stone of sacrifice. After raising *pulque* four times in dedication, the captives were forced to drink and climb onto the round stone, where they were tied with a "sustenance" rope to the center of the stone and forced to fight a series of Aztec warriors while the community watched. The text reads,

> Then they fought each other, they kept menacing each other . . . they
> looked at each other well (to see) where they would smite each other,
> would cut each other in a dangerous place . . . and if some captive was val-
> iant, courageous . . . He met all four of the ocelot [and] eagle warriors, he
> fought them. And if they could not weaken him, then there went one
> who was left-handed. Then this one wounded his arms; he felled him, he
> felled him flat. This one appeared as [the god] Opochtli. And although
> the striped one already faltered, already weakened, also he quite acquitted
> himself as a man; he still acquitted himself as a man.[27]

In this stirring scene, the combat of the battlefield is represented
before the populace of the city but without the variables, accidents,
and defeats of the battlefield, or in modern terms, without the fog of
war. This elimination is a crucial factor in the achievement of what
J. Z. Smith calls a "controlled environment." The Aztecs had constructed a dramatically controlled environment in which the spec-
tators could perceive the perfect power of their warriors in a condensation and idealization of Aztec warfare. This condensation of
battlefield to city was further represented in the use of the ritual "eagle vessel," the *cuauhxicalli*, a circular wooden or stone vessel in which
the heart and blood of the sacrificial warrior was placed. In a display
of the spreading of charismatic power, the vessel was carried throughout the city and symbolically saturated space. The text tells us that it
was carried "to every place. Nowhere did he forget in the *calmecacs*
in the *calpulcos*. On the lips of stone images, on each one, he placed
the blood of his captive. He made them taste it with his hollow cane."

Once the victim had been sacrificed and skinned, the skins were
worn by the captor's assistants in prodigious displays of male power
and success. As these skins worn by Aztec males moved through the
city, the experience of the ideal battlefield permeated the public
spaces of Tenochtitlan and transformed the neighborhoods into miniature battlefields. Mock battles broke out, but the texts indicate that
anger, wrath, wounds, capture, and ransom were serious parts of the
play. Groups roved through the streets looking for the men wearing
Xipe's skin, to attack and attempt to snatch a piece of skin from the
navels of the hanging skins. The concentration of mock war into the
space of the neighborhoods was repeated again in one of the closing
acts of the month. After the family ritual meal had taken place and the
xipeme deposited the skins in a ritual cave, bathed themselves (they

hadn't bathed for twenty days and the text tells us the sound of slap-
ping their skins to clean off the grease was "like the breaking of ocean
waves"), the captor chose a man, reminiscent of the festival of Toxcatl, "pleasing to look upon, acceptable, strong," and adorned him
with another skin, the skin of trees, or paper worn by Xipe. He broke
out into the streets "dispersing people, . . . vexing them, rattling his
rattle board." As he fought people who pelted him with stones, he
captured some, took their capes, and returned this collection to his
captor's house as though returning from distant lands to his own city,
with booty.

THE BODY AS CHARISMA

As Alfredo López Austin shows in his discussion of the correlation
between the human body and the universe, the objects of the Aztec
material world were charged and animated with supernatural forces,
penetrated by celestial beings, receptacles of "divine fire." Possession,
or the transformation of a person's body into a container of a god's energy, was not just an illusion of a small group of priests, but the
worldview and ethics of the entire community. He writes,

> For the Nahuatl man, some of the supernatural beings had a reality as
> present, as immediate, as daily as he could capture through his senses. The
> supernatural was judged to be material, potentially visible, tangible and
> audible. It was remote from man because of man's limitations but man
> was immersed in the supernatural. When the human being believed he
> could not break his own barriers of perception, he thought the world re-
> vealed itself to him more fully.[28]

This crossing of the membranes between the visible and invisible world is reflected in Tlacaxipeualiztli in the extraordinary array
of physical objects sought after, touched, smelled, seen, carried,
snatched, killed for, distributed, or eaten. And no object is more powerful, visible, or changed than the human body. The hair is grabbed
and cut, bodies are ransomed, draped, and striped, the legs are
wounded, the corpse dragged, thrown, and dismembered, the heart is
extracted, the head is paraded, the blood is spread, and, most impres-
sively, the skins of sacred men are worn and displayed throughout the
city. Also, military "emblems" are eagerly sought out, worn, and even

draped over the skins to be displayed. These layered symbols (skins decorated with emblems) are used for the collection of food and gifts from neighborhoods and royal houses. Furthermore, people are transformed into surreal images of other bodies consisting of butterflies, fish, corn, nets, gods, and warriors.

I find this pattern of the concentration of cosmo-magical power in selected material objects reminiscent of Stanley Tambiah's study of the Buddhist saints of the forest and the cult of amulets, where the transmission of charisma is accomplished through special treatment and display of material objects associated with sacralized human bodies. Charisma, whether seen from the point of view of Max Weber, Edward Shils, or Clifford Geertz, or of their informants, for that matter, is understood as a unique magical quality *perceived* to reside in an extraordinary person, place, or thing, contributing to its being revered as a locus of ultimate value and supernatural energy. Tambiah writes about charisma in Thai Buddhism,

> Sacralized amulets in the form of small images of the Buddha or famous saints or of medallions struck with the faces and busts of the same, and amulets of other shapes and representations are an old phenomenon in Thailand. There are classical and medieval classifications and systems of names for this fecund variety of sacred objects—relics, statues, images, *stupa* monuments, etc. and complex explanations of their roles and uses. These explanations range from their pious considerations as "reminders" to their awed treatment as "sacra" radiating fiery energy and protective or fertilizing powers. In fact, one finds on pursuing this question that the beliefs and attitudes surrounding amulets are virtually of the same kind as those surrounding famous Buddha statues which are credited with supernormal powers.[29]

While I cannot go into a full exposition of Tambiah's interpretation here, suffice it to say that charisma embodied in amulets, statues, and the bodies of those who wear them communicate two kinds of vital knowledge—cosmological and social knowledge. Tambiah has shown how performative knowledge includes both cosmic symbolism and social symbols of hierarchy. These " 'sacra' radiating fiery energy" communicate both the "immanent ordering principle of the cosmos" and "an expression of the differential potencies and power relations emanating from a society's classified positions." That is, charisma becomes power perceived as both cosmic orientation and social status.[30]

Tambiah offers a valuable lead for a new understanding of the tie between Tlacaxipeualiztli, warfare, and cosmology. But in Aztec society the charisma, or the objectification of power so that it can be perceived, was expressed in a fecund variety of sacred objects, one of the most powerful being the sacrificed human body and in particular the skin and body parts of the sacrificed warrior. Human skin, the container of all that is human, is taken from the body, worn by other humans, and paraded through the city to evoke mock combats, trigger gift exchanges, and most of all to communicate information about the power of social order and the cosmos. The skins are seen, smelled, heard, touched, grabbed, and transformed. In a gesture reminiscent of the desire for brief intimacy in our own culture, the citizens of Tenochtitlan act out "give me some skin" as they snatch at the navels of skins worn by young warriors boasting their own power in vivid displays. The nature of power associated with skins is reflected in Durán's "discovery" of the meaning of the name Totec as "Awesome and Terrible Lord Who Fills One Up with Dread." And we can see that the acquisition of charisma starts at the moment the Aztec warriors cut hair from their captives. The text reads that the captor was being transformed through this cutting into an "eagle man," one who moves upward to the sun. The text also states, "it was as if he took 'contleiocujliaia' [i.e., fame, glory, or grandeur] from him" resulting in the subsequent acquisition of other objects, "flowers, honor, tobacco, cloaks."

As the skins move, along with the other parts of the warrior's body, so charisma moves and maps out a ceremonial landscape that transforms the people and the city. I want to emphasize that it is not just the skins, but the changing of skins, coverings filled with the charisma of sacrificed warriors and the sacrifice, that enables people to "change place." On the one hand, social place is transformed when the wearer of skin is socially elevated through the acquisition of charisma and displays of public courage. Upstart local warriors also gain social status by acquiring some of the skin under their fingernails. On the other hand, ontological place, or cosmological rank, is changed as humans become god images. The sacrificed warriors become "eagle men," and as the text says about eating the flesh, the family of the captor is "considered as gods." We are witness to a performance that communicates two kinds of knowledge and changes social position and cosmological understanding.

PIVOTING THE SACRED: THE CAREER
OF THE HUMAN BODY

In reviewing the career of the human body in this festival, I am impressed with the number of transitions and types of changes it undergoes. From the moment of the captive's appearance as a whole body to his last manifestation as a thigh bone, a "god mask" in the captor's domestic space, he undergoes a process of fragmentation and transportation. He is, literally, redistributed throughout the ceremonial landscape. The enemy warrior is first changed into a captive who has lost his social identification, symbolized by the cutting of his hair. This cutting begins the process of fragmentation and reduction that leads to a radical change in his mode of being. The intention of the change is indicated in his new name, a *tototecti*, or the Dead in Honor of Totec. Even while alive he is already considered dead, a walking corpse among walking people. It could be said that he is the ideal enemy—already dead, whose shell and innards belong to the god and the city. Then he is painted in red stripes, as he is to lose his own corporeality and become incorporated into Aztec ceremonial space and eventually into the bodies of the Aztecs. The physical reduction continues when he is cut open and his heart extracted to nourish the sun. This change gives way to a gesture of symbolic transcendence when his heart is lifted up as his body falls down, and he is designated an eagle man. "Hence it was said: 'The eagle man is taken upwards,' because indeed he who died in war went, went looking, sat resting in the presence of the sun. That is, he did not go to the place of the dead." Rather, he acquired the quality of lightness, the power to rise up. His blood is symbolically sucked up by the gods when the hollow tube is placed in his bloody chest cavity. The transformation continues when he is thrown down the steps of the Great Temple, his bones breaking to pieces. His shell is completely broken open when he is skinned and remains a completely vulnerable corpse. Durán writes, "Other men donned the skins immediately and then took the names of the gods who had been impersonated. Over the skins they wore garments and insignia of the same divinities, each man bearing the name of the god and considering himself divine."[31]

These skins are taken over by Aztecs at many levels of the hierarchy, the king, the priests, seasoned warriors, and novices. The skins of enemies mark and link up different levels of the social order, while the structure of the hierarchy is maintained as Moctezuma and the nobles wear and dance in the more powerful, valuable skins.

The pivoting of the sacred is stepped off in a ritual episode linking the *ixiptla* to cosmic organization. Durán writes of this pivoting, which is directed toward the cardinal points of the Aztec world,

> Over the skins they wore garments and insignia of the same divinities, each man bearing the name of the god and considering himself divine. So it was that one faced the east, another the west, another the north, and still a fourth the south, and each one walked in that direction toward the people. Each of these had tied to him certain men as if they were his prisoners, thus showing his might. This ceremony was called Neteotoquiliztli, which means Impersonating of a God.[32]

Yet there is one more decisive act of sacred transition and incorporation, the ingestion of the captive's substance into the Aztec body. But the route of incorporation, even to the stomach, is not primarily through the mouth, but through the senses, through a process similar to what is called synesthesia. Before discussing the eating of charisma, let us turn to this idea.

SYNESTHESIA

A recent development in the study of theater and ritual gives emphasis to the anthropology of experience and especially the process of synesthesia, which awakens, in the ceremonial atmosphere, the whole human organism to the ontological and political message of rituals. While some studies define synesthesia as the unity of the senses, which enable the unity of meaning to be understood and internalized,[33] another approach emphasizes the relationship between sensory perception and a moral factor, the awareness of moral action and responsibility. Following Smith's definition of ritual, synesthesia awakens one to the controlled environment so that a controlled message of right conduct, or right performance of duty and meaning, can be held together. In this view, notions akin to justice, responsibility, and ethical conduct become accessible not only to the mind, but to the entire sensory equipment of the species. Awareness is joined to oughtness and power to behavior. An example appears in Durán's account of "a great sermon . . . pronounced by one of the dignitaries" after the enormous displays of skins, emblems, and body parts. The speech was filled with a series of elegant metaphors and delivered in an elegant style. The orator referred to "our human misery, our low state, and to how much we owe to Him who created us. . . . He extolled fear, reverence, modesty, breeding, prudence, civility, submission and obedience, charity toward poor and wandering strangers."[34] In the midst of the grand theatrical displays comes a message that joined the senses to the moral responsibility of the populace.

Consider the interrelationship of control and synesthesia in the visual and olfactory career of Tlacaxipeualiztli. When the captives were brought into the city, they were paraded and distributed throughout the barrios of the city. These captive warriors within the city made an immense impression. Their reputations certainly proceeded them, as nearly berserk men whose powers of expression seemed on the edge of the sheer ideal. Consider this description by the "Anonymous Conqueror" of enemy warriors in the field.

> One day an Indian I saw in combat with a mounted horseman struck the horse in the chest, cutting through to the inside and killing the horse on the spot. On the same day I saw another Indian give a horse a sword thrust in the neck that laid the horse dead at his feet. It is one of the most beautiful sights in the world to see them in their battle array because they keep formation wonderfully and are very handsome. Among them are extraordinary brave men who face death with absolute determination. I saw one of them defend himself courageously against two swift horses, and another against three and four, and when the Spanish horseman could not kill him one of the horseman in desperation hurled his lance, which the Indian caught in the air and fought with him for more than an hour, until two foot soldiers approached and wounded him with two or three arrows. He turned on one of the soldiers but the other grasped him from behind and stabbed him. During combat they sing and dance and sometimes give the wildest shouts and whistles imaginable, especially when they know they have the advantage. Anyone facing them for the first time can be terrified by their screams and their ferocity. In warfare they are the cruelest people to be found, for they spare neither brothers, relatives, friends nor women even if they are beautiful they kill them all and eat them.[35]

The image of these berserk warriors who would be progressively reduced to their skin and bones in the shackles of the Aztecs demon-

strated superior power and a moral order to the populace of Tenochtitlan. The ultimate expression of a controlled environment, where
power was perceived as ontological and hierarchical, takes place at the
gladiatorial stone—a miniature magic circle of warfare. It is here that
synesthesia is concentrated and a fusion of senses is achieved. All the
forces of the Aztec world gathered to watch the perfect battle. Even
the gods descend from above, being led by the warriors out of the
shrines, as if from the sky, and come to circle the gladiatorial stones.
These spectacular images, specters even, apparitions of the great gods
appear at the site of sacrifice. They are openly seen and display themselves while the rulers from other communities are hidden, masked
by a membrane or skin of branches and leaves. Beyond this inner circle the "entire city was present at this spectacle."

In the action that ensued, all the variables and dangers for the
Aztecs were gone. The dangers of the battlefield were eliminated as
the enemy weapons were dismembered of their obsidian blades and
replaced with the swaying feathers. Then the attack took place in a
five-to-one ratio in which the enemy was worn down, weakened,
wounded, killed, and his heart was "torn from him." All this was surrounded by a dancing, drumming, whistling, horn blowing ensemble
of warriors, priests, gods, and lords, amidst a display of shields. The
senses were awakened to more than they could handle, and the message was monumental. The text emphasizes not just the defeat of the
enemy, but his defeat, surrender, sacrifice, and transcendence into the
Aztec cosmos. The text tells how he is finished off when "he throws
himself down as dead, he wished . . . he might perish," which he does
when the deity impersonator, the left-handed one, extracts his heart
and "giveth the sun to drink."

EATING CHARISMA
This concentrated play of conflict, victory, sacrifice, and offering, the
seeing, hearing, and smelling of death is spread, vividly, through the
city in at least two ways. First, the blood of the victim is carried to
many temples in the city, saturating space with the charisma of the eagle man to all the *calmecacs*. The blood is spread, touching the stone,
wooden, and perishable images of gods. The sacred circle pivots and
moves with the precious blood. Second, the circle of a controlled environment expands and sways through the city as the skins are worn,

fought over, and seen. The message of this synesthesia is "we capture the enemy, we humiliate him, we sacrifice him, dismember him, and incorporate him into our cosmos, we wear him and now we ingest him."

In this sequence, we see a ritual of complete *absorption and incorporation*. This intimacy is what is reflected in that puzzling ritual exchange of close kinship when the captor and captive are *supposed* to acknowledge that they are father and son. While the details of this cannibalistic meal are sparse, it is clear that a careful distribution or, in fact, a redistribution takes place. The body is relocated from the sacrificial stone to the neighborhood of the captor and then to his home "in order to eat him. There they portioned him out. They cut him to pieces and they distributed him." This distribution has hierarchy in it for "First of all, they made an offering of one of his thighs to Moctezuma. They set forth to take it to him." While the thigh is in movement, the blood relatives of the captor travel to his house and "there they made each one an offering of a bowl of dried maize called tlacoalloi. They gave it to each one. On each went a piece of the flesh of the captive."

The final gesture of control and incorporation appears when the captor sets up his "pole of the flaying of men" in his courtyard, a display for his neighbors that he has flayed a captive. But this pole is transformed when an image of the god, in the form of the captive's thigh bone, is masked with a "sleeveless knotted cord jacket" and a small spray of heron feather and paper is attached. This complex image is called a "god captive." Interestingly, the thigh is skinned of any flesh before display, a miniature example of the earlier flaying.[36]

A CAREER OF SKINS
The patterns of metamorphosis are clearest in the movement of skins, fluid signs of Aztec warfare, and the charismatic body. They move, provoke, invite gift exchanges, and deteriorate. They are worn by various groups—beggars, warriors, warrior's helpers, and even the ruler. Many people are transformed, momentarily, into Xipes, but Xipes of different rank. They are not just worn, however, they travel. For days they are paraded through the neighborhoods, seen and touched by mothers and children, revealing to the populace the destiny of the enemy warrior and, by association, the destiny of the Aztec warrior sac-

rificed in enemy towns. These images of the gods enter into homes, circumambulate the courtyards as if sacralizing the space into a magic circle, and receive gifts.

We cannot overestimate the visual power of this ceremony. It is the seeing of power that dominates the final stages of the month. In this case, what the population sees are layers of charisma, in the forms of various coverings, sacred membranes, skins, and emblems. They see the impersonators wearing the costumes of gods. They see the emblems of war, the images of successful violence covering some of the skins of sacrificed beings, and transformed enemies who were slain by men wearing skins of bears, eagles, jaguars. All these layers are permeable membranes, projecting and releasing the powers of gods, courage, sacrifice, and animals into the atmosphere of the city and its cosmos.

AUTHORITY AND WAR

Given the dynamic and complex relationship between war beyond the city and the ritual performances of warfare within the neighborhoods, I wonder about the efficacy for understanding empire using Ross Hassig's persistent dichotomy of politics/religion and ideology/practical necessity. Did the Aztecs view the world, or act within their world, as if what we refer to as war, religion, ideology, force, power, and empire were separate entities? I do not think so. One scholar who has a different view of the relationship between ritual and warfare is Johanna Broda, who illuminates the *expressive* relationships between religion and war, ideology and force. Throughout her work she shows how either/or dichotomizing restricts rather than expands our understanding of Aztec warfare. For example, in her "Relaciones políticas ritualizadas: el ritual como expresión de una ideología," she examines the tissues of relations between myth, cult, economic expansion, and warfare under the authority of Aztec *tlatoque*. She writes,

> Myth and cult form a unity with very complex interrelationships that often cannot be explained in a logical manner; also this ensemble has been historically constructed. We have seen that the ceremonies analyzed in my work were intimately connected with social stratification and with relationships of domination and power. The cult provided an ideological justification for these phenomena. Also the cult gives a justification for the imperial expansion and for war as an instrument to establish power.

> Through their participation in the ceremonies, the commoners and the lords accept the government of the ruler and they are confirmed in their position as vassals, while the foreign lords accept the supremacy of Tenochtitlan and are assured in this way of their own superiority as a dominant class.[37]

My work here attempts to further develop Broda's insistence on the tissues of relations between war and religion, ideology and cult. One vital element in her discussion, which is largely ignored in Hassig's work, is the pervasive role of authority and especially royal authority grounded in religious belief and myth. It is true that Hassig writes informatively about specific rulers and their campaigns, but we learn very little about the conceptions undergirding rulership and its prodigious cult, power, force, and sense of destiny. In my view, it is the metamorphic careers of these warriors' bodies that reveal the *expressive relations* of the Aztec capital in ways that have not been seen. It is the case, as Broda states, that ritual is an expression of an ideology of warfare. It is also the case that warfare is nurtured and directed by rituals like Tlacaxipeualiztli.

A MOVABLE CENTER

The Feast of the Flaying of Men is a story of the metamorphosis of the body of the captured warrior as it moved throughout the ceremonial landscape, a landscape marked and linked by the passage and contact with charismatic objects associated with war, conquest, sacrifice, and transcendence. The gorgeous and terrible displays of warriors draped in the dripping skins of sacrificial victims and the *cuauhxicalli* filled with blood moving throughout the city show that Tlacaxipeualiztli was a story the Aztecs told to themselves about their triumphant wars, in the way they wanted it known.

In this sometimes terrifying and visually striking ceremony, we are presented with a process of metamorphosis of place and power. Although it is a controlled environment, it is not stationary or permanent. In fact, it is a fleeting, decomposing, perishable world. There are transformations within transformations, a magic circle that pivots, dashes, and circumambulates. In my view, this entire festival linking the ceremonial center with the battlefield gives new meaning to the celebrated idea of an *axis mundi*. In several theories of sacrifice, the magic circle, sacred ground, or controlled environment is either an end point (the perfect kill, hunt, or gift) or the starting point (the sympathetic magical place that is to influence the kill, hunt, or gift exchange). In the first approach, the sacrifice completes, while in the second, it produces. Yet each approach tends to look at the ritual from the perspective of the priest or the academic. When we change the perspective from the priest to the observer, deity impersonator, mother carrying child, teenager in the street, or novice in training, the ceremony as a perfect battle *is a middle place, the pivotal place in a process of production and completion.* It is both the end point and the starting point. It is a perfect battle after the war and a magical display to the citizens of how things should go in the next war. It is a public victory within the city and a preparation for a future battle. It is an ideal recollection and an anticipatory ceremonial practice because it provides a clear cognitive and experiential system or map. The vital element in this notion of middle place—at once a statement of how it should have gone and of how it should go—*is the public accumulation of charisma.* The synesthesia of smelling, seeing, smearing, wearing, and touching takes the dynamics of the battlefield and changes it into the dynamics of the ceremonial center where it spreads to the dynamics of everyday life in preparing for the next expansion of the magic circle and wearing of skins. As Ross Hassig states, power perceived is empire, but as Tlacaxipeualiztli shows, power in the Aztec world was perceived as much in ceremonies of sacrifice and their charismatic transformations as in the stomping, moving hoards who blazed like a sacred fire in the lands beyond the capital city.

CHAPTER 6

Cosmic Jaws
We Eat the Gods and the Gods Eat Us

By the time the Spanish army led by Fernando Cortés fought and talked its way into the Halls of Moctezuma in 1519, some Europeans had become aware that Indians periodically ate parts of human beings. Christopher Columbus had reported that one island he explored was "inhabited by a people who are regarded in all the islands as very fierce and who ate human flesh."[1] Amerigo Vespucci claimed that he had actually met a cannibal who told him he had eaten more than two hundred human beings. This encounter, plus the lack of set mealtimes among the natives, was supposedly proof that the Indians lacked real civilization! These and other reports were partially based on "fact" but also upon the time-honored European interpretive framework, which since the time of Herodotus turned the inhabitants living at the edge of the known world into one kind of monstrosity or another.[2] One fifteenth-century account of cannibalism that may have influenced the perceptions of both Columbus and Vespucci as well as their translators (later translators claimed Vespucci's native had eaten three hundred bodies) was John Mandeville's popular description of the world outside the West, which reads as something like what we might label the first Barnum and Bailey Circus. Anthony Grafton writes in *New Worlds, Ancient Texts*, "In Mandeville's account Christian miracle working monks coexist with Pliny's monstrous races, the anthropophagi, Amazons, one-eyed men, blemmyes, and dogheads, one legged men whose feet were so large they could be used as parasols against the blistering sun."[3]

Addressing the problem of cannibalism directly, the anonymous author known as Mandeville wrote, "But in that country there is such

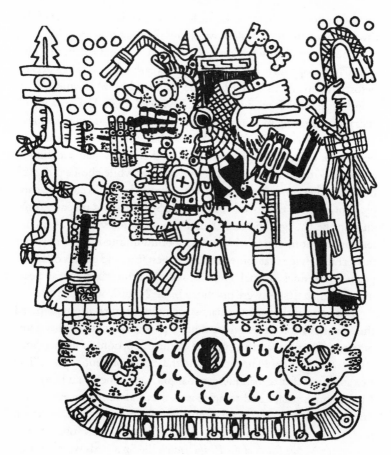

The gods of death and life, Mictlantecuhtli and Quetzalcoatl Ehecatl, are joined at the spine and hover over the earth's "cosmic jaws" in this scene from the *Codex Vatincanus B*. Also note the emphasis on the mouths of the gods, one shown as a hungry skull mouth and the other as wind trumpet. (After Laurette Séjourné, *El pensamiento náhuatl cifrado por los calendarios* [Mexico, 1981], courtesy of Siglo Veintiuno Editores, S.A.)

a cursed custom, for they eat more gladly man's flesh than any other flesh. . . . Thither go merchants and bring with them children to sell to them of the country, and they buy them . . . And they say that it is the best flesh and the sweetest of all the world."[4] This surprising avowal, that the tastiest meat in a world of committed meat eaters is human flesh, was joined by the author to the widely held view of the times, that eating human flesh was a morally distasteful practice.

These attitudes toward New World cannibalism were more widespread in Europe than we may think, for as early as 1505, over a decade before the Spaniards arrived on the mainland of Mesoamerica, an Augsburg publisher produced a widely viewed single-leaf drawing of Indians celebrating in a cannibal feast. There they stand in nakedness, decorated with leaves and bespeckled with feathers, female breasts exposed—one for a suckling infant and others for visual suckling—conversing, touching, and eating one another while choice pieces of human bodies, a head here, an arm there, and a buttocks close by, dangle above from a freshly cut arbor while Spanish ships prepare to anchor in the background and change the scene forever.[5] This single-leaf publication, along with others, communicated the simple but powerful message that some of the strongest fears and desires of Europeans—nakedness, sexual freedom, and the dismemberment and eating of human flesh—were practiced in the New World.

But none of these texts, images, accounts, or fabrications prepared the Spaniards for either Moctezuma's lavish banquets or the Aztec practice of human sacrifice and the eating of portions of human bodies that they witnessed in and around the capital of Tenochtitlan. The extraordinary feasts, banquets, ritual practices, smells, and tastes of Moctezuma's palace and temples were beyond compare. As the influential anthropologist Lewis Henry Morgan was to report in 1876 in his "Montezuma's Dinner," a 43-page book review of Hubert Howe Bancroft's *Native Races of the Pacific States,* the Spaniards were both attracted to and repelled by Aztec food, at once a royal feast and in Morgan's exaggeration a residue of human carnage.[6] The best though problematic description of this complex meal, that is, "Montezuma's Dinner," comes from Bernal Díaz del Castillo's eyewitness account of the banquet. The footsoldier, now grown old and writing as much to discredit other writers as to provide a record of his memories, remembered that Moctezuma was fed thirty different dishes, all kept warm for his inspection, and that he ate behind a screen decorated with gold images of "idols," sitting at a table with a table cloth and "rather long napkins" where four beautiful, clean women and four old chiefs served him in red and black Cholula earthenware, while he was entertained by hunchbacks, jesters, and dancers. Then, the ominous hearsay passage,

I have heard it said that they were wont to cook for him the flesh of young boys, but as he had such a variety of dishes, made of so many things, we could not succeed in seeing if they were human flesh or of other things, for they daily cooked fowls, turkey, pheasants, native partridge, quail, tame and wild ducks, venison, wild boar, reed birds, pigeons, hares and rabbits, and many sorts of birds and other things which are bred in this country, and they are so numerous that I cannot finish naming them in a hurry; so we had no insight into it but I know for certain that after our Captain censured the sacrifice of human beings, and the eating of their flesh, he ordered that such food not be prepared for him thenceforth.[7]

Elsewhere, apparently more sure of himself, Díaz del Castillo describes the process of sacrifice and cannibalism, "Then they cut off the thighs, arms and head and eat the former at feasts and banquets, and the head they hang up on some beams, and the body of the man sacrificed is not eaten but given to these fierce animals."[8]

Fifteen years ago, these descriptions and practices were the center of an academic firestorm that still simmers today. On the one hand, a few anthropologists like Marvin Harris and Michael Harner offer the sensational and silly argument that Aztec cannibalism was a solution for protein deficiency within a material world of population pressures and famine. The result was the creation of the "cannibal kingdom" of the Aztecs.[9] A series of critical essays appeared in *Science, Natural History,* and *Human Nature* and in the letters to the editor section of the *New York Review of Books* and the *Mexico City News,* which effectively demolished this interpretation.[10] And privately, angry letters dashed back and forth across the country between old friends and new adversaries about issues of withholding, distorting, and ignoring data and projecting theories. A second group of scholars and critics led by Marshall Sahlins took the position that a ritual explanation was adequate to explain the Aztec purposes and meanings expressed in large-scale sacrifice and ritual cannibalism. In my view, a more contextual approach, sensitive to certain discoveries in the history of religions and organized by the study of Aztec cosmovision, provides another road to understanding some dimensions of Aztec eating and cannibalistic practices. This approach is akin to Stanley Tambiah's view of rituals as "amalgams or totalities constituted of both word and deed . . . " influenced to a large degree by cosmology. Tambiah insists that cosmology is

... embedded in ritual action. Cosmologies (and cosmogonies) nearly always, and classifications frequently, tend to be viewed as enduring arrangements of things and persons, their underlying premises and initial ordering seen either as having an existence outside the flux of ordinary and everyday changing events and expectations, or as motivating and generating to some degree the surface everyday phenomena of the present time.[11]

In order to understand the prominence of jaws, mouths, tongues, eating gestures, and the rituals of using the mouth to eat human beings and, in the case of at least one god, to eat the sins of human beings, I will follow Tambiah's lead and seek out the mythic materials that point to the "underlying premises" and "enduring arrangements of things and persons" reflected in Moctezuma's Dinner. As we shall see, the Aztecs were obsessed with the problems and possibilities of eating almost anything, and they developed a sophisticated cosmology of eating in which gods ate gods, humans ate gods, gods ate humans and the sexual sins of humans, children in the underworld suckled from divine trees, gods in the underworld ate the remains of humans, and adults in the underworld ate rotten tamales! It is also important to note that at certain points in their sacred history, the Aztecs conceived of beings in their sky as a devouring mouth and the earth as a gaping jaw.

In this chapter, I explore the theme of cosmic jaws, in which the sky is a mouth and the earth is a jaw, by examining four types of evidence: (1) pictorial images of mythic or cosmic events, (2) sculptural and written images of Tlaltecuhtli, the Earth Lord, and the Sun God, Tonatiuh, (3) prayers and songs depicting eating in the underworld, and (4) the ritual practice of using the mouth to confess sexual sins, which are then eaten by the goddess Tlazolteotl who punishes the tongues of humans. This will allow us to gain some insight into ways in which the "mythic structure" of Aztec cannibalism was embedded in rituals of eating human beings and gods.[12] In my view, these myths and practices show a powerful tension at work in Aztec life, a tension between their realization that life was inescapably tied to the laws of decomposition and putrefaction, while at the same time, humans and gods, in order to survive for "a little while here," were constantly in the hunt for vital forces embedded in the bodies of gods, humans, and plants.[13] A clue to the urgency of the cannibalistic meal caused by these contradictions, an urgency that cemented the "enduring arrangement of things and persons" together, can be glimpsed in this claim by the Dominican priest Diego Durán, who grew up in Mexico in the decades immediately following the military conquest of Tenochtitlan. He writes, "The flesh of all those who died in sacrifice was held truly to be consecrated and blessed. It was eaten with reverance, ritual, and fastidiousness—as if it were something from heaven."[14]

As we shall see, the Aztecs claimed, and to a real extent believed, that the flesh they were tearing from the bodies of warriors was a sanctified substance, the flesh of the gods, or as they referred to the warrior's heart, "a precious eagle-cactus fruit."[15] In addition, I will explore one of the most interesting Aztec oral acts, the guilty rhetoric of sexual sinners whose words were eaten by the sacred force of the earth. My task in this chapter is to outline and interpret some of the enduring ideas, myths, and beliefs that brought about the magical transformation of a human body into a divine body so that part of it could be eaten and used to sanctify the mouth that ate.

MYTHIC MORSELS

> The cosmological perspective implies that ritual acts cannot be fully comprehended except as part of a larger frame of cultural presuppositions and beliefs which provide the phenomenological and subjective basis for engaging in the ritual in question.[16]

The mythic episodes, or morsels of gods eating gods or human beings, can be found in a variety of Mesoamerican texts, including pictorial, architectural, and ethno-historical data. The title for this section, "Mythic Morsels," comes from a fragment of research carried out by the anthropologist Tim Knab among the Nahua Indians of San Miguel in the Sierra del Puebla, Mexico. His work gives us a contemporary clue to the larger frame of cultural presuppositions of Aztec cannibalism. Knab records,

> The earth, the most holy earth, *santisima tierra, talticpac wan talocan,* is the source of life for the people of San Miguel. As they themselves say:
>> We live HERE on the earth (stamping on the mud floor)
>> we are all fruits of the earth
>> the earth sustains us
>> we grow here, on the earth and lower
>> and when we die we wither in the earth

> we are ALL FRUITS of the earth (stamping on the mud floor).
> We eat of the earth
> then the earth eats us.[17]

I am impressed with two themes in this song: the theme of *duality*, in which the earth is both edible and an eater, and the theme of the *exchange* relationship between the earth and humans. These themes of exchange and the duality of eating stand at the center of the meaning of mythic cannibalism in other parts of Mesoamerica.[18]

Perhaps the most extravagant image of the earth eating a human being, or the earth as an "eating landscape" as Phil Arnold has it in his study of the sacrifice of children in the month of Atlcahualo,[19] comes from the sarcophagus lid of the Maya Lord Pacal's tomb. Pacal was a seventh-century Maya ruler in the Classic ceremonial city of Palenque. He reigned for sixty-eight years, from 615 to 683 c.e., and his death marked a serious crisis in the royal succession. He was buried within, actually *beneath*, the Temple of the Inscriptions, hidden away in a sealed chamber within the earth. The elaborately carved sarcophagus lid is focused by a central image, that is, Pacal falling into the underworld in the form of a huge gaping jaw. The art historian Linda Schele describes the scene:

> On the top of the lid, Pacal himself is shown teetering at the beginning of his fall into the Maw of the Underworld, which is represented by two great dragon skulls set with their lower jaws joined below him. He poises, half sitting and half reclining, atop the head of the Quadripartite Monster, the symbol of the sun. In death, Pacal falls into Xibalba, along with the setting sun. Pacal and the Sun Monster have fallen down the axis mundi, the World Tree at the center of the world, represented by cross symbols rising above Pacal in the center of the sarcophagus lid. The branches of the tree terminate in bloodletting bowls and streams of blood, represented by square-nosed dragons with jade beads in their mouth. The trunk is marked by God C, another symbol of blood; in this instance God C also refers to the sap of the tree. Sacrificial blood, then, is likened to the sap of the tree and is the medium through which the souls of the dead move from level to level in the Maya universe.[20]

There are two notions in Schele's description that I want to emphasize. First is the cosmological status given to the image of eating. In the Maya case, the eating earth is part of the vertical cosmos along which the action takes place. This cosmos is ordered by a World Tree

that represents the three levels of the Maya cosmovision—the Over-
world, the Earthly Level, and the Underworld of Xibalba. Royal
death is placed within this larger frame of reference, and the jaws of
the underworld constitute, *literally*, the underlying premise of the
scene. Second, the act of swallowing the dead ruler is the start of a
journey through the Maya underworld, the world of Xibalba, which
in Pacal's case is like the sun's journey—it promises to end in a rebirth.
The earth is like the entrails of the cosmos, and a mythic digestion
is taking place in which Pacal is swallowed and travels through the
various locations, compartments, and houses of the underworld. As
Schele observes, "The image of death has cosmic implications. Pacal
falling down the axis mundi is metaphorically equivalent to the sun at
the instant of sunset. Like the sun, which rises after a period of darkness, he will rise after his triumph over the Lords of Death."[21]

These associations of a cosmic mouth, the world tree, and a sacred
bird are repeated with striking differences in the frontispiece of a central Mexican pictorial manuscript, the *Codex Féjérváry-Mayer*. In this
typical cosmogram, familiar to the Aztecs, the world is depicted as a
quincunx, a five-part universe with four trapezoidal-shaped regions
corresponding to the cardinal directions surrounding a central ceremonial area and image of a warrior god. Significantly, each of the four
quarters is *centered by a blooming cosmic tree with a sacred bird on top*, reminiscent of the image on Pacal's tomb. And like the Maya image, each
of the cosmic trees appears to grow out of, or at least emerge from, another cosmic structure. The eastern tree emerges from a temple with
a sun disk on top. The northern tree grows from a ritual bowl used in
sacrifice, and the western tree emerges from the head of a Tzitzimitl,
a celestial figure fallen to the earth. When we turn to the southern
part of the universe, we again see the gaping jaws of a crocodilian
monster giving way to a blooming tree with Mictlantecuhtli, the
Lord of the Underworld with his skull mask, facing Centeotl, the
maize god. This quadrant showing the image of the earth as a gaping
jaw suggests that the cosmic jaw was a widespread motif in Mesoamerican religion.

THE PRIMORDIAL MOUTH

We have a vivid written account of the earth as a primordial mouth in
the *Histoyre du Mechique*'s series of creation myths. In a section entitled
"De la opinión que ellos tenían de la creación del mundo y de sus di-

oses, y de la destrucción del mundo y de los cielos," we are told that before there was an earth, a great crocodilian creature was floating in a watery space. This goddess, named Tlaltecuhtli, whose joints consisted of eyes and mouths, gnawed with sharp teeth and snapped "like a savage beast."[22] Two sky gods, Quetzalcoatl and Tezcatlipoca, descended and declared that they needed to make the earth. They transformed themselves into two great serpents and each seized one side of Tlaltecuhtli, and squeezing with intensity, they tore her apart right down the middle. One half of her dismembered body became the earth, and the other half rose into the sky. Then, all the gods, in order to compensate her for the damage done to her body, descended to console her, and they ordered that from her body would grow all the fruit necessary for human life to exist. Her hair became the trees, plants, and grasses; her skin became the flowers and herbs; her eyes became the springs, pools, and caves; rivers and large caverns were formed from her mouth; and her nose became the valleys and mountains of the earth. From this cosmogonic ripping, opening, and dismemberment comes the surface, interiors, shapes, and waters of the earth. In a sense, her torn open body becomes a mouth, or a cornucopia of the earth's fruits.[23]

The relationship between the body and mouth of the deity and the bodies and mouths of the humans who worshiped her was explicit in some of the prayers and rituals of the Aztecs. Doris Heyden notes that of the eighteen major festivals of the Aztec, ten were dedicated to the earth and fertility, especially the plants of maize, amaranth, and flowers.[24] In the month following the festival of Tozoztontli, the month of planting, the people hung small effigies of clay and cloth to watch over the new lives of plants. The farmers, perhaps repeating the mythic episode of the gods tearing apart the body of the earth goddess, went "shouting and yelling, tearing out one or two stalks of maize, offering them to the temples as the first fruits. The men played flutes and women cried out, 'O lady come quickly.'" Echoing the earlier song of "we eat the earth and the earth eats us," these farmers were "speaking to Tlaltecuhtli, the earth whose skin and hair covered everything, the cornfields, the hills, the valleys, the springs, the caves, and all the vegetation."[25]

The image of the earth goddess with, or as, a menacing mouth appears in iconographic form in a number of sculptures and pictorial manuscripts. In one impressive version, we see the face of the goddess

Cihuateotl as a skull with large staring round eyes and an open mouth with a set of prominent teeth. In several surviving images, the teeth are often *the* key characteristic of the god's image. In fact, in the recent discovery of a statue at the excavation of the Templo Mayor, we have a dual image of devouring mouths. Nelly Gutiérrez Solana, in her "Relieve del Templo Mayor con Tláloc Tlaltecuhtli y Tláloc," describes the puzzling posture that two gods share, in which one appears to be lying on top of the other.[26] The most noticeable image the two share is in the region of their mouths. One god's head, identified by the gaping teeth, appears to be either emerging from the other god's mouth or in the process of being devoured into the mouth of the more prominent god.

COSMIC ENTRAILS

Direct and indirect associations were made between the digestive system of humans and the body of the earth. Relationships existed between the practice of ritual disembowelment, warfare, the digestive system, and concepts of the afterlife in a number of Mesoamerican artistic traditions. These include images of Tezcatlipoca-Ixquimilli disemboweling a sinner in the *Codex Borgia*, images of ritual disembowelment as a punishment for sexual misconduct, the throwing of the intestines of sacrificed Spaniards to the animals in Moctezuma's zoo, and the display and use of disemboweled intestines of enemies after battles. There are also scenes on several columns, stelae, and in codices of individuals losing their entrails in the underworld. Speaking directly to a concern for the influence of cosmovision and the parts and uses of the human body, Cecelia Klein writes,

> Sahagún's descriptions of the Aztec underworld imply, moreover, that it was structured much like the digestive system. The Aztec underworld was located deep in the "bowels" of the earth, which took the live form of either a large crocodilian creature or a monstrous amphibian who floated like an island in the middle of the ocean. The interior of the earth shared with the human body's interior an irregular, twisted, duct-like form. According to Sahagún, ". . . the sea enters within the land; its water passages, its ducts stand: they extend. It goes in all directions within the land in the mountains. Wheresoever it finds large spaces (or) small ones, there it makes its first beginning, perhaps somewhere on the plains, perhaps on the mountains."[27]

Caves, which permeated the Mesoamerican landscape, were likened to orifices leading to the underworld. In several pictorial images, the caves are drawn as gaping mouths with teeth, serving as places of emergence or devouring ancestors and humans. The "oral" significance of these caves is not limited to eating or digestion. They were a favorite place for oracles, the speaking and singing of divine messages. The relationship of these images to the stage of creation is made in the medical incantations recorded in Nahuatl by Hernando Ruiz de Alarcón in the seventeenth century, where "the mouth, the rectum, and the belly are referred to as Chicomoztoc, the seven caves," the place of origin and emergence of the Aztec ancestors.[28]

HUMANS AS DIVINE FOOD/
THE SUN AS A HUNGRY MOUTH

These fragments of myth and image revealing the primordial connections between the bodies of animals, humans, and creator gods show that eating, and especially the mouth, achieved cosmic status in Mesoamerica. What needs to be discussed is the cosmological imperative for eating human beings and the eating of gods and humans in the afterlife and in the underworld. After the cosmos with its flowering earth had been created from the split-open body of Tlaltecuhtli, the creation myth tells of a need, a thirst, a pressing obsession of the earth goddess. In her howling cries in the darkness, we hear of the cosmic imperative for divine cannibalism. The passage tells us that the goddess cried out, expressing her desire to eat the human hearts, and that she would not be silent unless she was "irrigated" with the blood of men. This statement of divine hunger appearing at the close of the cosmogonic episode, that is, at a point in the creation of the world that heralds the onset of human social life, is often repeated in other places. The point is that the dynamics of the Aztec cosmos included the need for gods to ingest and be nurtured by human substances, a kind of divine cannibalism of human beings. The cosmic jaws that populate the body of the earth goddess must be flexed and fed, in other words, irrigated with human blood, in order for the fruits of the earth to grow and feed human beings.

This notion of divine hunger for human bodies and substances is a central idea in what Alfredo López Austin calls the "ideological platform" of the Aztecs, which was used to wage war and motivate commoners to farm, fight, support armies, and participate in the spectacles of human sacrifice and cannibalism. The Aztecs imagined "bellicose deities who were hungry . . . whose existence depended on humans." While the earth was sometimes imagined as a gaping, howling, demanding mouth, the central Aztec deity who demanded human food was the sun, the "Fifth Sun" of the Aztecs, who was destined like the other suns to die in a cataclysm because he was part of the grand cycles of creation and destruction. In my view, Aztec cosmology represents an important variation on the nature of creation mythology as many historians of religions have interpreted it. From Mircea Eliade to Charles Long to Kees Bolle[29] and authors of numerous other studies, creation mythology has too often been depicted without acknowledging the destructive actions of cosmological systems. In the Mesoamerican case, the emphasis, outcome, and overarching destiny appears to be destruction, collapse, and chaos. There is also a tendency toward regeneration, but the emphasis on repeated cataclysms is very remarkable. It would be as correct to entitle a study of Mesoamerican mythology "Omega" as it is to refer to it as stories of "Alpha." López Austin writes about the Aztec case,

> The fundamental principle was the need to strengthen a hungry god, one in need of food, a god whose existence depended on humans. This was the Fifth Sun, who was condemned, like the sun that had preceded him, to die in a cataclysm. As long as men could offer blood and the hearts of captives taken in combat, his power would not decline, and he would continue on his course above the earth.[30]

The most vivid image of the Sun as a demanding mouth is, of course, depicted in the so-called "Aztec Calendar Stone," which is actually a cosmovision of universal time carved in stone. In the center of a circular symmetry of boxes, circles, signs, and images of animal and human parts stares the face of Tonatiuh, the Fifth Sun, whose open mouth yields a tongue in the form of a sacrificial knife symbolizing the imperative to acquire human beings for sacrifice and divine food in the form of blood. This theme is repeated in a number of codices, including the *Borgia*, where the sun god is lavishly dressed and seated on a throne, drinking a rich stream of blood flowing from a buzzard sacrifice. A more crudely drawn image appears in the *Florentine Codex* where a priest holds a human heart above the body of the victim,

pointing toward the face of the sun, which appears to wait in anticipation. The celestial space contained a hungry mouth in the Aztec
imagination.

This association of the sky, or at least the sun, with eating humans
is altered in at least one instance where the souls of certain warriors eat
divine food in the paradise of the sun. As Alfredo López Austin shows
in his study of ideology, myth, and the human body, among the
different worlds of the dead was one called "Tonatiuh Ilhuicac,"
where an abundance of trees covered a great plain divided into two
parts, a western and eastern half. "Each morning, the warriors killed
in combat received the Sun with all the panoply of war, raising their
voices and their shields as they accompanied him."[31] These warriors
transferred the Sun at midday to women who had died in their first
childbirth, and they carried him on a quetzal feather litter on till
sunset when he was handed over to the beings of the underworld. After four years of this divine service, the warriors were transformed
into birds and butterflies and given the freedom of flying back and
forth from "Heaven to the surface of the earth to sip the nectar of
flowers."[32] The souls of these dead humans continue to eat in the afterlife.

EATING IN THE AFTERLIFE
One of the Nahuatl phrases for "to die" was *itech naci in Tlaltecuhtli*, or
"I join Tlaltecuhtli," the earth monster goddess described earlier. In
some cases eating continued in the afterlife, as the insatiable gods devoured the remnants of humans. The Aztecs responded to this in such
ritual actions as feeding the ever-hungry Mictlantecuhtli by pouring
jars of blood over the head of his image.[33] It is important to acknowledge just how persistent these deities were in their demands for human bodies and blood. In an elegant prayer spoken or chanted to Tezcatlipoca, Lord of the Smoking Mirror, on the event of the ruler's
death, it is said that Mictlantecuhtli, the Lord of the Underworld,
pants with hunger for human remains:

> He [the ruler] knew, he hath followed our mother, our father
> He [the ruler] knew, he hath followed our mother, our father
> Mictlantecuhtli, Tzontemoc
> Cuezalli have a great thirst for us

they are always hungry for us
they keep on panting, always insisting
they never rest. By night, by day
they are always sighing, shouting.[34]

As we have seen in the case of the celestial warriors who travel from heaven to earth to suck on the nectar of flowers, the souls of some of the dead continued to eat in the afterlife. So it was with certain children. Elsewhere in the *Florentine Codex* we find a remarkable description of the eating habits of children who died in infancy, especially those who died while nursing before they had eaten corn. They lived in the "house of Tonacatecuhtli and suckled on the tree of life or sustenance."

It is said that when
little children die,
they become green stones,
they become precious
turquoise, they become
bracelets. When they die they do
not go to the terrible place of the
icy winds, to Mictlan. They go
there, to the house of
Tonacatecuhtli. They live at the
place of the tree of our sustenance.
They sip the flowers of our
sustenance. There they live at the
tree of our sustenance; they nurse
from it.[35] (italics mine)

However, the cuisine of the underworld was not usually delicious. The Aztec juxtaposed this image of eternal suckling from the tree of sustenance with the feasts of the charnel house awaiting the dead in Mictlan, where adults devour the worst of foods and are continually eaten by Mictlantecuhtli. Consider this description of divine cannibalism beneath the earth, where the dead eat excrement and refuse.

Mictlantecuhtli
Mictecacihuatl, there
in Mictlan they eat

feet, hands. Their food
is the black beetle;
their gruel, pus. They drink it that way,
from a skull. They eat many
stinking tamales in Mictlan. The
tamales are the waste matter from
black beetles.
. . . Everything which
on earth is not eaten is food in
Mictlan.
And it was said: "Now
nothing is eaten, Much
poverty is suffered there in
Mictlan."[36]

COSMOS AS A COMPOST HEAP

As I have noted elsewhere,[37] the cosmovision of the Mexica emphasizes the more dangerous phases of the life cycle—the phases of
threat, death, decomposition, and eccentric periodicity. From the
grand cosmogonic episodes of repeated creations and destructions to
the names given to the world ages, that is, the names of the destructive
forces, to the episodes of sacred history in which great kings or
culture heroes abdicate their authority, to the images of the sun and
earth as hungry mouths, Mesoamerican myths and the rituals they
were embedded in portray a tense, unstable, dynamic, and perishable
world. Nevertheless, these episodes of collapse, gloom, and devour-
ment were perceived as necessary stages in the *recomposition* of the
world and the recreation of the cosmos. Our challenge is to understand the Mexica theory of cosmo-magical power, that is, how life
was sustained and rejuvenated in the face of this emphasis on destruction.

One of the most compelling images of a theory of cosmo-
magical regenerative power comes from Thelma Sullivan, the distinguished *nahuatlato* who describes the earth and its decomposing parts
as a compost heap. Sullivan is focusing on the earth goddess Tlazolteotl, the eater of filth, associated with the earthiness of sexual life,
sexual license, and the confession of wrongdoing. In return for confessions, Tlazolteotl, one of the earth goddesses, will "eat" the sexual
sins of humans and digest evil sexual energy so that the sinner can be
restored to a moral equilibrium. What seems most interesting is the

prestige that revitalization continues to have within this clearly negative valuation of cosmic and human existence. Sullivan writes that
Tlazolteotl-Tlaelquani was

> the goddess of the fertile earth, and symbolized, too, the earth that re-
> ceives all organic wastes—human and animal excrement, vegetable and
> fruit remains, fish, fowls, and animal bones, and so forth—which when
> decomposed are transformed into humus. Humus in Nahuatl is called
> *tlazollalli*—from *tlazolli*, "filth, garbage," and *tlalli*, "earth" (Sahagún II:
> 251). In the same way that Tlazolteotl caused the symbolic rebirth of the
> transgressor by eating the ordure of his wickedness, she also symbolized
> the transformation of waste into humus, that is, the revitalization of the
> soil.[38]

This view of the earth and some of its deities as a cosmic compost
heap, eating the refuse of humans, animals, and vegetation to restore
vitality to the earth, reflects a cosmovision of power and vital energy
that is both specifically Aztec and shared with many traditional societies. This cosmo-magical view presupposes an intimate parallelism
and, in fact, *transferability* between the vital forces of humans and the
realms and personalities of the gods. The Aztecs believed that rulers
could acquire the vital force of other men who were sacrificed by
eating parts of their bodies, thus prolonging their own lives on earth.[39]
And the blood of sacrificed victims was sprinkled over the bodies of
visiting ambassadors for the same reason. It also appears that at least
some Mesoamerican farmers were particularly committed to the idea
of the transferability of power between humans, gods, and the spirits
of the fields. There is a cohesion and interchange between vital forces
of cornfields and, in particular, very productive cornfields. An especially productive cornfield was given the name *miccamilli*, or "cornfield of death." This meant that one of the family members of the
field's owner was going to die, as his or her vital energy had been
transferred into the field's generous yield. One vivid example of this
cosmo-magical view of the acquisition of power through sacrifice and
eating can be found in another oral expression, the guilty rhetoric of
Aztec sinners who confess to a goddess who then eats their lust and requires the painful bleeding of the sinner's tongue and genitals.

SPEAKING IN TONGUES TO *TLAZOLTEOTL*

The Aztec sense of orality and eating takes a fascinating turn in the
grand confession to the earth goddess Tlazolteotl as reported in Book

I of the *Florentine Codex*. For in this confession we find that the use of the human mouth to confess sexual sins, what I call guilty rhetoric, results in the use of the divine mouth to eat those sins. In what follows, I want to emphasize the performative force of the sacred actions and especially the flow of words that constitute the confession, or *neyolmelahualiztli*, which translates as "the act of straightening the hearts." There are a series of complex interrelated parts to this performance, which at the beginning, middle, and end depend on the ability of words to symbolically strip a person of one identity and assist in the creation of a new one. It is not only words, but certainly the tongue that is the focus of the action, the tongue that at one moment is homologized with the penis, and the tongue that must create the oral words that set one's heart straight. In order to gain perspective on this complex rhetorical moment, I want to briefly discuss the Aztec sense of "heart" and read the ritual confession in seven parts, focusing on the (1) notion of the goddess's realm; (2) naming of the goddesses and the verbal cosmic setting of the confession; (3) ritual construction of space and time for the confession; (4) invitation to confess, to open one's heart; (5) opening of one's heart; (6) punishment against the stomach, the tongue, and the penis; and (7) retreat to silence and confidentiality.

In the Aztec conception of the human body, the most vital and vulnerable aspects of the cosmos were concentrated as animistic entities or souls in the skull, the heart, and the liver. The soul of the head was the *tonalli*, which provided warmth, vigor, valor, and growth to the person. The soul of the liver was the *ihiyotl*, which provided passion, feeling, and sometimes dangerous emanations for human beings. The third animistic entity, and the most important for our topic, was the heart, the place of equilibrium. *Teyolia*, or heart, derives from *yolia*, or "he who animates," and *yol*, or "life," and was the location of vitality, thought, fondness, and rationality. Animals, towns, lakes, sky, ocean, rulers, and many other objects had *teyolia*. Each town had a heart called the *altepeyollotl*, or "heart of the town." *Teyolia* appeared in the mother's womb as a gift from the gods, and it was hot during life and cold during death. Human hearts received the divine force of *teyolia* when they accomplished the extraordinary in war, art, poetry, politics, or science. Certain very extraordinary individuals had enormous amounts of *teyolia* and enjoyed public prestige. But the *teyolia* could be seriously damaged through sexual misconduct. In fact, if one member of a family committed adultery, the *teyolia* in the family was damaged and eventually had to be treated ritually when the adulterer confessed to the eater of filth, Tlazolteotl, who demanded painful autosacrifices. As mentioned, this confession was the "act of straightening the heart."

The Realm of the Goddess

> As to her being named Tlazolteotl: it was said that it was because her realm, her domain, was that of evil and perverseness—that is to say lustful and debauched living. It was said that she ruled and was mistress of lust and debauchery.[40]

It is impressive that this goddess rules a geography, a realm, but the realm *is not so much a space as it is an action*, a sexual action. She is identified as the cause of lustfulness as well as the cure! One of the best expressions of her rulership of this realm comes when we are told that "Tlazolteotl offered one, cast upon one, inspired in one," this debauchery. It was typical in Aztec thought for a god to rule a specific domain. One god governed the domain of war, another governed the domain of art, still another controlled the waters. This goddess ruled sexuality and in so doing provided from within her own substance the forces of sexuality, for good or ill, that is, she cast lust upon humans, like casting a net over them. But her influence was also internal, as she "inspired in one" or breathed into a person sexual misconduct. She also provided from within her own substance the release and cure from this excessive lust. Tlazolteotl provoked sinful sex but could also take it away. As we shall see, she ate the substance of sexual lust committed by humans, thereby taking it back into her divine body.

The Naming of the Goddess/A Verbal Cosmic Setting

> And as to her name Ixcuina: it was said there were four women—the first named Tiacapan (the first born or leader), the second Teicu. . . . Each one of these was called Tlazolteotl.[41]

It is impressive that spoken language creates the setting of the confession by first multiplying the names of the goddess into four. This cosmological setting for the straightening of one's heart reflects the Aztec pattern of the one and the many. Various gods could be concentrated into one single god, and one god could be multiplied into various gods. Some of the chief gods such as Tlaloc, Ehecatl, and Xiuhtecuhtli were often converted into four gods in order to live in each of the cosmic trees. The same pattern was expressed in the goddess of sexual love, who had four sisters, each one located in the four corners of the universe. In a sense, this multiplicity meant that there was no escape from the sexual complexities of human existence.

One of the names of the goddess was Tlaelquani, or "Eater of Filthy Things." The goddess inspired lust and ate it. I am impressed with the oral focus of so much of this ritual performance, as also expressed in the passage "because one told, one recited before her all vanities; one told, one spread before her all unclean works, however ugly, however grave . . . Indeed all was exposed, told before her."[42] This oral discourse between human and goddess depends on the action of the mouth from start to finish.

The verbal action is reiterated when the penitent goes to a soothsayer "in whose hands lay the books . . . who preserved the writings, who possessed the knowledge . . . the wisdom which hath been *uttered*."[43] Utterances are not only made by the penitent's mouth, they wait for him or her embedded in the pictorial manuscripts! It is for this reason that the penitent announces, "I wish to go to the master, our lord of the near, the nigh. I wish to learn of his secrets."[44] The passage emphasizes the penitent's desire to be both very close to the deity and to seek protection from the divine figure in order to acquire virtue and become upright. One's guilt and sin have become enclosed in names and signs, which have been uttered.

The Ritual Construction of Space

> The soothsayer said; "Thou has done a favor." He instructed him when
> he should come he chose the day. He consulted his sacred almanac . . .
> when it was already the appointed time . . .[45]

In order for the ritual transformation and exchange of guilty and cleansing rhetoric to take place, a sacred space and time must be identified. The soothsayer was the go-between or conduit between the goddess and the penitent, and he had to identify the space and rhythm of time suitable for the powerful event. A "good day, good time" was chosen, the home of the penitent was swept clean, and a new reed mat, which was the specific setting of the confessions, was laid down near the new fire that was lit. Incense was cast into the flames of Xiuhtecuhtli and the first words were uttered, reflecting the duality we have seen to be so crucial in Aztec thought, "Mother of the gods, father of the gods, the old god, here hath come a man of low estate . . .

he hath lived in filth, . . . hear the torment of this lowly one."[46] These phrases show a spatial relationship between a person speaking from a lowly, earthbound position to a god who is old, honored and at the center of the universe.

Although it is not made explicit in this text, the use of the home as the site of confession and cleansing may be said to symbolize the communal nature of guilt. The sexual misconduct of one member of a family could spread illness and harm to others. According to the research of López Austin, one person's sexual sins could harm all members of the family, *living and dead.* This is due, in part, to the power of the disequilibrium of one of the souls. For instance, a moral life produced a *cemelli,* a unified liver. But immoral sexual activity altered the liver, which then erupted with emissions of *ihiyotl.* These emissions could injure the health of others, including animals. An adulterer would emit noxious forces that could infect the spouse, and this disease was called *chahuacocoliztli,* or "illness due to adultery."[47] Children and other innocent bystanders were especially susceptible to these influences.

The Invitation to Open/Clean One's Heart/Confess

Thou hast . . . come to tell him, to deliver thyself of, thy evil atmosphere . . . to open thy secrets.[48]

This passage indicates the formal invitation to the penitent to open himself (earlier the phrase "the heart was opened") through narration of his sexual history. The soothsayer implores, "uncover thy secrets, tell thy way of life, in whatsoever way thou art moved . . . pour forth thy vices . . . and tell thy sorrows to our lord of the near and nigh, who stretching forth his arms to thee, embraceth thee and carrieth thee on his back."[49] It is noted that this action, which apparently could take place only once in a lifetime, took courage, "be not timid because of shame . . . be daring."[50]

The Opening/Cleaning of the Heart

. . . "I take off my clothes and uncover, in thy presence my nakedness" . . . then he began the tale of his sins, in their proper order, in the same order as that in which he committed them. Just as if it were a song . . . in the very same way he told what he had done.[51]

This passage tells of the narrative structure of the confession, which is likened both to a song and to a journey, "as if on the road he went following his deeds,"[52] and resonates with some aspects of contemporary psychoanalytic technique. In contemporary therapeutics, the analysand is instructed to relive the road of his or her life as a means of creating a catharsis and a clear pathway to see the impulses, forces, and sources of complex, troubling feelings. For the Aztecs, the confession, which is the cleaning of one's heart, has to address the amount of phlegm and soil that has covered the heart. It was thought that too much weight of guilt on the heart would drive a person crazy.

The Punishment

When the Ciuapipiltin descend, . . . thou shalt starve thy entrails.[53]

Following the narration of the path of one's sexual misdeeds, the soothsayer delivered the punishment according to the severity of the story or the volume of guilt. The intensity of punishment is reflected in the reference to the descending Ciuapipiltin, who are the women who died during their first childbirth. After death, the souls of these women ascended to the western sky of the sun and formed five groups whose function was to accompany the sun during the first half of its celestial journey. These beings descended to the earth every fifty-two days, with permission to occupy invisible houses and punish wrongdoers, or just anyone they chose. For example, a beautiful child was paralyzed and deformed. It was on the date of their descent that the penitent was to carry out at least two painful kinds of ritual cleansing.

First, a serious fast was undertaken. This fast signified the withdrawal from eating things of the earth, a reversal of human growth and human nature and the involvement in *in teuhtli in tlazolli*. López Austin has noted that the first disequilibrium, or sin, was committed the first time a child ate from the body of the Earth Mother, typically a corn pabulum.

> When a child eats the substance that comes from the interior of the earth, the child ingests the weight and quality of death. All that comes from the Earth Mother comes from the death that produces life. In this way, the life that is maintained at the cost of death has to be transformed into death. If a human eats corn, he is required to pay his debt to the earth by giving his own body when he dies. Throughout life, the human being is sinning on the earth, is building up a debt to the earth. This debt is disequilibrium, which must be paid or set right. This payment, in Aztec

thought, is done with offerings, with autosacrifice, with human sacrifice, with dances, and finally with the surrendering of one's body to the earth.[54]

This confession is just such an "offering" and the next requirement introduces the painful practice of autosacrifice, which is a debt payment.

Second, the penitent is told, with very specific instructions, that he must "pay in blood." During the fasting period, the tongue receives harsh treatment as straws and sticks are drawn through it. Straws, reeds, and sticks are drawn "through the middle, thou shalt break it through from the under side"[55] of the tongue or in some cases the ears. But it is not only the protuberance of the tongue that told the guilt that is pierced and bled, it is also the protuberance of the penis, which committed, in part, the sexual action, that is bled. The penitent is also required to draw sticks, reeds, and straws through his penis many times. "Thou shall pass them through singly, or pass them through as one, binding them together, be they four hundred or eight hundred sticks which thou shalt pass through."[56] In this way, the faults are overcome.

Autosacrifice was carried out by all members of Aztec society at some point in their lives. As Cecelia Klein shows in her critical work "The Ideology of Autosacrifice at the Templo Mayor," depictions of people engaged in self-sacrifice greatly outnumber the images of human sacrifice, at least on the stone monuments that have survived. It appears that from very ancient times, the piercing of one's own body with spines, obsidian blades, or other instruments promoted agricultural and reproductive fertility and good health. These acts of bleeding the self seem to be closely connected to the concept of paying a debt or making an exchange for supernatural aid. Parents bled their children during the month of Tozoztontli to protect them from illness and spiritual danger, and children were bled during the New Fire Ceremony. Describing the ideology of autosacrifice, Klein summarizes,

> Since both sexual transgression and overindulgence in food and drink were closely associated with moral and physical weakness, sexual abstinence and fasting usually accompany bloodletting. Conversely, those who had behaved asocially in this manner often sought to restore their

strength by offering their blood. Adulteresses and priestesses who broke
their vows of chastity are specifically reported to have done this . . . Human blood could be shed on behalf of plant and animal life, as well, with
the understanding that it in turn would benefit people.[57]

These practices among the priesthood could reach extraordinary
proportions, reflecting the Aztec and our concerns with guilty rhetoric, guilty tongues. They actually tied knots in the cords that were
pulled through their tongues and, according to Diego Durán, some
priests not only bled their virile members but split them in two to insure impotence and the complete avoidance of sexual relations!

The Retreat into Silence/Confidentiality

The soothsayer before whom sins were laid nowhere spoke of what
had been placed before him, of what had been said . . . For the sins
were given—they were told—to him of the near, the nigh, whom
mortal man might not see.[58]

I am impressed with the closing comments about silence and confidentiality. Once the guilt had been confessed, relived through the
telling, and cleansed through the fasting and autosacrifice (lesser
offenses required singing, dancing, or the making of images), the
penitent was required to do penance at the temple at night while na-
ked, wearing only the emblem of Tlazolteotl on his loins and buttocks. He then returned home and silence was required of both penitent and soothsayer.

This ritual silencing of the guilty rhetoric now ingested by the
goddesses was intensified by certain priestly groups who drew large
numbers of knotted cords or thorns through their tongues. "According to Motolinía, one physical effect of this practice was considerable difficulty in speaking. The Cholulan priests who offered their
own blood to Camaxtli drew the rods through their tongues every
twenty days, he tells us, precisely so as 'to keep their tongues from
murmuring.'"[59] During one eighty-day fast in honor of the god Camaxtli in the region of Tlaxcala, the head priest who sang "could
scarcely move his tongue." This is a radical way of silencing the flow
of guilty rhetoric and reminding the penitent of the seriousness of
the offense and blocking the allure of the sin.

BETWEEN TWO WORLDS

In Aztec thought, human life was a tender, perishable combination of the Above and the Below, the Four Quarters, and the Dualities of the cosmos. Cosmic Jaws as celestial, terrestrial, divine structures were vital points of transformation that linked these realms to the fate of human life. These jaws were part of the underlying premises and orderings of the world that generated the everyday phenomena for humans to work with. Perhaps the final word on the profundity of this cosmic pattern of eating the gods who eat us should be given to that greatest of Aztec messengers, the Mexica midwife, as she addressed the four-day-old baby in the naming ceremony. The cosmic jaws were now reduced to the beloved mouth of an infant. Just before sunrise, she took the newborn child in her arms, faced west, and began to bathe the child. Cooing, she told the male child he had been sent from the gods Ome tecutli, Ome ciuatl who lived in the highest heavens, gave him a taste of water, the blue water, the yellow water in order to purify the heart. Then she said,

> My youngest son, my youth, take, receive the water of the lord of the earth, our sustenance, our refreshment, which is that which cleanseth one, that which batheth one. May the heavenly water, the blue water, the deep green, go into thy body; may it remain in thy body. May it remove, may it destroy the manner of things thou wert given with which thou wert arrayed in the beginning—the bad, the evil; for we are still left in its hands; we merit it, for even before, our mother Chalchiuhitli icue, knoweth of it.[60]

CHAPTER 7

The Sacrifice of Women
The Hearts of Plants and Makers of War Games

> A human's life is a continuous debt to the gods. Humans eat, and when
> that happens, they take on an obligation. It is the gods' obligation to
> nourish their creatures. The hands of the gods are symbols of their
> capacity to create and sustain, but the human consumption of food
> must be reciprocated. The gods give sustenance on loan.
>
> Alfredo López Austin, *Tamoanchan, Tlalocan: Places of Mist*

> When they had gone reaching the place of the skull rack, then (the
> wearer of Toci's likenesses's skin) tramped upon her drum. And the sea-
> soned warriors already stood awaiting (Cinteotl). For there he departed
> with his thigh (skin) mask in order to leave it in enemy land.
>
> Bernardino de Sahagún, *Florentine Codex*

It is in the ritual killing of females where we gain unique information
about Aztec ritual sacrifice, social order, and, to some extent, gender
relations. This statement may come as somewhat of a surprise because
the sacrifice of enemy male warriors has traditionally been the focus
of study. However, a closer reading of the ritual performances as described by Sahagún and others shows that women were ritually
slaughtered in one-third of the yearly festivals. If we want to gain
more understanding of the Aztec cosmo-magical practice of sacrifice,
the ceremonial landscape of the festivals, and the social ordering of
male and female relations, a revealing place to look is in the short and
long descriptions of four ceremonies in Book 2 of the *Florentine Codex,* where young women were explicitly the victims.[1] In what follows, I will attempt an alliance between verbal picture making and an
interpretation of selected materials, primarily from Book 2 of the
Florentine Codex, as a means of giving the reader a richer understand-

At the height of one sacrificial festival, a young female *ixiptla* of a corn goddess is sacrificed and flayed. Her skin is worn by a large male priest whose ritual identity is transformed into the corn goddess. Note how her skinned hands are hanging in front of the ritual skirt. (From the *Codex Borbonicus.* After Laurette Séjourné, *El pensamiento náhuatl cifrado por los calendarios* [Mexico, 1981], courtesy of Siglo Veintiuno Editores, S.A.)

ing of how the sacrifice of women among the Aztecs of Tenochtitlan strove to combine, in distinctive ways, the religious commitments to the regeneration of plants with commitments to the regeneration of warfare.[2] While others have noticed the combination of plant renewal and warfare in these rites, I hope to carry the discussion further by illustrating the meanings of this dual focus of the sacrifice of women.

It is in the Aztecs' consistent, sometimes desperate, ritual search for plant regeneration that we gain some access to their understanding of the nature of human existence. They were a people obsessed with the structured nearness of death,[3] but who also possessed the ritual techniques to manipulate, dance with, and periodically transform death into the forces of life. Those sacrifices, referred to as *nextlahual-tin* (the debt payments), were the ritual magic to this mystery of metamorphosis. The sacrifice of women, as much as any other kind of sacrifice, dramatized for their priests and citizens and served up to their gods the hope that they could use ritually controlled death to regenerate their plants, their children, and even their forces of war, which brought death to enemies. In what follows, I will employ the notion of the "cosmo-magical circle"[4] from the perspective of the history of religions in order to develop a kind of ritual and social map of the sacrifice of women. We will see that the rituals of sacrificing women were highly mobile ceremonies marked by cosmo-magical circles— symbolic spaces where gods and humans actively exchanged their coessences in order to participate in the rejuvenating forces of earth, animal, plant, and sky. By using cosmo-magical circles, I mean to emphasize the circular shape of these rites, that is, the rejuvenating purposes of these rituals, the flow of exchange between cosmic levels of sky and earth, male and female, life and death, and the focusing style of sacrifice inclined to collect in various concentrated moments and spaces the crucial elements of sacrificial change. I am also emphasizing another feature of the notion of ceremonial landscape, namely that in the Aztec imagination, all these elements—people, plants, ritual buildings, costumes, hills—were perceived as living participants, each with a spiritual identity, power, and volition.

As the surviving narratives make clear, these cosmo-magical circles gathered the sacred symbols, potent cosmic forces, and key participants together in groups along a prescribed ritual route so that the debt payments could be accomplished and the populace could witness and participate in the rites of passage. In the sacrifice of women, the female body, marked by sexual and regenerative powers, layered with cosmic colors, jewelry, and mythic and memory clothing[5] was one such circle. The sacred women who gathered around her, sometimes dancing, sometimes whispering, and sometimes waving hands, were another cosmo-magic circle. The temples they visited, the places of sacrifice, the marketplace, the ruler's palace, and the spot on the enemy frontier where her skin is deposited were also magic circles, or parts of larger cosmo-magical places. All of these were the places of crucial religious change that released, confined, and focused sacred forces in order to regenerate plants and warriors. This sense of circular rejuvenation, focus, and place linking at least plants and war is reflected well in the ritual procession of the Xilonen *ixiptla* who visited four cosmic locations, which were also associated with the cyclical motion of the four sacred year-bearers. "These just sustained, just carried along the four year-bearers—Reed, Flint Knife, House, Rabbit; thus do the year-bearers go describing circles, go whirling around (as they measure time)."[6]

COSMOVISION AND COSMO-MAGICAL

> The need to maintain harmony between the world of the gods and the world of men—what A. J. L. Wensinck called the dramatic conception of nature—required that man should participate in cosmic events by accompanying them with appropriate rituals.[7]

A word about terminology will help the reader. Scholars of Aztec religions use the term *cosmovision* to refer to the "worldview," or coherent and rational arrangement of space and time communicated through religion and mythology.[8] I have found this term and the discourse around it to be useful for describing the indigenous models of space and time as represented in rites, architecture, and mythology. But I frequently also use the term cosmo-magical[9] to emphasize two *dynamic* aspects of the more general cosmovision. First, there is the capacity of rites and places to dramatize, with maximal potential sacredness, the interactive relationships people in the social realm have with the gods and creative forces of the cosmos. In this sense, cosmo-magical draws attention to the parallelism between various levels and realms of the cosmos as well as the power of rites to bring these di-

verse realms into contact and exchange. In other words, cosmo-
magical means that divine energy and force inhabit buildings as well
as people, hills as well as temples, graineries as well as pyramids, costumes as well as animal skins and feathers, stones as well as bones—
and that all these elements and others participated, and performed
in the ritual life of the ceremonial landscape of the Aztecs. Second,
cosmo-magical refers to the creative juxtaposition of opposites in
which the *destruction* (by knives, fire, water, arrows, etc.) of sacred objects contributes to the *recreation* of the forces of fertility in the underworld, on earth, or in the heavens. In both cases, the term *cosmo-
magical* forefronts the metamorphosis of ritual action, and the present
study seeks to draw the reader's attention to the dynamic dimensions
of these rituals.

SACRIFICIAL THEORY AVOIDS AZTECS AND SAHAGÚN

The startling practice of the sacrifice of women is one of the major
religious patterns of central Mesoamerica that anthropologists and
historians of religions have often avoided in their constructions of
theory and approaches to ritual life. It is remarkable that even the
most recent compelling theoretical statement on sacrifice, Nancy
Jay's *Throughout Your Generations Forever: Sacrifice, Religion and Paternity,* makes only passing reference to the vivid descriptions, practices,
and logic of the killing of young women by male priests at the Templo Mayor and other ceremonial centers. Why would a major comparative study from the perspective of feminist scholarship, which
strives to "illuminate aspects of sacrifice that have been regularly left
in darkness," turn its back on the Sahagúntine corpus, the most detailed and reliable record of real sacrifices, especially sacrifices that
speak to the issue of patriarchal control of creative forces? Perhaps Jay,
like many of us, is struck dumb, hermeneutically speaking, in the face
of the direct, sustained, vivid descriptions of the preparation of
young women's bodies for sacrifice, the ritual deceptions and mas-
querades they were led through, the occasional sexual use of these
young women by warriors and rulers, and the brutal ways they were
stretched out on sacrificial stones by male priests who beheaded them
with the beaks of swordfish, extracted their hearts, and sometimes
wore their skins. [10] Jay, like the rest of us, is apparently unable to deal
directly with the Aztec's sustained concentration of mind, resources,

and physical action on the powers of blood and body parts as cosmo-magical objects of change. Why the development of ritual techniques of cruelty? Why the cultivation of the public eye for horror? But is it the meanness of these people's practices alone that stops scholars and laypeople from looking into these narratives? Or is there something delicate, optimistic, and disapproving in our own historical views, understandings, and commitments of what religion and the history of religions is? Or, to move in another direction, have the indigenous sacrificial practices of the Americas been left out and ignored by theorists of sacrifice for intellectual, chauvinistic reasons? Or is our refusal to look at the Aztec record of sacrifice in general and the sacrifice of young women in particular a refusal to acknowledge with René Girard that, in part, the secret heart and soul of the sacred, if not human culture, is violence? Is the Aztec grossness really grossness or just a more complex, sobering, and terrible story about some dimensions of the history of religions that is too hard to tell and very much too hard to sell? Or is there a level of sacred cruelty in Tenochtitlan that shocks our most effective categories of understanding?

A METAMORPHIC VISION OF PLACE AND RITUAL

I do not know the answer to these questions, but I believe they are important for the study of Mesoamerican religions and cultures. It has taken me a long time to come around to reading with some intensity the existing record of these ritual debt payments in the forms of the public ritual killing of adolescent girls, and still more remains to be done in reconstructing the text and tracing the pictures of the Aztec slaughter of children and women. And I still find profound puzzlement and a sense of mystery in the sacrificial story. One useful entry into the meanings and purposes of these practices, and especially those involving the ritual movement of females and the dismemberment and movement of their body parts and skins, can be found in using the "metamorphic vision of ritual and place" that I have written about elsewhere.[11] Metamorphic vision of place is a useful alternative to both Mircea Eliade's notion of "central place" and Jonathan Z. Smith's insistence on the "locative" and "utopian" models of place that guide ritual action. In the Mesoamerican world, human understanding of the cosmovision was informed by a metamorphic vision of place that had at least six major facets. Alfredo López Austin, writing about patterns of regeneration associated with the mythical places of Tamoanchan and Tlalocan, has outlined these facets, which I have reduced to six for the purposes of this chapter. Metamorphosis depends on (1) the dynamic coessence of the gods,[12] in which gods can change into humans, animals, and plants, and animals can change into humans; (2) the sexual activity of the gods, which enclosed earthly beings in heavy, mortal skins and introduced death into the world; (3) the ways in which gods and humans nourished each other through providing food and practicing sacrifice; (4) the *axis mundi* of the cosmic tree/cosmic mountain, which provided abundant "hearts" or animistic powers for agriculture, humans, and gods, in other words, it was the source of metamorphosis; (5) humans who constructed microcosms of the divine society of the gods in their ceremonial centers, which house symbolic "hearts" and ritual actions that animate those "hearts;" and (6) the chief representatives of divine hearts, who are the *hombre-dioses, ixiptlas,* rulers, and artists who contain divine duality within them.[13] As one scholar writes of these various kinds of replications and their cosmo-magical power, "the images do not represent the gods; they are not symbols of the gods. They are *containers of the divine essence.* Rock formations have shapes where an ancestor (a 'giant,' 'old one,' or 'wealthy one'), who was trapped there at the moment of the Sun's original appearance, can be seen. Fossils, archaeological objects, rock crystals, and rocks with particular shapes are 'containers' of the 'ancients.' When a native priest finishes cutting a paper figure, the image is not animated, but the priest invokes the divinity, raises the moveable sheets of the figure, and anoints it with blood of a domestic fowl in order to give it energy" (italics mine).[14]

It is with this model of cosmo-magical metamorphosis in mind, with its emphasis on divine coessence, sexuality, nourishment through sacrifice, the cosmic mountain, and the human containers of divine essence, that I turn to four of the festivals dedicated to the sacrifice of women. The young women we are about to track in their swaying, singing, running, whirling vortex toward death were understood as the human coessences of the vital maize plant, whose hearts had come alive through visits to the symbolic cosmic mountain that prepared them for an ultimate transformation in sacrifice. In my reading of these ceremonies, female capacities to transform and participate in the transformation of plants opened out into their powers to inspire and participate in the transformation of boys into warriors and to stimulate, in at least one ritual, the militarization of society.

TELLING A STORY AND MAKING A PICTURE
OF SACRIFICING WOMEN

I read the four festivals related to female sacrifice in the *Florentine Codex* as a *cumulative text,* that is, as though there was one narrative tradition about the treatment of women's bodies in sacrifice woven through different rituals and disclosed gradually in the interviews and manuscript preparation. While I am certain this is a scholarly device that serves at least my own interests, it reflects the evolving disclosure of some important details about the sacrifice of women. Specifically, the portion of the codex relating the first festival of female sacrifice (Huey Tocoztli, "Great Vigil," fourth month) describes the young woman's appearance on the ritual stage and her transformation through adornment and dancing into a *teotl ixiptla,* but avoids any reference to her death or the use of her body. We are also introduced to the male–female tensions and antagonisms that play important roles in these sacrifices. The second festival of female sacrifice (Tecuilhuitontli, "The Small Festival of the Lords," seventh month) repeats the repertoire of the first festival but adds a more vivid description of the girl's change into the goddess and a dramatic presentation of her death. But it is not until we read the fourth festival of female sacrifice (Ochpaniztli, "The Sweeping," eleventh month) that we discover how her body was ritually treated *after* her death. We also learn new details about what women's bodies meant to the Aztec priests, warriors, and king. Women were the supreme givers; they gave words, seeds, virginity, hearts, and skin in order to regenerate plants and stimulate males to war.

It is also remarkable that we are given contradictory images of the purposes of these sacrifices in the short and longer descriptions in Sahagún. If, as one scholar argues, rituals "focus" social energy and attention, the short descriptions of chapters 1 through 19, at the front of Book 2, differ in focus from the elaborate narratives of these ceremonies, chapters 20 through 38. The short accounts state repeatedly that the focus is the ritual death of the *ixiptlas.* The longer accounts, several of which do not describe killing, focus not on prodigious acts of slaughter, but on adornment ceremonies; movements according to etiquette; singing choruses; mock battles in the streets; swerving entourages; offerings of blood, plants, and foods to gods; vigorous dances and dashes; periods of profound silence; human touching; and displays of human compassion. We do not find descriptions of wild orgies of aggression and murder. These longer accounts displace the act of killing to a peripheral, if potent, role and emphasize the pivoting of the cosmo-magical circles of ritual change around the ceremonial landscape of the city and even beyond its confines.

Children First

To more fully understand the sacrifice of women, we must first discuss briefly the ritual killing of children, who were sacrificed in the first quarter of the Aztec year. For here we will see evidence of several basic patterns that prepare us for the encounter with the beheading and skinning of the female deity impersonators. All the sacrifices appear as complex, dynamic rituals within rituals. During the first month of the year, called Atlcahualo, or Abandoned Water, in which the children were killed, we read that "There was much compassion. They made one weep; they loosed one's weeping, they made one sad for them, there was singing for them."[15] These sounds of sorrow may show that the Aztecs had profound emotional responses to the ritual dramas of killing children. That the Aztecs felt ambivalence as well is suggested in the report that offering priests, especially the elder ones, left the scene at certain moments. "And if any of the offering priests avoided them, they would call them 'abandoned ones.' No longer did one join others in singing; nowhere was he wanted; nowhere was he respected."[16] The Spanish gloss on this text emphasizes that the priests did not return to the place where the killing of children was carried out. On the one hand, this may refer primarily to the inability of priests to carry out the rigors of the rite, which demanded long hours of walking, chanting, concentration, and staying awake. Not keeping the vigil meant the priests were castigated. But the text is also telling us that the killing of the young children was painful and a heavy sorrow for priests and others to witness and participate in. Too often scholars emphasize that the Aztecs sacrificed children during this first month, starting the year with the freshest, youngest, and most potent humans. But the texts tell us that some children were killed during the first four months of the year, "some in each month . . . so that until the rains came in abundance, in all the feasts they slew children."[17] No doubt the sorrow and feelings of avoidance were experienced during this entire time.

Enter the Women Changing into the Hearts of Corn

> They formed her image as a woman. They said "Yea, verily, this one is our sustenance"; that is to say, indeed truly she is our flesh, our livelihood; through her we live; she is our strength. If she were not, we should indeed die of hunger.[18]

In the fourth month of the year (the fourth twenty-day period, or *veintena*), the Aztecs celebrated Huey Tocoztli, or the Great Vigil, in which we see the dramatization of two of the chief characteristics of human sacrifice; the prime importance of the cycle of debt payment referred to by López Austin in the quote that opens this chapter, and the practice of cosmo-magically dressing humans so they can die like gods die and regenerate the "hearts" of plants. We also see evidence, which increases in later rituals, of male and female aggression.

The animation of plant forces begins when young men set up sedges covered with blood, taken from their legs and ears, in front of images of the gods in the homes of the populace.[19] In the morning, the priests spread out in the city, "they went taking all the roads to the houses," going from house to house asking for alms.[20] The introduction of male competition and aggression associated with these ceremonies appears in the ritual walks that followed. Apparently, the priests of each temple priesthood had their assigned routes for these ritual walks and if they met another group, there was "ill-feeling over it, they were disliked because of it, there was continued wrangling over it." After returning to the temple with the day's offerings, the priests went out into their fields "to get Centeotl" (Maize Cob Deity), in the form of a stalk of green maize that they took back to the temple and decorated with flowers. The god was nurtured with an offering of five foods in a basket upon which stood a "hard-baked frog, hard, stiff, its face painted blue, a woman's skirt about its hind quarters." The frogs and blue paint symbolize the cosmo-magical force of the precious first rains, which frogs announce with their first croaks.

This plant-nurturing symbolism is extended to young females who carried the "cobs of maize in groups of seven" on their backs to the temple of Chicomecoatl (Seven Serpent). In effect, the young girls are equal to the young maize seeds and together they represent the earth, the feminine part of the cosmos, which stores and releases the powers of growth in the plants. This cosmo-magical change is intensified when the young girls and cobs of maize are adorned and painted red. The corn is wrapped in reddened paper and the girls' arms and legs are pasted with red feathers.

Powerful Female Words

As living fertility images, these girls walk in the city toward the temple of Chicomecoatl, attracting the faces and the occasional taunts, but, we are told, *not* the eyes of young males. This edgy situation introduces suggestions of important gender relations between males and females. On the one hand, the story told to Sahagún reveals that a prescribed set of verbal insults were sometimes spoken to the girls as they walked in the city. On the other hand, Aztec girls had sets of verbal flourishes to admonish flirtations or insults spoken in their direction. One such insult is recorded:

> And if someone joked with one of them, they chide him. One said to him: "He with the occipital tuft of hair can speak! Canst thou talk? Be thou already concerned over how thy tuft of hair will fall off, thou with the little tuft of hair. It is an evil-smelling tuft of hair, it is a stinking tuft of hair. Art thou not just a woman like me? Nowhere hath thy excrement been burned.[21]

More important is the passage stating that men's insults were weak in comparison with what women could produce. Elderly women's words had the power to criticize masculine weakness and stimulate demonstrations of strength and the warrior potential. "For verily thus the women could torment (young men) into war; thus they moved them; thus the women could prod them into battle. Indeed we men said; 'Bloody, painful are the words of the women; bloody penetrating are women's words.' "[22]

The girls walked in procession to the temple and granary where two more changes took place. First, the ears of maize "were made hearts. They became their granary hearts. They laid them in the granary."[23] In Aztec botanical thought, the maize seeds were composed of two elements; the visible seed and the invisible substance called the "the heart of maize." The hearts of maize, animal species, and plants were recycled through a great granary in the underworld of the dead, the place called Tlalocan, a colossal receptacle enclosed in the cosmic mountain. López Austin summarizes these places of abundance.

> The gods' dwelling . . . is a great hill. Inside the hill enormous agricultural wealth, animals, minerals, and currents of water are kept . . . The wealth of the hills is a collection of "seeds"; they act as the invisible source of the classes. When they are brought into the world, they can reproduce their respective classes. The great hill is, at the same time, the "heart" of the Earth. Contemporaneous Nahua call it Talokan, and other groups identify it as a Table of Gold. It is the great source from which the "seeds" come, and to which they return when they have completed the terrestrial part of their cycle. One of the great hill's representations is a tub, an image that is also used for the hill's goddesses.[24]

For a grain of maize to be converted into an active seed, it had to be united with the "heart" through the work and technique of rituals. This procession of the young girls, living symbols of corn, to the temple and granary, and the rites that take place there, achieves this union and constitutes cosmo-magical circles. The physical and spiritual corns come together and we are told that "when the seed was sown, when it was time for planting, thus they sowed."

In this first action at the temple, we see the repetition of the archetype—the archetypal hill is symbolized in the temple granary and the earthly seed is a repetition of the seeds from Tlalocan, the watery underworld that supplies the forces of life. The second change comes when one of the girls is magically transformed into the *teotl ixiptla*, the living receptacle of the "heart" of the goddess, by being adorned with cosmic symbols, though the description here is muted. She is dressed "all in red—completely red on her arms, her legs, her face"[25] and becomes the image of Chicomecoatl, the heart of the corn. Her powers are prodigious for Chicomecoatl "made all our food—white maize, yellow maize, green maize shoots, black maize, black and brown mixed, various hued; large and wide; round and ball-like; slender maize; long maize; speckled red and white maize as if striped with blood, painted with blood . . . then the beans . . . amaranth . . . chia."[26] This is a goddess who *makes.*

In the longer narrative of this sacrifice in Sahagún, there is no description of the killing of the girl, though it did in fact take place. Women have appeared on the ritual stage and possessed the sacred power of words and plants. They have been gradually transformed into the "heart" of maize, the invisible substance that gives corn, amaranth, beans, and chia the power of regeneration. We see the cosmomagical correspondence that young women, under the spell of ritual, become young corn. We know that this woman has been dressed to be killed, and that her death pays some kind of debt that restarts the germination of plants, but it is only when we turn to the seventh ceremony, beginning forty days later, that we are told of the actual ritual slaughter of girls.

We Are Told How the Woman Is Killed: She Dies Like a God

And they bore down upon her neck with the beak of a swordfish.[27]

The red woman of the Great Vigil is replaced by a yellow and green woman in Tecuilhuitontli, "The Minor Festival of the Lords," where we find a luscious image of the dressing of the female *ixiptla*. We are told in Dibble and Anderson's translation that a young woman "dies a sacrificial death." But the Nahuatl term is *teomiqui*, which means to "die divinely" or to "die as a god," as though one were the incarnation of the god. In this case, the *teotl ixiptla* was the female receptacle of the heart of the goddess of salt, Huixtocihuatl, the elder sister of the rain god, and she was sacrificed, or died, for the goddess *in order for that goddess to be regenerated*. She first was dressed from head to foot with an organized array of cosmic symbols of the sea, sky, felines, plants, birds, and flowers. Yellow ocher the "color of maize blossoms" was painted on her face below a vivid green paper cap with many outspread quetzal feathers in the form of maize tassels. Golden ear plugs flashed on the sides of her face like "squash blossoms," and she wore a shift designed with waves of water and an image of green stones and billowing clouds. This image of water and sky was repeated in the skirt, which partially covered the calves with bound jaguar skins covered with bells. Her ankles wore golden bells so that when she walked she rustled, clattered, and tinkled. She moved on "foam sandals" lined with cotton yarn. All this color, design, and symbol was the bright backdrop for her shield with water lily flowers and leaves painted on it. This fertility image was adorned with yellow parrot-feather pen-

dants made into tassels "like the forepart of a locust" and eagle, quetzal, troupial, and the ruddy tail feathers of parrots.

She went dancing for ten days with women wearing artemisia
flowers and linked together by the *xochimecatl*, a flower rope. "She
kept swinging the shield around in a circle, with it she crouched, she
walked leaning on the staff, she walked thrusting it into the ground"[28]
as though opening the earth for planting. Gender relations are hinted
at again, as this prodigious show of female power, talent, and arrangement with a goddess in the center was led by old men, the conductors
of the procession; "they went directing them . . . the chief men of the
calpulli . . . they were named keepers of the god(dess)."[29] In fact, an
old man carried a brilliant feather ornament, called Huixtocihuatl's
brilliant plumage, in front of the goddess. After ten days of dancing
there was an all-night dance at which the old women kept the girl
dancing so she would not sleep.

Following these delirium-producing rites, the sacrifices began
when war captives, who had also been transformed into gods' images,
were forced to dance all night and were referred to as her "funda-
ment." These individuals served as beds, or supports, for the goddess
after she was sacrificed. When the goddess's image died, she had companions who died just moments before. Their bodies were located as
beds, or foundations, and her body was placed on top of them. But
before the killing began, the participants underwent changes of name
and place. First, the captives and the priests were given the names of
huixtotin, or salt people. This naming signified a metamorphosis of
place within the ritual, for these participants were "considered as belonging to a remote archetypal place which is located on the sea coast,
the mythical place of origin of the salt people."[30] Their mythic identities were symbolized by their head insignias of claws of eagles, quetzal
head feathers, and eagle down. Second, this powerful, mythical entourage walked in a procession through the ceremonial center to the
cosmo-magical circle of the temple of Tlaloc and ascended to the
summit. The drama and tension that had been building were now released in a short, compact, and explosive description of the sacrifice.
First, the fundaments were put to death, and then the goddess was
brought out to the sacrificial area. "And when this was done, thereupon they laid her down on the offering stone. They stretched her out
upon her back. They each laid hold of her; they each pulled tightly

her hands, her feet. They bent her breast up greatly; they bent down her back. And her head they pulled tightly so that they took it nearly to the ground."[31] This female example of total vulnerability, this heart of the goddess, was then beheaded. "And they bore down upon her neck with the beak of a swordfish, barbed, serrated, spiny-spiny on either side."[32] Why the swordfish? The use of the swordfish as the instrument of death brings forward the mythic episode in which the great aquatic figure of Cipactli, the creator goddess who inhabited the sea, was torn apart to create elements of the earth. When she was torn apart, she screamed at the universe. In fact, the female body, now gushing with blood, was further torn apart. This was a cosmo-magical moment when a parallelism was established between an event in mythic time and a contemporary event in ritual space. "And the slayer stood ready; he arose upright for it. Thereupon he cut open her breast. And when he had opened her breast, the blood gushed up high; it gushed far. It was as if it rose; it was as if it showered; it was as if it boiled up."[33]

The heart was taken from the body and placed in a *chalchiuhxicalli,* a green stone jar that had cosmic images carved into it. The explosion of the chest and the recovery of the heart of the goddess must have been the cathartic release of the profound tensions, hopes, and fears building since the goddess was adorned as a cosmic image of fertility two weeks prior. But it is striking that only three small paragraphs are dedicated to the action of killing. Was this Sahagún's repulsion, or the circumspection of the informants? Or is the point that the ceremony, for the participants, was as much about the many rites of transformation leading up to this explosive finale as the act of death itself?

Trumpets announced the swift taking of the goddess's heart and the regeneration of the spirits of the corn. Then, her body was covered with a precious cape and brought down from the summit of the temple in the early dawn. And the salt people returned to their neighborhood for feasting, heavy drinking, skirmishes, insults, shared exhaustion, apologies, pardons, and muddled amnesia.

In this second sacrificial ceremony focused on women, we see again the themes of women as hearts of plants, the enhanced picture of the *ixiptla's* cosmo-magical costume, suggestions of gender control, and the additional violent imagery of the thrusts of the sacrificial knives and the profound release of tensions in the drunkenness and feasting afterward. But the most thorough picture of the ritual use of the female body awaits us in the ceremonial feast of Ochpaniztli, where we learn astonishing things about the complex use of the body *after* the sacrifice. Yet before that revelation of ritual metamorphosis, let's turn briefly to the eighth month, or Huey Tecuilhuitl, when the tender maize goddess Xilonen is regenerated through sacrifice. For in this ceremony the male pursuits of female sexuality are important elements to take note of.

We Are Told How They Lord It Over Her

>   . . . the masters of the youths . . . asked for the women only in secret, not in front of others.[34]

The Aztec focus on the ritual regeneration of the hearts and matter of vegetation deepened in Huey Tecuilhuitl, the Great Festival of the Lords.[35] And one significant narrative episode describes the techniques of male sexual dominance and the manipulation of moral codes between males and females. The dancing women were gathered together into a kind of female herd, for the masters of youth "grouped them, rounded them up, placed them together, grouped them together, indeed hunted them out, lest one might go somewhere, lest one be forced to accompany someone, lest some perverse youth might take one away."[36] This speaks to a control of adolescent male and female passions, and it is likely that both males and females were looking for ways to get at each other. Yet male privilege had the upper hand, for the noblemen spoke to the female guardians, asking for access to the girls. "Nonetheless, the noblemen addressed the matrons that they might go releasing some [of the women] . . . And when they released them [the girls] were given gifts . . . food . . . and gifts were given of the . . . matrons." This gift exchange, sex with young women for gifts for older women, was carried out in secret. The front-rank nobles "asked for the women only in secret . . . he went to await her in his home . . . they ate in secret."[37] The eating in secret refers no doubt to sex as well as food. The text reads, "And the woman came forth only at night, she spent only the night (with him); she departed when it was well into the night."[38]

This ambivalent moral code protecting young women and then dispensing them in secret for sex and food was surrounded by strict prohibitions for those who flaunted or made these liaisons the basis for public discussions. Scandals led to assemblies in the song house where culprits were identified for punishments that included beatings, stripping of warrior rank, blistering of the body with fire, or total social rejection. A similar punishment went to the woman for "nevermore was she to sing and dance with the others; nevermore was she to hold others by the hand."

The central female was then cosmo-magically transformed into the goddess Xilonen by ritual dressing, dancing, and "entering the sand" in four directions.[39] Entering the sand was a symbolic act of dying, joining the water and earth as a passageway into the underworld. She traveled with a consort of women to four sacred sites associated with the four year bearers. The text describes these cosmo-magical circles as "Reed, Flint knife, House, Rabbit; thus do the year-bearers go describing circles, go whirling around (as they measure time)."[40] She participated in collective dances with offering priestesses who "went encircling here . . . went enclosing her." The priestesses, who were called "the hanging gourd," conducted her to the temple of sacrifice. Along with offering priests blowing trumpets, she scattered powdered *yauhtli* into the presence of the fire priest who awaited her at the spot of sacrifice with the "mist rattle board."

In a remarkable display of physical dexterity, he lifted her up on his back, her body bent backward over his body bent forward, and she was sacrificed in this posture. The phrase used to refer to this death was "she performed her service," *njman ye ic tlacoti*, meaning as a slave she had made the payment of the debt by completing the circle of reciprocity crucial to the regeneration of plants and foodstuffs that drove this month's events. Her heart was extracted and placed this time in a blue gourd (a symbol of the cosmic mountain, perhaps), and her head was severed. Then, the telling phrase follows immediately upon this destruction of her body: "And at this time were eaten for the first time, tortillas of green maize. For the first time was offered, for the first time was chewed the cane of green corn. And for the first time were cooked amaranth greens. And for the first time the sweetness of flowers—tagetes, tobacco flowers—was smelled."[41] It is the emphatic series of "first time" references that reveal the creative power of this act of "dying like a goddess dies." It brings the green maize to life for humans and therefore signifies hope for human life to continue. The ceremony ends with descriptions of intense drinking bouts and punishment for unlicensed drinking by anyone except the elder women and men.[42]

We Are Told How She Is Skinned, Transforms a Man into a Goddess,
and Leads War Games—She Gives!

> They banished her sorrow, they kept gaining her attention, they kept
> making her laugh that she might not be sad . . . And when they flayed
> her, then a man (a priest) quickly put on her skin. He was called Tecciz-
> quacuilli—a very strong (man), very powerful, and very tall.[43]

The most spectacular display of the female in service of dying like a
god appears in the month of Ochpaniztli, in which we discover several gruesome uses of her body after death. We again find that sex was
a crucial part of the rite. These sexual and militant uses of her body
reveal the combined commitments to the regeneration of plants and
warfare, female and male cosmic forces. I will focus on two aspects of
the ritual—the deception of the young girl by her handlers and the
movement of her skin in the social order of the city and into the foreign geography of the empire. We are taken on a tour of cosmo-
magical circles, places that are sacred or sacralized by her presence and
her actions of *giving*. In each of her ritual stops, at each magic circle,
she gives. She gives her seeds in the marketplace, she gives up her virginity in the palace of the *tlatoani*, she gives up her life at the temple,
and she gives up her skin to the males who carry it into the heart of
the warrior society and to the edge of the empire! All this "giving" is
forced on her by the males who are driven by their privilege of gender
and force her to conform to the cosmo-magical imperative I have
outlined. The ritual use of her skin helps to transform the city into a
site of war games and contributes to the militarization of society.

The central image in this complex, dynamic rite is Teteo innan,
"Mother of the Gods" (also known as Toci, "Our Grandmother," and
Tlalli iyollo, "Heart of the Earth"), who appears on the ritual stage
after five days of silence. Following the hand waving dance that involved rows of circling dancers and "perverse" drunken youths, a
four-day mock battle breaks out between various groups of women,
including women physicians, pleasure girls, and older women. The
women are divided into two equal groups and dash after each other in
the streets, hurling balls of reeds, cactus leaves, and tagetes flowers.
These battles serve to mentally focus the women on the purpose of
the ritual, which is to sustain a heightened, positive mood in the
group and especially in the Teteo innan *ixiptla*. "Thus they banished
her sorrow, they kept gaining her attention, they kept making her

laugh that she might not be sad. But if there were weeping, it was said it would be an omen of evil."[44] If this elevation of mood was not achieved, the consequences were disastrous and the disasters would spread to agriculture and warfare. For it was said that if she wept, "many eagle-jaguar warriors would die in war or that many women would become *mociuaquetzque* when from their womb (children) would go."[45]

The dancing women escort her to two important locations before she is killed. First, she is escorted, "the women physicians came encircling her," to the marketplace where she scatters cornmeal in order to ensure fertility. This scattering of her seeds undergoes a dramatic reversal in the next stop of her tour toward death. She is taken aside "to where she was guarded in her temple" and the women physicians deliver a portentous message. She is told, "My dear daughter, now at last the ruler Moctezuma will sleep with thee. Be happy." It was likely assumed that this announcement of royal sex and the dissemination of his seed would ensure her elevated mood, and it may have initiated the reenactment of a mythic *hieros gamos*, the sacred sexual union of the Sky, in the form of the Chief Speaker, and the Earth, in the form of the goddess. Moctezuma's powers, and perhaps his mood, are elevated by the juices of the earth and his seed is scattered within the "heart" of the plants that she embodies.

There is deception woven into this sexual union of an adolescent girl/goddess with the adult male god/king because the next line in the text states, "They did not tell her of her death; it was as if she died unaware. Then they adorned her, they arrayed her."[46] The coincidence of meanings here is enigmatic, for does having sex with the ruler, him penetrating her body, become an imitation sacrifice of the final penetration ahead? Or is the sex a prophylactic to sorrow? For both adult ruler and adolescent goddess, this was a numinous sexual act. For the girl, it was undoubtedly an overwhelming experience of being opened up by the most holy man in the society, distracting her up until the last moment of life from feelings of sorrow. But are we really to imagine that the young woman felt only happiness and no confusion, panic, or sorrow in being forced into sexual intercourse with the ruler? The purpose of this distraction was to protect the ruler's representatives of battle, the jaguar and eagle warriors *and* women in childbirth.

When Sahagún's informants described the killing scene, the details are few. The decapitation, heart extraction, and skinning take up less than four lines. What does receive extensive attention, and demands ours, is the ritual use of her skin after death. Gender identities are confused and a masquerade takes place that helps us understand why these women were ritually transformed, deceived, penetrated, and killed. She was killed and her body was used to provoke and prepare men for warfare. "A very strong (man), very powerful, and very tall" puts on her skin and is given the name Teccizquacuilli (*tonsurado del caracol grande*). From this moment on, as long as *he* wears the skin, *he* is understood as *she,* that is, the living goddess image. One *ixiptla's* death has given birth to another *ixiptla,* though the second is a male transformed into the female deity.

Immediately, another human circle is formed, which takes on a militaristic style that spreads out into the city. The male who is now a female begins to act; "As she quickly placed herself here (on the edge of the pyramid), it was with great speed. Then she quickly came down. They followed her swiftly . . . offering priests went helping her . . . they went guarding her. And a number of nobleman and great brave warriors were awaiting her. . . . Much did they run . . . as if they flew."[47] But Teccizquacuilli does not wear the entire skin. A crucial subtraction takes place when the thigh skin of the goddess is cut away to generate yet another god. The thigh skin is taken to the community of Pochtlan where another impersonator, a male impersonator of the maize god Centeotl ("Maize Cob Deity"),[48] the son of the goddess Toci, is given and wears what is called the "thigh (skin) mask."

These two god-images, empowered by the skin fragments of the sacrificed girl, eventually meet at the Temple of Huitzilopochtli, but only after the Toci impersonator hurries down the pyramid guarded by offering priests, and together they dash through the streets followed by groups of great warriors and noblemen. Then "they fight with grass" meaning they fight with brooms. "They flew . . . they went striking their shields . . . they swiftly turned to her . . . crowding . . . pressing as they ran."[49] Then he, who is a she-god, appears before the populace with the nobles/warriors spreading the imagery of the complete metamorphosis of a teenage girl into the covering of a strong warrior, minus the thigh piece but enlarged by the sounds and gestures of attack. We are told, "there was much fear; fear spread over the people; indeed fear entered into the people."[50]

This rushing procession ends at the foot of the Great Temple where Toci met her son Centeotl. When the Toci impersonator stands at the foot of the temple, she raises her arms and spreads them and spreads her legs out as though embracing the god. Years ago, Eduard Seler suggested that this gesture was a simulation of sexual intercourse that commemorated the historical union of the Culhuacan princess and the Aztec leader during the early years of Mexica wanderings.[51] If so, the triad of plants-sex-war appears at this cosmo-magical circle of the temple. The Centeotl impersonator is wearing his peaked cap, which has the name "curved obsidian knife," the god of frost. The two go side by side to Toci's temple and "[take] their places there."

The following day, the sacrality of Toci is heightened when all the noblemen greet her and provide her with another layer of cosmo-magical skin. They attach feathers and soft eagle down to her arms and legs, paint her face, and dress her in a shift with an eagle design and a painted skirt. Quail are beheaded in her honor and incense is set before her, all in a series of swift gestures. Then several layers of "great vestments" are draped on her, including her paper crown, five marketplace banners, and a row of maguey leaves for a headdress. All of this layering of sacred powers, the skin of the goddess, the colors, feathers, and great vestments transforms the impersonator into a sacrificer. She, who was sacrificed to pay the debt, is now the sacrificer who collects it back. She is now dressed to kill others as four captives are brought before her(him). She slays them by opening the chest cavities and extracting the hearts.

She retrieves her son, Centeotl, and together they travel, spreading their cosmo-magical dual imagery of plants and war across the ceremonial pathways to one of the most impressive ceremonial centers, the skull rack. This grand trophy case of the head-collecting aspect of Aztec religion becomes the launching ground for the most eloquent statement of center-periphery dynamics of the ritual. Centeotl prepares to leave the Aztec city by "tramping on his drum" and is joined by seasoned Aztec warriors for a symbolic journey outward to the frontier of enemy territory. Surrounded by a troop of strong, agile, swift warriors, the male wearing (or carrying) the female skin thigh mask leaves the city, crosses the lake, departs the valley, and goes high into the mountains. He travels to the "land of the foe" on one of the side peaks of Iztac tepetl (literally, "White Mountain," the female mountain) and implants the thigh mask at the frontier. This provocative, bold display, in which a piece of female skin is planted in the face of the enemy, is not without human cost. Enemy scouts set upon them and "on both sides there were deaths."

While this marking of the frontier with the thigh skin mask and the blood from the skirmish takes place, the mother of Centeotl, the impersonator of Toci, returns to her home at Atempan, a neighborhood on the shore in the capital. Meanwhile, the bravest warriors, "the leading warriors, the generals, the commanding generals . . . the respected brave warriors, those valiant of their own will, who set no value upon their heads, their breast, the fearless of death who in truth hurled themselves upon our foes"[52] all gather before Moctezuma. All the warriors are placed in rows before Moctezuma who, seated upon the flayed skins of eagle and jaguars, dispenses the sacred war devices, the adornments, the costly array of gold and quetzal feathers, the insignia of great achievements. There are salutes, dances, displays of bright powerful warriors who "[move] like flowers" around the temple. The beloved old women raise a ritual tearful cry about the warriors who, like the Centeotl impersonator, will soon be going out to the periphery of the empire to do terrible battle in the conflagration of war.

The ceremony begins to disperse when Toci, with her Huaxtec handlers, sings in a high falsetto (like women's voices) till sunset. Among the other gestures of the closing ceremonies in the next several days is the public display by dancing of the arrayed warriors, with Moctezuma "in great glory." The devices gleam and scintillate in the sun. There are processions from the temples and the strewing of seeds of maize in the streets and from the heights of temples.

This grand, athletic display of goddesses dismembered and recreated on the bodies of males, one who becomes a female and one the son of the female, these processions and sacrifices and ġift giving to warriors, this display of the dancing king comes to a close with one final public skirmish between the goddess Toci and the city. Brave warriors race away from the main temple in search of feathers until they come to the figure of Toci who enters into a collective, combative race in which her own entourage battles others. Moctezuma, at an appointed spot, enters the race for a brief spell and then slips into a nearby temple. The offering priests lead the impersonator to a final cosmo-magical circle, a sacred wooden building where s/he is stripped of the adornments and the skin. The skin is placed on a wooden support with its head looking forward into the city. The metamorphosis is now complete. The vital hearts of plants are restored and the warriors are prepared to launch themselves outward to that frontier marked with blood and skin. The metamorphic vision of place recedes and the locative view of the world is revived in the final phrases, "And when they had gone setting it in place, then there was a turning about; there was a quick departure."[53]

CONCLUSION

I have attempted to combine verbal picture making and interpretation, from the perspective of the history of religions, of selected Sahagúntine materials in order to enlarge our understanding of how the sacrifice of women strove to combine ritual cosmo-magical efforts to regenerate plants and warfare in Tenochtitlan. Using the model of the "metamorphic vision of place and ritual," I have attempted to map out the ritual movements of women's bodies through a series of cosmo-magical circles that transformed them into the hearts of plants and the inspirations for war. The routes of these women, which, in a cumulative sense, move from house to temple to granary to marketplace to stone of sacrifice to the palace to the military frontier, spreading sacred powers and changing their cosmos, were managed by male warriors, priests, and the ruler. It is significant that while women play important roles in the sacrifices of women, males direct them, seduce them, insult them, sacrifice them, and wear them. Women, when they have power, express it in their capacities to, among other things, become hearts of corn or "torment young men into war." In my view, these sacrifices of women illustrate that females were not only travelers along a route of cosmo-magical circles, or sacred circles themselves, but that they were the living pivots, especially in the rite of Ochpaniztli, linking the hearts of plants with the preparation for war and the striving for the glamor of war by the males. It will take future studies to clarify whether this male management of female powers was primarily a strategy to take female creative energy associated with the earth, plants, and fertility and redirect it, in certain cases, through ritual metamorphosis, into military needs, styles, and purposes.

CHAPTER 8

When Warriors Became Walls, When the Mountain of Water Crumbled

. . . and a great brave warrior . . . became a wall.

In a space of just four pages at the end of the *Florentine Codex* describing the whirling, ferocious battles between the Spaniards and their Indian allies against the Mexicas, the reader finds over ten references to walls that symbolize the city of Tenochtitlan. Houses become walls, canals are referred to as walls, and most poignantly, warriors become the final walls of the city. Among the references we find "they abandoned the wall," "all of the houses . . . became a wall," "Chalchi-uhtepeua hid himself behind a wall," "they went forcing them to take a stand at Copalnamacoyan where stood a wall," and "the canals were considered to be like great walls." The Aztecs, like Gilgamesh who attempted to win security against chaos and death by maintaining the walls of Uruk,[1] strove desperately to keep their imperial enclave upright and their symbolic world in order. But to see these references as forefronting the locative nature of the city's final narrative would be a mistake. The story at the end of the empire is, in some ways, the same story that has been performed all along—the interplay between the metamorphic vision of space, the symbolism of the center, the locative vision of place.

The fate of these walls, as with the warriors who stood on them and became them, was a terrible metamorphosis. All that had been taking place for the two hundred years of Mexica dexterity, cunning, brilliance, and cruelty changed places, and the great *altepetl* that was at the heart of the empire collapsed and underwent a furious, dreadful,

The Aztec capital was conquered by the combined Spanish/Indian assault.
Aztec warriors become a part of the walled defense of the island city of
Tenochtitlan in this scene from the *Florentine Codex*. (After Paso y Troncoso,
courtesy of the University of Utah Press.)

and, eventually from the Spanish perspective, glorious change. These
combinations of dread and glory, commitments to symbolic order
and the vertigo of change during the city's final resistance are depicted
in Sahagún's last volume and symbolized in the following scene. We
are told that the Mexicas have their backs literally up against the few
remaining walls when, in their own words, "step by step the Spaniards gained more ground and captured more houses. They forced us
backwards" until the Mexica rulers chose to dress a "great brave war-

rior" in the most potent battle array they could gather, the "Quetzal-Owl" uniform, filled with the divine fire of gods and kings. The last Aztec ruler, Cuauhtemoc, Diving Eagle, spoke of the royal uniform to the gathered warriors at the hasty investiture in this way: "This regalia belonged to my father, the great warrior Ahuitzotl. Terrify our enemies with it. Annihilate our enemies with it. Let them behold it and tremble."[2] The ruler placed in the warrior's hands the "magic object," the most potent mythical weapon in the Aztec arsenal, the "Serpent of Fire," which we remember was Huitzilopochtli's divine weapon that severed the head and body of Coyolxauhqui at Coatepec, Serpent Mountain (in chapter 2). The warrior, dressed in the quetzal-owl uniform, became an inspiring sight for "he indeed looked marvelous." It was felt that he had become possessed by the god Huitzilopochtli and the ancestral rulers of the Mexicas and was sent forth to confront the Spaniards: "Mexicanos, the power of Huitzilopochtli, resides in this finery. Loose the sacred arrow at our enemies, for it is the Serpent of Fire, the Arrow that Pierces the Fire."[3] The impression was stunning and symbolized the drastic, even apocalyptic, changes everyone was facing. Accompanied by four captains, now representing as a group the five sacred directions, the great warrior's quetzal feathers spread out around him, increasing the size and terror of his appearance. The elders remembered with pride the effect it had on the Spaniards, "When our enemies saw him approach, they quaked as if they thought a mountain were about to fall on them. They trembled with dread, as if they knew the finery could work magic."[4] This *ixiptla* of Huitzilopochtli and warrior kings initially overwhelmed Spanish and Tlacaltecan warriors and then, under intense attack from his foes, he seemed to disappear into the battle air. "And then he dropped from the roof terrace. He did not die . . . the battle just stopped; thus silence reigned; nothing took place . . . Thus night fell."[5] But in fact, something consequential was taking place, for the mountain that was crumbling was not the Spanish mountain but the Aztec "mountain of water," the great *altepetl* of Tenochtitlan, and it was falling on the people of Tenochtitlan.

It is for these reasons that we might consider retitling Miguel León-Portilla's celebrated book, which in the Spanish was entitled *Vision de los Vencidos,* for we are not witnessing so much the vision of the vanquished as a dynamic vision of a vanquished place! From the first page to the last sentence of Book 12, entitled "The Conquest," the narrative is dominated by the transformation, conflagration, shrinkage, collapse, and ruin of a supreme social place, the crystallized image of the Aztec world where once "no one fears to die in war" but now allies stream in to the ceremonial precinct, crying to the ruler Cuauhtemoc, "O my beloved noblemen, with a little we have come to help the city." The city is narrated as changing from the quintessential center of the world into a pulsating "conflict zone" where arrivals led to murders, conversations led to misunderstandings and betrayals, rulers were utterly changed through desperate cremations, treasure houses and females were looted, and the walls and warriors who were walls were reduced to skeletal structures upon which the Spaniards built the capital of New Spain.

In what follows, I will interpret this change from *axis mundi* to conflict zone by focusing on several episodes in the interpretive and military games of critical arrival[6] each side played, the shrinkage of the city, and the final narrative attempt by Spaniards and Mexicas alike to resurrect the capital, in a shared image of nostalgia, into a city of gold. We will see how the combination of interpretation and aggression played crucial roles in the conquest of the city and how its collapse was understood and memorialized.

THE CONTACT ZONE/CONFLICT ZONE
AT THE PERIPHERY AND CENTER

From first page to last word, the final tome of the *Florentine Codex* is about the destruction of a city. The place where "eagles roared" and that Bernal Díaz del Castillo compared to "the wonders they tell of in the tale of Amadis" is progressively reduced to a fragmented landscape, as the Aztec poets soon lamented,

> We are crushed to the ground,
> we lie in ruins.
> There is nothing but grief and suffering in Mexico and
> Tlatelolco,
> where once we saw beauty and valor.[7]

The title page to Book 12 announces that it narrates how "the Spaniards conquered the city of Mexico," and the first chapter heading reiterates this urban focus by stating that what follows "telleth how war was waged here in the city of Mexico." The initial sense of place in the text is of the empire and city as a contact zone—a zone of physical and symbolic contention, maneuvering for advantage, spying, and fear. Mary Louise Pratt defined a "contact zone" as a "social space where desperate cultures meet, clash, and grapple with each other, often in highly asymmetrical relations of domination and subordination,"[8] and while she intends this guideline for reflections on other types of cultural exchanges, the definition works well for the early exchanges, especially on the shores of Anahuac in 1519. For here we find bodies, languages, interpretations, and elites struggling for the upper hand and always in shifting scenes and relations of greed, misunderstanding, and the lust for dominance. But this contact zone soon evolves into something more powerful, dangerous, zealous, and fervent. The contacts become conflicts that lead to heroic, intensely destructive, sometimes self-destructive and chaotic actions. The temples, palaces, causeways, and neighborhoods become the sites of terrible wounds, sacrificed Spaniards and their horses, murdered rulers, dismembered priests and women, drowning soldiers, and demolished walls and homes. The city of Tenochtitlan became the *conflict zone* of European/native American contact par excellence and the ramifications of what happened in and around the city in 1519–1521 are embedded in Mexico and the Americas of today. And the narrative of this war in the conflict zone began at the periphery of the empire, out on the water. Let us look at three episodes of contact and conflict in which interpretations and aggressions were interwoven into the game of arrival.

Following a description of the omens that announced the conquest (discussed in chapter 1), the "first boat" arrived, and the Indians went out to meet it, spy on it, and exchange with it. The first words reportedly spoken between the contending parties leads to a designation of place. The Spaniards call out, "Who are you? Whence have you come? Where is your home?" and the Mexica merchant spies answer, not naming themselves but their home, "It is from there in Mexico that we have come."[9] Soon, gifts come from Mexico's ruler for the strangers on the shore, and we see evidence of the Aztec's first interpretation of the encounter. We read that when Moctezuma hears the details of the first exchanges between Spaniards and his spies, he "thought that the new arrival was our prince Quetzalcoatl," the ancestral priest king of the great city of Tollan who had departed Mexico, promising, in some accounts, to return one day and restore his kingdom. The Aztecs thought that these people were somehow "like us," and we have an interpretive tradition for such an arrival. The Aztec ruler, trying to project his interpretation forcefully onto the scene, sent "the treasure of Quetzalcoatl," which consisted of the regalia of the Toltec god-king. Fortunately, we have a list of these gifts and the details of the regalia that was meant to cover Cortés from head to toe. The first item on the list was a mask, a divine mask, "a serpent mask inlaid with turquoise." The Aztec ruler, in his attempt to embroider the Spanish arrival with his own symbols and signs, included the rich regalia of two other gods, Tlaloc and Tezcatlipoca, *and* a second collection of Quetzalcoatl's "divine adornments."[10] In the Aztec memory of this early symbolic contact, Moctezuma had his interpretive way when Cortés put on the mask of Quetzalcoatl and dressed as the god.

There are several possibilities of the meaning of Moctezuma's efforts. In effect, Cortés was being dressed as the *ixiptla*, the living image of one of the Aztec gods. On the one hand, this action has usually been interpreted as elevating Cortés to the level of Quetzalcoatl, the patron god of cities and rulers, as part of Moctezuma's eventual drama of abdication. On the other hand, from our study of sacrifice, we know that all sacrificial victims, especially those of high honor, were dressed as gods prior to being sacrificed. Is Moctezuma playing a sacred game, a sacred joke on Cortés by preparing him, at least in the eyes of understanding Aztecs, for the sacrificial stone? What seems clear to me is that the Aztecs were striving to impose their own indigenous interpretation on the encounters, as if to say, we rule by ritual and symbols as well as by brutality. But in the Aztec account, Cortés resisted the game of being put into a vulnerable position and dressed with this incredible list of riches and offered an insult, "And is this all? Is this your gift of welcome? Is this how you greet people?" The implication is that if the Aztecs had brought this extraordinary finery to his feet and body, then there must be more up there in that great city of Mexico.

This "contact zone" quickly became the "conflict zone." While the distance from the waters to the capital were great over land, it was a short distance in conversation, and the goal of traveling to the capital and confronting the ruler grew immediately in Spanish minds. Following the drama of gift exchange and as the rumor of Quetzalcoatl's return unfolded, the Spaniards began their bloody, cunning, and single-minded pursuit of the capital.

These exchanges became laced with violence as each side strove to gain the upper hand, the more powerful symbolic statement and military display. One scene in particular revealed the passing back and forth of the interpretive advantage. As the Spaniards steadily approached the capital, Moctezuma sent emissaries and magicians with food for the visitors, but in a fashion that would "use their wizardry upon them, cast a spell over them, that they might perhaps blow upon them, enchant them . . . so that they might take sick, might die, or else because of it turn back."[11] To bring this reversal of fortune about, Moctezuma put the Spaniards into physical, visual, and olfactory contact with their cuisine of violence. The Mexica king sent a cornucopia of foods that not only included eggs, turkey hens, sweet potatoes, plums, guava, avocados, tuna cactus fruit, custard apple, but also captives, with the instruction that the Spaniards should sacrifice them and *drink their blood*. In fact, the emissaries had soaked much of the food in blood and the result was potent on Spanish noses and stomachs, "They were nauseated. They spat; they closed their eyes tight, they shut their eyes; they shook their heads . . . For strongly did it reek of blood."[12] The Spaniards were temporarily repulsed and, as with the masks of the gods, it seemed as though the Aztecs had made the more persuasive move. But the struggle of cruel wizardry was lost, for when the messengers returned to the capital, they announced to Moctezuma, "We are not their equals; we are as nothing."[13]

A third episode deepens our sense of the conflict zone in the march to Mexico-Tenochtitlan by revealing ancient quarrels among native groups, inter-Indian rivalries that suggest an indigenous conflict zone had been long in place. It is also the first image of walls burned to the ground. The Spaniards were relentlessly marching toward the city, attacking, repelling attacks, and making native allies along the way. Moctezuma sent out his sorcerers to set up a magical wall to block the way, to "contend against the (Spaniards)." These sorcerers were confronted by another native sorcerer in the form of a vision, sent not by the Spaniards but by a rival Indian community. In this vision, which appeared collectively to Moctezuma's magicians, a

Chalcan drunkard leading the Spanish vanguard blocked their path, possessed of the god of *pulque* and bound by eight grass ropes around his chest. The Chalcans were one of the most successful of the Aztecs' enemies, resisting for years the Mexica attempts to dominate their *altepetl* located in the southern region of the lake area. The Aztecs had previously lost military campaigns to the Chalcans before finally subduing them late in the fifteenth century. The Chalcan sorcerer-ghost arrived spewing hatred and insults against Moctezuma, of whom he asked, "Is he then perchance now overcome by a great fear? He hath committed a fault; he hath abandoned the common folks; he hath destroyed the people. Because of him they have been struck on the head; because of him they have been wrapped (in wrappings for the dead). They have been laughed at. They have been mocked."[14] This onslaught of verbal abuses, accusations of a ruler overwhelmed by fear and committing sins against his people whom he has, by his frail leadership, condemned to derision and death, reflects an inter-native conflict zone that both preceded the arrival of Spaniards and extended long after the war of conquest, when native informants from various communities reported their memories at Sahagún's round table interviews. As if the Chalcan's condemnations were not enough of a sign of inter-Indian conflicts and Tenochtitlan's fall, the enemy sorcerer announced that it was the people's city that was in certain peril, "Nevermore will there be a Mexico; it is already (gone) forever. Go hence; it is no longer there. Turn about; look at what cometh to pass in Mexico—what thus already cometh to pass!"[15]

With their backs toward the city, Moctezuma's men turned about, and when they did, the city of the omens of the conquest rose up before them in a wall of fire, "They beheld that already all the temples, the *calpulli* (buildings), the *calmecac* (buildings), all the houses in Mexico were burning; and it was as if already there was fighting."[16] The report of this encounter and its visions of the end of the city resulted in Moctezuma's "head hanging down. No longer did he speak aloud . . . as if he had lost hope."[17] One of his last acts of resistance before the Spanish arrived at the edge of the capital was the construction of a pathetic "wall of maguey plants" across the road.

The story of inter-*altepetl* native rivalries intensified as the Spaniards penetrated the city's confines, walls, temples, palaces, and women. False allies, such as the Xochimilcans, offered help to the

Mexicas only to betray them at the crucial hours of battle. The narrative of Book 12 favors the heroism of the Tlatelolcan warriors and rulers over the weaker Tenochcas under Moctezuma's fading leadership. Native rulers were murdered, some say by the Spaniards and others say by the natives themselves. The royal bodies were cremated amidst native eulogies and insults. The most complex symbol of the indigenous rivalries and the collapse of the city is, of course, the native woman Doña Marina, or Malinche, whose trilingual tongue (she spoke Nahuatl, a Maya language, and was learning Spanish in various ways, including through her intimacies with Cortés) and body serve as the dynamic contact zone between Aztec and Spanish meanings. She was Cortés's mistress and bore his favorite son, and it was she who translated, or mistranslated, the words of exchange between Cortés and Moctezuma. Was she a traitor of the Aztecs, as has been memorialized down through the centuries, or was she a spy for the natives while sharing the secrets of the Spanish advance? We are told emphatically that "when Moctezuma's address which he directed to the Marquis was ended, Marina then interpreted it, she translated it to him. And when the Marquis had heard Moctezuma's words, he spoke to Marina; he spoke to them in a barbarous tongue."[18]

THE CITY IN BITS AND PIECES

This barbarous Spanish tongue ordered a ferocious series of attacks by thousands of native warriors and hundreds of Spanish soldiers against the city. The last twenty chapters of Book 12 narrate the violent fragmentation of the capital and the lost cause of the valiant native defenders. The struggle and metamorphosis of place is described in terms of the destruction of barrios, buildings, alleys, homes, walls, women, and children. We are faced with a crescendo of place names—neighborhood after neighborhood, wall after wall—that collapsed in the face of attacking cannons, catapults, swords, arrows, bodies, and shrieks. Ayotzintepec and Chinantla fell to the enemy, as did Tepeyacac. Canals were breached at Tecpantzinco, Tzapotlan, and Atenchicalco. Having gained precious ground, the Spaniards were terribly, but only temporarily, defeated in the Noche Triste and retreated to Teocalhueyacan to regroup and reload. The degree of ferocious violence, slaughter, and death suffered by the Spaniards is vividly described in one episode of this retreat on the Spanish night of sorrows. Cortés had ordered a retreat from the capital and the Spaniards attempted to sneak out in the night. The retreat was discovered and the Aztecs attacked along the Tlacopan causeway. The Spaniards were driven to the brink and forced to jump into the waters at the Canal of the Toltecs. The carnage is described, "The canal was soon choked with the bodies of men and horses. They filled the gap in the causeway with their own drowned bodies. Those who followed crossed to the other side by walking on the corpses." The dead bodies of the Spaniards and their Indian allies became a bridge to eventual safety. The Spaniards retreated and it is while they were recouping their losses and preparing for the siege of the capital that Moctezuma was killed and his body ritually cremated.

When the final siege of the capital began with the attack of the brigantines some time later, the attackers smashed through the walled and human defenses, they penetrated Moctezuma's palace and crossed Uauhquiyauac, and the city began to shrink and disintegrate from their pounding weapons, feet, and bodies. The Aztecs resisted mightily against the notorious Spanish captain Pedro Alvardo, who realized he had come to "arise against a stone" of jaguar and eagle knights. Nonoalco was taken, and the Aztecs were crouched in tight places, "the brave warriors crouched low at the walls and remained hidden (among) houses or walls," crying out to each other *"Mexicae ma ie cuel"*—"O Mexicans, courage!"[19] Skirmishes and hand-to-hand combats broke out in a thousand small contested areas animated by stomping, beating of breasts, and especially song! "The enemy Tlaxcallans . . . sang. Also the Mexicans sang. On both sides there was song. They intoned whatsoever they remembered. Thus it came about that they animated themselves."[20] In a scene depicted by the artists of the *Florentine Codex,* many Spaniards were captured and sacrificed along with their horses, and the heads of man and beast were strung up on one of the great symbolic structures of the conflict zone, the *tzompantli,* or skull rack, in a public performance of defiance and rage. But this display of decapitated horses and men only inflamed the enemy, who "pressed us back as if with a wall." The Mexicas were forced to abandon barrio after barrio, wall after wall, and were driven back into the last fortified enclaves near Tlatelolco, where they were forced "to take a stand in Copalnamacoyan, where stood the wall."[21] One of the last acts of defiance, described earlier, was when the

WHEN WARRIORS BECAME WALLS   221

quetzal-owl warrior, under furious attack, dropped from the roof terrace, out of sight, and into Mexica memory. Cortés's Indian and
Spanish warriors reduced the extensive space of the city to the Tlatelolco ceremonial precinct where they forced Moctezuma's nephew
and surviving ruler, Cuauhtemoc, who had previously sent out the
quetzal-owl warrior in sacred defiance, into submission. Today, at the
ceremonial center of the Plaza of Three Cultures, near the spot of the
surrender, stands a gray monument, a slab, a single symbolic wall with
these words carved on it, "On the 13 of August of 1521, heroically de-
fended by Cuauhtemoc, Tlatelolco fell to the power of Hernan Cortés." Then in a prideful assertion of the metamorphosis of place and
people that ensued, the monument reads, "This was not a triumph or
a defeat but the painful birth of the mestizo people which is Mexico
today."

CITY OF GOLD: SUM OF ALL WONDERS
Among the final scenes narrated to Sahagún are those describing the
Spanish lust for gold and for Aztec women. While Cortés was managing the surrender of the Mexica nobles, "everywhere on the roads the
Spaniards robbed people. They sought gold. They despised the green
stone, the precious feathers, and the turquoise."[22] They also rounded
up the pretty women, the most human of conflict zones, in a military
action. We are told that the Spaniards seized the pretty women,
"those whose bodies were yellow, the yellow ones," as they were also
robbing the people. Some women, fearful of rape and servitude,
worked frantically to make themselves appear old and unattractive.
"And some women, when they were to be taken from the people,
muddied their faces, and clothed themselves in old clothing, put rags
on themselves as a shift. It was all only rags that they put on themselves."[23]

This combination of women and gold takes on the meaning of a
sexual joke in the final dialogues of the *Florentine Codex*. You will remember from the introduction that the victorious Cortés gathered
the native rulers together to ask, "What of the gold? That which was
guarded in Mexico?" The surviving Aztec governor, the figure
known as the Cihuacoatl or Snake Woman, the second in command
behind the Chief Speaker, and Cortés traded barbs about who had
taken the gold, the Aztecs or their rivals, the Spanish allies of Tlatel-

olco. At a tense moment in the conversation, Doña Marina, Cortés's mistress, speaking for the Spaniard, ordered the Aztec spokesman, "The captain sayeth, 'You will produce two hundred pieces of gold this size.' She measured it with her hands; she moved her hands in a circle."[24] The Cihuacoatl's response was a clever, if lewd, countermove and reference to Cortés's and Malinche's sexual union, "Perhaps some poor woman put it (the gold) in her skirt. It will be sought. He will find it."[25] Then, as though to move swiftly past the double entendre of Malinche's circling hands and her skirt, and Cortés seeking gold there, another noble stepped forward and uttered the last words in the form of a eulogy of the Aztec city as a city of gold thriving *before* the Spaniards ruined it. He summarized the imperial pattern of Aztec conquest, tribute collection, and riches that poured into the "mountain of water," putting in words the painted scenes of centripetal control we interpreted in the first chapter of this book. He says that "when yet there was Moctezuma, when there was a conquest, the Mexicans, the Tlatilulcans, the Tepanecans, the Acolhuans moved together . . . and those of the floating gardens—all of us moved together when we conquered." The Mexica world was an integration of city-states that gathered the green stone, the precious feather, the gold, and beautiful bird feathers into the capital. In a sense, he was saying that the city as a whole, as a way of life, was precious *prior* to the arrival of the Spaniards. The implication was that if they wanted the riches of Tenochtitlan, they shouldn't have overrun the precious city. Now the city was fallen and what they sought had been ruined. In his final words, recalling the days before the invasion, "They gave it to Moctezuma. It arrived there together. All the tribute, the gold was together there in Tenochtitlan."[26]

The sum of all wonders.

Introduction

The opening epigraph is taken from Fray Diego Durán, *The History of the Indies of New Spain*, translated, annotated, and with an introduction by Doris Heyden (Norman: University of Oklahoma Press, 1994), p. 140.

1. René Gerard, *Violence and the Sacred,* trans. Patrick Gregory (Baltimore: The Johns Hopkins University Press, 1977), p. 31. The fuller statement by Gerard is: "The sacred consists of all those forces whose dominance over man increases or seems to increase in proportion to man's effort to master them. Tempests, forest fires, and plagues, among other phenomena, may be classified as sacred. Far outranking these, however, though in a far less obvious manner, stands human violence—violence seen as something exterior to man and henceforth as a part of all the other outside forces that threaten mankind. Violence is the heart and secret soul of the sacred."

2. While I claim the Chicago tradition of the history of religions as part of my heritage, this study offers a critique of the overly optimistic tone of interpretation found in the works of Mircea Eliade, Joseph Kitagawa, and Joachim Wach, where an overemphasis on the creative, uplifting, regenerative forces obscures the brutality, destructiveness, and horror also embedded in religion.

3. Mircea Eliade and Lawrence E. Sullivan, "Orientation," in Mircea Eliade, editor in chief, *The Encyclopedia of Religion,* vol. 11, pp. 105–106 (New York: Macmillan Publishing Company, 1987).

4. One scholar in particular, Charles H. Long, goes so far as to write, "For my purposes, religion will mean orientation—orientation in the ultimate sense, that is, how one comes to terms with the ultimate significance of one's place in the world." See *Significations: Signs, Symbols, and Images in the Interpretation of Religion* (Aurora, Colo.: The Davies Group Publishers, 1999), p. 7.

5. I use the Nahuatl term *altepetl* to refer to the Aztec city. *Altepetl* means literally "Water Mountain" and signifies the religious origin of the community as a union of divine powers dwelling in earth and water. In Remi Simeón's useful dictionary, the term *altepetl* refers to city, state, people, and community, and the word became synonymous with human settlement. In indigenous beliefs, the patron deities lived

in the surrounding hills and a number of Mesoamerican pyramid temples were *imago mundis*—humanly constructed images of their water mountain.

6. There are a number of Nahuatl terms that refer to sacrificial rituals and human sacrifice. The broadest term is *tlamictliztli*, or ritual slaughter. This word is found in the *Primeros Memoriales* of Sahagún, folio 255r, among a list of ritual forms. Two important works on Aztec sacrifice are Yólotl González Torres, *El sacrificio humano entre los mexica* (Mexico City: INAH/FCE, 1985), and C. Duverger, *La flor letal*, trans. J. J. Utrilla (Mexico City: FCE, 1983). Sometimes, the term *teomiqui* is used, which translates "to die divinely" or "to die as a god dies." The most common sacrifice was autosacrifice, or *izo*, "to bleed," or *tetequi*, "to cut." Another term, *nextlahualtin*, means "payments," signifying a repayment to the gods through ritual slaughter for the gift of life previously given by the gods.

7. Alfredo López Austin argues that the explanation for the astonishing increase in human sacrifices "must be sought in the inefficiency of the conquerors to dominate the peoples who had fallen before their army." This means that sacrifices increased as ways to control newly acquired territories and to diminish potential rebellions (*The Human Body and Ideology: Concepts Among the Ancient Nahuas* [Salt Lake City: University of Utah Press, 1988], p. 380).

8. See "Sacrifice" by Jill Robins, in *Critical Terms for Religious Studies,* ed. Mark C. Taylor (Chicago: University of Chicago Press, 1998), pp. 285–297, for an example of this problem. The critical discussion of sacrifice is largely confined to biblical materials and never mentions the Americas or Mesoamerica, where one of the most elaborate records of sacrifice is available.

9. Italo Calvino, *Invisible Cities* (San Diego: Harcourt Brace Jovanovich, 1972), p. 14.

10. During a research project in Japan, I visited and witnessed a number of small- and large-scale pilgrimage routes and sites that sometimes involved challenging mountain terrain. I was impressed with the dynamic changes in the natural and cultural landscape of these pilgrimages, which varied in elevation, foliage, physical challenge, and an ever-changing vista and sense of one's body moving through a ceremonial landscape where muscles, vision, sound, taste, smell, and mind are changed. While in Japan and reading a number of Sahagún's descriptions of Aztec sacrificial ceremonies, I began to discern a similar dynamic and diversity in the processions through the ceremonial landscapes of the Basin of Mexico, and I could begin to map the intense metamorphoses of physical and mental awareness that were described. These experiences and comparisons helped in the development of an altered model of the ceremonial landscape within and beyond the built form of the capital city. I began to think of Aztec religion as not only focused on the "centered mass" of the Great Temple and the capital city but more in terms of a "sensitive grid" through which ritual processions moved between related and sometimes competing ceremonial centers, terrains, and geographies. I developed an alternative model to both Mircea Eliade's "center space" and J. Z. Smith's "locative vision of place," which argued that religious performances renewed and created cultural

meaning through exercises of "changing place." The key idea is that the Aztec world was ordered by what I call the "metamorphic vision of place." This model of metamorphosis, usually dependent on sacrifice, is presented in chapters 4, 5, and 6.

11. Clifford Geertz, *Local Knowledge: Further Essays in Interpretive Anthropology* (New York: Basic Books, 1983), p. 22. In Geertz's words, "Because theory, scientific or otherwise, moves mainly by analogy, a 'seeing-as' comprehension of the less intelligible by the more (the earth is a magnet, the heart is a pump, light is a wave, the brain is a computer, and space is a balloon), when its course shifts, the conceits in which it expresses itself shift with it." In this series of essays, I employ two such analogies to attempt comprehension of the Aztec city, i.e., the city as symbol and the city as performance.

12. Italo Calvino, *Invisible Cities*, p. 14.

13. Toby Cole, *Venice: A Portable Reader* (New York: Frontier Press, 1979), p. 145.

14. Ibid., p. 60.

15. Bruno Bettelheim, *Freud's Vienna and Other Essays* (New York: Alfred P. Knopf, 1989), p. 7.

16. Raymond Williams, *The City and the Country* (New York: Oxford University Press, 1973), p. 154.

17. Ibid., p. 155.

18. Concerning my interest in viewing cities as performers, one could turn to a number of other novelists whose cities do much more than stand as grand symbolic designs for the life of characters but rather act as major characters themselves. Consider Toni Morrison's New York in *Jazz*, or Carlos Fuentes's Mexico City in *Where the Air Is Clear*, or Tomas Eloy Martinez's Buenos Aires in *Santa Evita*, or the greatest city, Macondo (well, it becomes a city), in Gabriel García Márquez's *One Hundred Years of Solitude*. The city is forced again and again into the consciousness of the characters and the reader, or it inspires or limits consciousness (and sometimes the city *is* consciousness) in ways that make it akin to a great god of the earth and air. And who has not noticed in film after film about political and governmental culture in the United States the architectural performance of the national mall in Washington, D.C. (*No Way Out, True Lies*), stretching from the capital building down the open spaces between the Smithsonian museums and reaching past the Vietnam Memorials (*JFK, The Firm*), past Lincoln's memorial (*In the Line of Fire*), to the National Cemetery (*Courage Under Fire, Gardens of Stone, The Rock*)? In scores of films, our cities and their monuments, streets, and ceremonial centers are backdrops, tropes, characters, symbols, and actors, suggesting that these urban spaces not only perform North American culture, they exist as an urban unconscious that infiltrates our secret wishes, desires, and dreams.

19. Charles H. Long, "Toward a Post-Colonial Theory of Religion," unpublished manuscript, p. 6.

20. Charles H. Long, *Significations*. Regarding the pervasive and profound powers of

colonial expansion, Long writes, "The other critical element (besides Enlightenment thought) in the discussion of religion in the modern world is related to the
Western exploration of the world that is symbolized by the voyages of Christopher
Columbus in the late fifteenth century. From that time until the twentieth century,
the Western world, through conquest, trade and colonialism, made contact with
every part of the globe. These encounters and confrontations with other cultures
raised again the issue of religion. Did all peoples possess religion or were there cultures that were devoid of the religious sentiment? If religion was a form of human
meaning that might be dispensed with, what status should one allow the religions
of these other cultures? . . . Is it possible that there can be a general category of religion given the many varieties of this phenomenon?" (p. 3).

21. Calvino, *Invisible Cities*, p. 5.

22. Sahagún, *Florentine Codex*, 12:126.

23. Ibid.

1. City as Symbol in Aztec Thought

Regarding the title of chapter 1: some readers will discern a connection between
the method of this chapter and Carlo Gingberg's essay on the conjectural paradigm
elucidated in his "Clues: Roots of an Evidential Paradigm," in *Clues, Myths and the
Historial Method* (Baltimore: The Johns Hopkins University Press, 1989), pp. 96–
126. By "clues" I mean signs or symbols that open out from themselves into overt
and covert linkages with other signs and symbols and lead us on a tour toward a view
of the whole image, or problem in the case of this chapter, of the religious world of
the Aztecs as reflected in the *Codex Mendoza*. This is a document that has seldom
been recognized as yielding clues about the religious nature of the Aztec city. But in
fact, like Gingberg's insistence on "privileged zones" of minor details that lead us to
the "idea of totality," I view the many minor details of the *Codex Mendoza*'s frontispiece as an emblematic statement about Aztec religion. In a sense, it is a privileged
zone about the Aztec's most privileged zone—their cosmo-magical vision of the
city. Gingberg wrote, "Though pretensions to systematic knowledge may appear
more and more far-fetched, the idea of totality does not necessarily need to be abandoned. On the contrary, the existence of a deeply rooted relationship that explains
superficial phenomena is confirmed at the very moment it is stated that direct knowledge of such connection is not possible. Though reality may seem to be opaque,
there are privileged zones—signs, clues—which allow us to penetrate it" (p. 123).

The first epigraph is taken from Paul Wheatley, *The Pivot of the Four Quarters: A Preliminary Enquiry into the Origins and Character of the Ancient Chinese City* (Chicago:
Aldine Publishing Company, 1971), p. 441.

The second epigraph is taken from Italo Calvino, *Invisible Cities* (San Diego: Harcourt, Brace & Jovanovich, 1972), p. 10.

1. Morgan and his energetic disciple Adolph F. Bandelier were engaged in a hot and belligerent critique of the romantic image of Aztec society as articulated in William Prescott's "cunningly wrought fable," *History of the Conquest of Mexico* (New York, 1843), and Hubert Howe Bancroft's *Native Races of the Pacific States* (New York, 1875). Following the leads of E. B. Taylor, who argued that the white race was best endowed for civilized life, and Robert Wilson, who categorized the Aztecs in his *Mexico and Its Religion* (New York, 1855) as an "ordinary tribe of North American savages," Morgan reconstructed a view of Aztec society as much to save the reputation of American ethnology as to force his view that there was an essential "Indianness" shared by all New World aborigines, which bound them to the middle status of barbarism—in the middle, that is, between the savages below and the civilized peoples above. His famous scheme of society's progress appears in the first chapter, "Ethnical Periods," of his *Ancient Society* (Cambridge, Mass., 1967). For a cogent analysis of this debate, see Benjamin Keen, *The Aztec Image in Western Thought* (New Brunswick: Rutgers University Press, 1971), esp. chapter 12, pp. 380−411. According to Morgan, the "Aztec Romance," which pictured the Aztecs as civilized, was the "most deadly encumbrance upon American ethnology . . . that must be got rid of." Attacking directly the writers of this encumbrance, he states that "it caught the imagination and overcame the critical judgment of Prescott, our most charming writer, it ravaged the sprightly brain of Brasseur de Bourbourg, and it carried upon a whirlwind our author at the Golden Gate [Bancroft]" (Keen, p. 392). For an elaborate view of his position, see Lewis Henry Morgan, "Montezuma's Dinner," in *North American Review* 122 (1876), pp. 265−308. Throughout the long response to his opponent, Morgan presents an arrogant anthropological interpretation of Aztec life. Riddled with overt racial discriminations, Morgan's method was to quote generously from eyewitness and secondary-source descriptions of the Aztec capital and to ridicule those parts that did not fit into his view of Aztec barbarism as libel, lies, and "gossip of a camp of soldiers suddenly cast into an earlier form of society, which the village of Indians of America, of all mankind, best represented." The palaces described by Cortés and Díaz del Castillo were similarly dismissed, "Upon this rhapsody it will be sufficient to remark that halls were entirely unknown in Indian architecture." The report that Montezuma has military guards posted at his dinner was pure invention, as "it implies a knowledge of military discipline unknown by Indian tribes." That the barbarian chief Montezuma might have eaten at a table with a tablecloth scandalized Morgan ("Montezuma's Dinner," p. 308).

2. Ibid., p. 308.

3. One valuable general approach to urbanism is found in Louis Wirth, "Urbanism as a Way of Life," *American Journal of Sociology* 44 (1938): 3−24. See Paul Kirchhoff, "Mesoamérica, sus límites geográficos, composición étnica y carácteres culturales," *Acta Americana* 1 (1943): 92−107, for a groundbreaking discussion of what cultural and geographical characteristics made up Mesoamerica. For an assessment of Paul Kirchhoff's contributions, see Yólotl González Torres, "Paul Kirchhoff (1900−

1972)," in *Anales de Antropología*, vol. 11 (Instituto de Investigaciones Antropoló-
gicas, UNAM, Mexico, 1974), pp. 415–421. A concise discussion of more recent
descriptions of "what is Mesoamerica?" appeared in Richard E. Blanton, Stephen
A. Kowalewski, Gary Feinman, and Jill Appel, *Ancient Mesoamerica: A Comparison of
Change in Three Regions* (Cambridge: Cambridge University Press, 1981); see especially the final chapter on comparisons and conclusions where the authors describe
Mesoamerica as an "elite-rank" empire in which the only "requirement was that
the participating societies have at least a chiefdom level of sociocultural integration"
(p. 246). Marxist studies combined with grand conceptual schemes appear in the
work of V. Gordon Childe, *New Light on the Most Ancient East* (London: Routledge
and Kegan Paul, 1952), and Karl A. Wittfogel, *Oriental Despotism: A Comparative
Study of Total Power* (New Haven: Yale University Press, 1957), who articulated theories of urban revolutions and specialized bureaucratic elites that have been applied
and tested with surprising results by Americanists concerned with reconstructing
the Aztec image. Specific applications to the Americas appear in Pedro Armillas's
pioneering work *Program of the History of American Indians*, trans. Glenda and Theo
Crevenna (Washington: Department of Cultural Affairs, 1958), and by the more precise study of Philip Phillips and Gordon Willey, *Method and Theory in American
Archaeology* (Chicago: University of Chicago Press, 1958), both of which describe
the urban character of Mexican civilization as ancient and pervasive. This material-
ist approach peaked in the penetrating analysis of Friedrich Katz; in the ecological
studies of William T. Sanders, Barbara Price, and their students; and in the series of
investigations in the Oaxaca, Maya, and Teotihuacan regions.

4. See Eric R. Wolf, ed., *The Valley of Mexico: Studies in Pre-Hispanic Ecology and Society* (Albuquerque: University of New Mexico Press, 1976), especially "The Model"
by Michael H. Logan and William T. Sanders, pp. 31–59, and other works by Sanders and his students, including "Classic Maya Settlement Patterns and Ethnographic Analogy," in Wendy Ashmore, ed., *Lowland Maya Settlement Patterns*
(Albuquerque: University of New Mexico Press, 1981), pp. 351–369. Also important as an overview is Sanders's and David Webster's "The Mesoamerican Urban Tradition," *American Anthropologist* 90 (1989): 521–546. Especially valuable is Sanders's
discussion of Richard Fox's model of urbanization, which argues that "cities can be
understood only in terms of the kinds of states in which they are embedded, and
that the primary business of most impressive preindustrial cities was government"
(p. 543). It is my contention that government in what Fox and Sanders call Mesoamerican mercantile, administrative, and regal-ritual cities depended upon and was
exercised through the daily, monthly, and yearly ritual expression of a system of symbols akin to what Paul Wheatley calls "cosmo-magical thought." Government was
sacred and the sacred was the ideological substance of government. An excellent
summary of recent scholarship on the rise of social stratification appears in Griselda
Sarmiento, "La creación de los primeros centros de poder," in *Historia Antigua de
México*, vol. 1, coordinators Linda Manzanilla and Leonardo López Luján (México,
D.F., Instituto Nacional de Antropología e Historia, 1994).

5. Blanton, Kowalewski, et al., *Ancient Mesoamerica*. The most important site for

understanding the evolution of urban societies is Teotihuacan. A concise summary of Teotihuacan studies up until 1981 appears in Rene Millon's "Teotihuacan: City, State and Civilization," in *Supplement to the Handbook of Middle American Indians: Archaeology,* vol. 1 (Austin: University of Texas Press, 1981), pp. 198–243. What is clear from 1980 on is the consensus, articulated by William T. Sanders, that Teotihuacan was a "true city." Millon notes that "Teotihuacan was truly a major urban center, whatever definition of non-industrialized city is used. More than this Teotihuacan now is widely recognized as a far more complex urban society than previously postulated by its most partisan advocates" (p. 198). For an excellent discussion of the state-of-the-art understanding of the waning and collapse of the great city, see Millon's "The Last Years of Teotihuacan's Dominance" in Norman Yoffee and George L. Cowgill, eds., *The Collapse of Ancient States and Civilizations* (Tucson: The University of Arizona Press, 1988), pp. 102–164. A new project, "The Classic Heritage of Mesoamerica" seminars organized in the Raphael and Fletcher Lee Moses Mesoamerican Archive, explores the geographical and historical influences of Teotihuacan. See especially the first volume, *Mesoamerica's Classic Heritage: From Teotihuacan to the Aztecs,* ed., Davíd Carrasco, Lindsay Jones, and Scott Sessions (Niwot: University Press of Colorado, 1999).

6. This approach has received a series of influential interpretations found in Linda Schele and Mary Ellen Miller, *The Blood of Kings: Dynasty and Ritual in Maya Art* (Fort Worth, Tex.: The Kimball Art Museum, 1986), and Linda Schele and David Freidel, *A Forest of Kings: Royal Histories of the Ancient Maya* (New York: William Morrow, 1991).

7. This point is well made by Sanders while using Fox's model, where the former states, "By broadening the definition of city to include all significant central places, we may envision all complex societies as involved in urban development. At one level, all cities are unique and have characteristics that must be explained by variables that are unique, namely, their own environmental settings and cultural histories. But on another level, we must compare and generalize, and Fox reminds us that we can do so productively, so long as we bear in mind the fundamental processes that affect urban development in larger sociocultural settings" ("The Mesoamerican Urban Tradition," p. 545).

8. Among the scholars who have concerned themselves with this relationship, one of the most outstanding is Walter Krickeberg, "Bauform und Weltbild im alten Mexico," in *Mythe, Menshe und Umwelt* (Bamberg, 1950), and *Las antiguas culturas Mexicanas* (Mexico, 1962). Also see Paul Westheim, *Arte antiguo de México,* trans. Mariana Frenk and Ursula Bernard (Garden City, N.Y.: Anchor Books, 1965). A number of more concise studies exploring the relationship of art and architecture to religious ideas have appeared, although it is not always clear that the sacred as a cultural force is affirmed by some of these studies. Revisions and amplifications of earlier works can be found in Esther Pasztory, *Aztec Art* (New York: Abrams, 1983); Elizabeth Baquedano, *Aztec Sculpture* (British Museum Publications, LTD, 1984); Eduardo Matos Moctezuma, *Vida y muerte en el Templo Mayor* (Mexico: Ediciones Oceano, 1986).

9. Outstanding examples include Wendy Ashmore's work on site-planning principles among the Maya and the exciting collaborative work of Alfredo López Austin, Leonardo López Luján, and Saburo Sugiyama, "The Feathered Serpent Pyramid at Teotihuacan: Its Possible Ideological Significance," *Ancient Mesoamerica* 2:1 (1991): 93–106. Also see Saburo Sugiyama, "Teotihuacan as an Origin for Postclassic Feathered Serpent Symbolism," in *Mesoamerica's Classic Heritage,* ed. Davíd Carrasco, Lindsay Jones, and Scott Sessions (Niwot: University Press of Colorado, 1999), and Carolyn Tate, *Yaxchilán: The Design of a Maya Ceremonial Center* (Austin: University of Texas Press, 1992).

10. Laurette Séjourné's *Burning Water* (Berkeley, Calif., 1976) discusses Aztec religion as a degradation and perversion of the golden age of pre-Hispanic thought that flourished, according to her, in Teotihuacan between 200 and 800 C.E. This position is elaborated in her stimulating *El universo de Quetzalcoatl* (Mexico City, 1962), which has an introduction by Mircea Eliade. Among the many works of Mesoamerican spirituality, see Miguel León-Portilla's still valuable, popular *Aztec Thought and Culture* (Norman: University of Oklahoma Press, 1963). León-Portilla takes the interesting tack of utilizing Walter Jaeger's *Paideia, los ideales de la cultura griega,* 3 vols. (Mexico City, 1942–1945), concerning Greek thought and culture as the norm to measure and interpret the cosmological, philosophical, and rational achievements of ancient Nahuatl thinkers. Burr Brundage's *The Fifth Sun: Aztec Gods, Aztec World* (Austin: University of Texas Press, 1979) is an articulate and vivid account of the interrelationship of Aztec myth, theology, and society. The best exploration of the Aztec state as a cosmic image is perhaps Richard Townsend's articles and especially his *State and Cosmos in the Art of Tenochtitlan* (Washington, D.C.: Dumbarton Oaks, 1979). Johanna Broda's intensive analysis of mountain ceremonial centers and the interconnections with urban settlements has resulted in a new hypothesis about cosmovision and ceremonial settlements; see "The Sacred Landscape of Aztec Calendar Festivals: Myth, Nature, and Society," in *To Change Place: Aztec Ceremonial Landscapes,* ed. Davíd Carrasco (Niwot: University Press of Colorado, 1992), pp. 74–120. Also see the vivid interpretations of Inga Clendinnen in *The Aztecs: An Interpretation* (Cambridge: Cambridge University Press, 1991).

11. This concern, initiated in another cultural area by Numa Denis Fustel de Coulanges in *The Ancient City: A Study of the Religion, Laws, and Institutions of Greece and Rome* [1984] (Baltimore: The Johns Hopkins University Press, 1980), has recently been tested indirectly against the Aztec materials by the urban ecologist Paul Wheatley and explored directly by Mesoamericanists Doris Heyden in "An Interpretation of the Cave Underneath the Pyramid of the Sun in Teotihuacan, Mexico," *American Antiquity* 40 (1975): 131–147, and "Caves, Gods, and Myths: World-View and Planning in Teotihuacan, Mexico" in *Mesoamerican Sites and World-Views,* ed. Elizabeth P. Benson (Washington, D.C.: Dumbarton Oaks, 1981), pp. 1–35; and Eduardo Matos Moctezuma in *Life and Death in the Templo Mayor,* trans. Bernard R. Ortiz de Montellano and Thelma Ortiz de Montellano (Niwot: University Press of Colorado, 1995). It is through Wheatley's work in particular, especially "City as

Symbol," his inaugural lecture at University College London on November 20, 1967 (London: H. K. Lewis, 1970), and his lengthy monograph *The Pivot of the Four Quarters: A Preliminary Enquiry into the Origins and Character of the Ancient Chinese City* (Chicago: Aldine, 1971), that the student of Mesoamerican religions can find a valuable theoretical and comparative framework for deepening our understanding of the relationships of the city and symbolic structures in Aztec Mexico. In "City as Symbol" and in another early study, *The Golden Khersonese: Studies in the Historical Geography of the Malay Peninsula Before A.D. 1500* (Kuala Lumpur: University of Malaya Press, 1961), Wheatley discusses the morphology and phenomenology of ceremonial centers, which were instruments for the creation of political, social, economic, and sacred spaces within and beyond the built form of the ancient city. Noting that the religious and cosmological dimensions of cities have been largely ignored by students of urbanism, he focuses his attention on a "genre of urbanism characteristic of the traditional world," a genre dependent upon and infused with "cosmo-magical thought." Cosmo-magical thought was the conceptual and mythical underpinning of traditional urban cultures. In the words of Wheatley, this type of thought "presupposed an intimate parallelism between the regular and mathematically expressible regime of the heavens and biologically determined rhythms of life on earth as manifested in the succession of the seasons, the annual cycles of plant regeneration, and within the compass of an individual life, birth, growth, procreation and death" (Pivot, p. 319). He argues that cosmo-magical thought gave form and structure to the ideal-type cities in the seven areas of pristine urban development (Mesopotamia, Northern China, Egypt, the Indus Valley, southwestern Nigeria, Mesoamerica, and Central Andes) by marking out social and ceremonial spaces and making them sites for the supreme manifestation of sacred authority, cosmic orientation, and political power in the plane of human affairs. He writes, "I am referring to the cosmo-magical symbolism which informed the ideal-type traditional city in both the Old and New Worlds, *which brought the city into being, sustained it and was imprinted on its physiognomy*" ("City as Symbol," p. 9, italics mine). In utilizing this kind of approach we can gain more understanding of the relationship between the historical and mythical past and the organization of urban space. For a cogent discussion about Maya culture see William L. Fash, *Scribes, Warriors, & Kings: The City of Copan and the Ancient Maya* (New York: Thames & Hudson, 1991). Also see Andrea Stone, "From Ritual in the Landscape to Capture in the Urban Center: The Recreation of Ritual Environments in Mesoamerica," *Journal of Ritual Studies* 6(1) (Winter 1992): 109–132.

12. Michel de Certeau, *The Practice of Everyday Life* (Berkeley: University of California Press, 1984), p. 129.

13. The first image of the *Codex Mendoza* is often called the "frontispiece," but Elizabeth Boone has rightly noted that it is not a prefatory or frontispiece but rather the first act in the drama of the story the native elders told the Spaniards.

14. Patricia Anawalt and Francis Berdan, eds., *Codex Mendoza,* 4 vols. (Berkeley: University of California Press, 1992), have achieved a watershed in the study of colo-

nial manuscripts that will be the standard for years to come. One area of interpretation that still needs amplification, however, is the ways in which the manuscript can serve as an extraordinary entrée into discussions of religion, religious action, and the pictorial events and discourses depicted in the manuscript.

15. I am indebted to Dana Leibsohn, "Primers for Memory: Cartographic History and Nahua Identity" in *Writing Without Words: Alternative Literacies in Mesoamerica and the Andes*, ed., Elizabeth Hill Boone and Walter D. Mignolo (Durham: Duke University Press, 1994), pp. 161–187, for leading me to this usage of de Certeau. In fact, de Certeau is well aware of the mixture of these two kinds of spatial stories, the tour and the tableau, and dedicates his chapter, in part, to "try and specify the relationships between the indicators of 'tours' and those of 'maps' where they coexist in a single description" (p. 119).

16. For a detailed and inspired analysis of the persistence and transformation of native Mesoamerican pictorial traditions, see Donald Robertson's *Mexican Manuscript Painting of the Early Colonial Period: The Metropolitan Schools* (New Haven: Yale University Press, 1959). A new edition, with a foreword by Elizabeth H. Boone, was published in 1994 (Norman: University of Oklahoma Press). A more recent, nearly exhaustive study appears in the four-volume *Codex Mendoza*, edited by Berdan and Anawalt. Anyone seeking to study space, tribute relations, costume, place names, or daily life in Tenochtitlan or the evolution of native pictorial styles, must refer to this splendid work.

17. Kathleen Stewart Howe, "The Relationship of Indigenous and European Styles in the Codex Mendoza: An Analysis of Pictorial Styles," in *Codex Mendoza*, 1:25.

18. Robertson, *Mexican Manuscript Painting* (1959), p. 2. It should be understood that Charles I was King of Spain but as emperor of the Hapsburg empire, he was known as Emperor Charles V.

19. A *nahuatlato* is an expert translator of the Nahuatl language. This type of individual was thoroughly bilingual and functioned in a variety of ways in Nueva España. *Nahuatlatos* translated Nahuatl speeches by Aztec priests for Spanish officials, interpreted pictorial signs, and assisted in the endless court cases that took place in the colonial period, quite often over land disputes. While there were many other Indian languages in Mexico, they were usually translated into Nahuatl before being translated into Spanish.

20. See H. B. Nicholson, "The History of the *Codex Mendoza*," for a thorough discussion of possible authors, contributors, and interpretations of the document's history. He keeps a number of questions open for future research. Berdan and Anawalt, *Codex Mendoza*, 1:1–11.

21. Robertson, *Mexican Manuscript Painting* (1994), pp. 61–62.

22. Robertson was not consistent in his attribution of this image as a representation of the capital, which may reflect the wider debate and confusion as to what a city was and what an image or map of a city consisted of. Later in his remarkable work he writes, "The frontispiece of Codex Mendoza, folio 2r is an example of the for-

malized map from the Nahua area. . . . There is nothing in this painting to be properly called an image of the city" (p. 182).

23. *Codex Mendoza,* 1:5.

24. Throughout this section, I have benefited greatly from the explanation of the pictographs and ideographs found in Donald Robertson's analysis and especially the collection of essays, commentaries, and descriptions in the Berdan, Anawalt edition. Also see the valuable English version of the *Mendoza, Codex Mendoza: The Mexican Manuscript Known as the Collection of Mendoza and Preserved in the Bodleian Library Oxford,* trans. James Cooper Clark, 3 vols. (Oxford: London, 1938).

25. See Elizabeth Boone, "The Aztec Pictorial History of the *Codex Mendoza*" in *Codex Mendoza,* 1:35–54, for this innovative reading of the image.

26. For a detailed reading of this page and its range of possible interpretations related to other manuscripts, see Rudolph van Zantwijk, *The Aztec Arrangement: The Social History of Pre-Hispanic Mexico* (Norman: University of Oklahoma Press, 1985), pp. 57–94. Van Zantwijk attempts to identify the associated directions of each quadrant and insists that the building in the upper quadrant is the *tecpan,* the government building.

27. The *tzompantli,* or skull rack, was a permanent part of the Aztec ceremonial center. It was, according to Diego Durán's informants, "a finely carved palisade as tall as a great tree. Poles were set in a row, about six feet apart. All these thick poles were drilled with small holes, and the holes were so numerous that there was scarcely a foot and a half between them. . . . From pole to pole, through the holes, stretched thin rods strung with numerous human heads pieced through the temple. Each rod held twenty heads. . . . One of the conquerors assured me that they were so numerous that they were impossible to count, so close together that they caused fright and wonder" (Diego Durán, *Book of the Gods and Rites and the Ancient Calendar,* trans. and ed. Fernando Horcasitas and Doris Heyden [Norman: University of Oklahoma Press, 1975], p. 79).

28. *Codex Mendoza,* 2:5.

29. There is more to this simple-looking mat than meets the eye. The woven mat, or *petlatl,* and the platform on which the *petlatl* sat, were the symbols of power and authority throughout many parts of Mesoamerica, but especially among the Mexicas.

30. The names and characteristics of the other leaders are as follows. The three figures seated behind Tenuch are Xocoyol (Foot Bell); Tecineuh (He Who Expels Someone), and Acacitli (Reed Hare). Note, however, that the interpreter mistakenly wrote Ocelopan (Jaguar Banner), who is actually immediately above Reed Hare in the upper quadrant with his ocelot banner name glyph. Facing Ocelopan, on the other side of the temple, is Quapan (Eagle Banner). In the right-hand quadrant sits Aguexotl (Water Willow) and Xomimitl (Foot Arrow). The lower quadrant contains Atototl (Water Bird) and Xiuhcaqui (Person Shod with Turquoise-Colored Sandals). In classifying the "writing" system used by the Aztecs, it is helpful

to refer to I. J. Gelb's *A Study of Writing* (Chicago: University of Chicago Press, 1963). It appears that in the case of the *Mendoza* we are dealing with what Gelb calls a semasiographic system of writing, which consists principally of two types of messages. First, we have pictographs, where the images of the objects referred to are used singly or in a series to tell something in general terms. Charles Dibble writes concerning this method of communication, "Animals, plants, birds, mountains, streams, and trees are recognizable as such; the scenes depicted are comparable to photographs of dances, processions, self castigation, sacrifice, or battles. Gods, goddesses or priests and common people are recognizable by their actions, their postures, their clothing, painting, and hairdress" ("Writing in Central Mexico," in *Handbook*, vol. 10, p. 324). Second, we have ideograph pictures in which images of objects stand for ideas associated with the images. For instance, a picture of a flower can represent a flower in the case of the pictograph, while in the case of the ideograph it means sacrificial blood. Likewise, a bundle of reeds may mean a bundle or reeds, as in a pictograph, but it means the tying up of a fifty-two-year cycle as an ideograph. Often both pictograph and ideograph occur on the same page in a codex and appear to be of equal antiquity.

31. Elizabeth Boone pointed out this complexity in a personal communication.

32. *Codex Mendoza*, 2:5.

33. *Codex Mendoza*, 4:7–8.

34. See note 11 in this chapter. It is important to emphasize that the term *city,* as used in Wheatley's work, does not refer solely to the built forms or material limits of the urban settlement. The significance of cities lies in the "way of life" they generated. Wheatley notes, ". . . the urban process is here to be understood as a complex nexus of functionally interrelated, parallel-trending changes by means of which increasing numbers of people in society at large become involved in some way in the affairs of the city. Whether or not they live within its physical purlieus, they come under the influence, and more often than not, the control of its institutions. This means that an urbanized society subsumes both a spatially urban and a spatially rural component. On the one hand there is the city-dweller proper, the resident within the urban enclave; and on the other there is the urbanized countryman who lives in terms of the city but not in it, who is bound to the city (or perhaps more accurately to the institutions of state located within the city) in an asymmetrical structural relationship that requires him to produce in one form or another a fund of rent payable to power brokers based, if not always resident, with the urban enceinte" (*Nagara and Commandery: Origins of the Southeast Asian Urban Traditions* [Chicago: The University of Chicago Department of Geography, Research Paper 207–2-8, 1983], p. 4). For applications of Wheatley, see Peter Wilson, *The Domestication of the Human Species* (New Haven: Yale University Press, 1988), and Davíd Carrasco, *Religions of Mesoamerica: Cosmovision and Ceremonial Centers* (San Francisco: Harper & Row, 1990). Stanley Tambiah's critique appears in *Culture, Thought and Social Action* (Cambridge: Harvard University Press, 1985). See Jonathan Z. Smith, *To Take Place: Toward a Theory of Ritual* (Chicago: University of Chicago Press,

1987), for a critical application of Wheatley's model of the city as a symbol. Charles Long's essay on human centers in *Significations: Signs, Symbols, and Images in the Interpretation of Religion* (Philadelphia: Fortress Press, 1986) also uses Wheatley's model for a new hermeneutical reflection. The most creative enlargement of Wheatley's work in hermeneutical terms is Lindsay Jones, *Twin City Tales: A Hermeneutical Reassessment of Tula and Chichén Itzá* (Niwot: University Press of Colorado, 1995).

35. See Jonathan Z. Smith's illuminating essay on rebellion and cosmic order, "Birth Upside Down or Right Side Up," *History of Religions* 9 (1970): 281–303, for an elaboration of the meaning of this term.

36. Wheatley, "City as Symbol," p. 7. We cannot overestimate the power of cities to influence and integrate the complex social and symbolic structures and dynamics of traditional societies. Wheatley describes these hyperpowerful centers in this way, "This particular hierarchical patterning of societal relationships is invariably accorded material expression in a localized nexus of built forms that is recognized in whatever cultural context it may occur, as a theater for the acting out of a distinctive manner of life characterized as urban. It is the forms and functions of these nexuses that constitute the subject matter of conventional urban studies, with inquires focusing on the built forms as (1) an arena for the interplay of both creative and destructive tension in the disposition of volume and space, (2) a locale promoting a characteristic style of life, of production, and of thought, and (3) a functional center of societal control, a creator of effective space as it has been called" (*Nagara and Commandery*, p. 1).

37. Wheatley, "City as Symbol," p. 10.

38. Paul Wheatley, "The Suspended Pelt: Reflections on a Discarded Model of Spatial Structure," in Donald R. Daskins, Jr., George Kish, John D. Nystuen, and Gunnar Olsson, eds., *Geographic Humanism, Analysis and Social Action* (Ann Arbor: University of Michigan, 1977). I quote this passage at length because it gives a different sense of the intellectual and spiritual enterprise involved in the construction of sacred space than the one implied when we utilize language like "imitation of the archetype." In Wheatley's formulation, the implication is clearly that the archetype is not only discovered, but also constructed; it reveals itself, but it is also mapped. Perhaps the notion of analogy is useful here. Man constructs the "analogy" and utilizes the active intellect and spiritual creativity to agree, imitate, and construct a resemblance of something that is both similar to and different from himself. Parallelism involves doing and interpreting a paradox. For a cogent criticism of this approach, see Stanley Jeyaraja Tambiah, "The Galactic Polity in Southeast Asia," in *Culture, Thought and Social Action: An Anthropological Perspective* (Cambridge: Harvard University Press, 1985).

39. Wheatley, "Suspended Pelt," p. 6.

40. Tambiah, "The Galactic Polity," p. 255.

41. Ibid.

42. Wheatley's model emphasizes the structuring of terrestrial space "in the image

of celestial space" and that these two types of space are related by the exact sequences of ritual and worship. But it is important to emphasize that in the Meso-american evidence there is great attention given to the dynamics of space—the use of space for ritual dynamics, which choreograph the motions and energies of celes-tial phenomena. Aztec cities were great theaters of motion, color, sound, and ges-ture. Even as we look at the image from the *Mendoza,* we are impressed with movement as well as with space. The plants are growing, the waters rippling, the speaker is speaking, and the eagle is landing. While Wheatley's work mentions this characteristic of ceremonial centers, much more needs to be done to understand the relationship of space and ceremonial motion. For a useful development of this per-spective, see Lindsay Jones, *Twin City Tales.* In my own writings, see "The Sacrifice of Tezcatlipoca: To Change Place," in Davíd Carrasco, ed., *Aztec Ceremonial Land-scapes,* with a preface by William Fash (Niwot: University Press of Colorado, 1999), pp. 31–57.

43. Calvino, *Invisible Cities,* p. 14.

44. Quoted in Miguel León-Portilla, *Pre-Columbian Literatures of Mexico* (Norman: University of Oklahoma Press, 1968), p. 87.

45. There have been a number of translators of this song from the *Cantares Mexi-canos,* with the work of Angel Maria Garibay K, *Historia de la literatura náhuatl,* 2 vols. (Mexico City: Editorial Porrua, 1953–1954), and *Poesía náhuatl,* 3 vols. (Mex-ico City: UNAM-IIH, 1964–1968). For a useful English translation, see *Cantares Mexicanos: Songs of the* Aztecs, translated from the Nahuatl with an introduction and commentary by John Bierhorst (Stanford: Stanford University Press, 1985). Also see Miguel León-Portilla, *La filosofía náhuatl estudiada en sus fuentes* (Mexico City: UNAM-IIH, 1959).

46. Lord Kingsborough, *Antiguedades de México,* ed. E Corona Nunez, 4 vols. (Méx-ico: Secretaria de Hacienda y Credito Publico, 1964–1967), 3:7–314. This image of the cosmic levels also appears in the "Historia de los Mexicanos por sus pinturas," in *Teogonia e historia de los mexicanos,* ed. A. Ma. Garibay K. (Mexico: Porrua, 1965), pp. 21–90, and "Histoire du Mechique," in idem., p. 103.

47. Alfredo López Austin, *Human Body and Ideology,* p. 54. H. B. Nicholson has per-suasively shown in various publications that the earth was considered one of the thir-teen cosmic levels. Thus, only twelve celestial levels are named in the text.

48. An excellent introduction to the sources relevant to the foundation tradition is Doris Heyden, *México: Origin de un símbolo* (Mexico: Colección Distrito Federal, 1988). Also see Elizabeth Boone, "Migration Histories as Ritual Performance," in *To Change Place,* pp. 121–152, and her "The Aztec Pictorial History of the *Codex Mendoza,*" in *Codex Mendoza,* 1:35–54.

49. Diego Durán, *The History of the Indies of New Spain,* trans. Doris Heyden (Nor-man: University of Oklahoma Press, 1995), pp. 43–44.

50. *Códice Aubin* (Mexico: Editorial Innovación, 1979), p. 95.

51. Rudolf van Zantwijk, "Principios organizadores de los mexicas: Una introducción al estudio del sistema interno del régimen azteca," *Estudios de Cultural Náhuatl* 4 (Mexico, 1963): 187–222. Van Zantwijk locates eight urban sections, or "ideal type sectors," and draws important connections between cosmovision and social organization.

52. Hernán Cortés, *Letters from Mexico*, trans. and ed. Anthony Pagden (New Haven: Yale University Press, 1986), p. 102.

53. Edward Calnek, "The Internal Structure of Tenochtitlan," in *The Valley of Mexico*, ed. Eric Wolf (Albuquerque, University of New Mexico Press, 1976), p. 296.

54. Durán, *History of the Indies of New Spain*, p. 46.

55. It was formerly believed that a *coatepantli*, or serpent wall, surrounded the precinct, but the excavations by Eduardo Matos Moctezuma have revealed this to be false; Eduardo Matos Moctezuma, *The Great Temple of the Aztecs: Treasures of Tenochtitlan* (New York: Thames and Hudson, 1988).

56. See Anthony F. Aveni, Edward E. Calnek, and Horst Hartung, "Myth, Environment and the Orientation of the Templo Mayor of Tenochtitlan," *American Antiquity* 53 (1988): 287–309.

57. Jorge Hardoy, *Pre-Columbian Cities*, trans. Judith Thorne (New York: Walker, 1973), p. 176.

58. For a cogent discussion of the Teotihuacan tradition of city layout and its influence on the Aztecs, see Leonardo López Luján, "Teotihuacan and Its Mexica Legacy," in *Teotihuacan: Art from the City of the Gods*, ed. Kathleen Berlin and Esther Pasztory (San Francisco: Thames and Hudson, 1993), pp. 156–165. There has been a recent challenge to this view by Saburo Sugiyama, who argues on the basis of his archaeological research that Teotihuacan was never a quadripartite city but a dual city, a city divided into two grand sections (personal communication).

59. The exact orientations of major sections of Tula are discussed in Leonardo López Luján, Robert Cobean, and Guadalupe Mastache, *Xochicalco y Tula* (Mexico: Jaca Books/Consejo Nacional para la Cultura y las Artes, 1996). These orientations include:

      before 950 the alignment was strictly north–south;

      950–1000 Greater Tula was aligned 15 degrees east of north;

      1000–1050 Apogee of Greater Tula 5 degrees west of north.

60. John Bierhorst, *Four Masterworks of American Indian Literature* (New York: Farrar, Straus and Giroux, 1974), p. 26.

61. Sahagún, *Florentine Codex*, 10:166.

62. Leonardo López Luján, personal communication.

63. A thorough analysis of the Aztec use of the pattern of four quadrants can be found in León-Portilla, *Aztec Thought*, pp. 44–50.

64. López Luján has made the relevant observation that there is a fascinating parallel

between Xiuhtecuhtli's position in the center of the cosmic image and his repeated appearance in the center of buried offerings at the Templo Mayor. Xiuhtecuhtli's location at the center of the cosmos was a widespread archetype of spatial orientation; see *The Offerings of the Great Temple*, chapter 8.

65. Durán, *History of the Indies*, p. 46.

66. Calnek, "Myth, Environment," p. 297.

67. See Frances F. Berdan's excellent "Glyphic Convention of the *Codex Mendoza*," *Codex Mendoza*, 1:93–102.

68. Elizabeth H. Boone, "The Aztec Pictorial History," *Codex Mendoza*, 1:48.

69. It should be noted that the conquests pictured in the *Codex Mendoza* represent only a partial list of the actual conquests of a number of the rulers. Perhaps these images represented the most important conquests.

70. Berdan and Anawalt, *Codex Mendoza*, 2:8–25.

71. Boone, "Aztec Pictorial History," *Codex Mendoza*, 1:51.

72. See the articles in *Codex Mendoza*, especially Berdan's "The Tribute Year to Year," 2:27–142, "The Imperial Tribute Roll of the *Codex Mendoza*, 1:55–79, and "Tribute Totals in the *Codex Mendoza, Matrícula de Tributos*, and *Información de 1554*," 1:158–159.

73. Berdan, "The Imperial Tribute Roll," in *Codex Mendoza*, 1:55.

74. The correspondence between the five tributary areas of the Mexica and their cosmology was first proposed by Paul Kirchhoff in his discussion of the Toltec empire in *Historia Tolteca-Chichimeca* (Mexico: INAH, 1976).

75. Johanna Broda, "El tributo en trajes guerreros y la estructura del sistema tributario mexica," in *Economía, política e ideología en el Mexico prehispánico*, ed. Pedro Carrasco and Johanna Broda (Mexico City: CISINAH/Nueva Imagen, 1978).

76. Carlos Fuentes, *Where the Air Is Clear* (New York: Farrar, Straus & Giroux, 1960), pp. 4–5.

77. Anthony Pagden, *Hernan Cortés, Letters from Mexico* (New Haven: Yale University Press, 1986), pp. 105–106.

78. There is some controversy over this list of buildings. Some scholars feel the abundant series of buildings actually refers to the major ceremonial structures dispersed throughout the city. Others believe the seventy-eight structures mentioned by Sahagún were located within the sacred precinct. The best study of the sacred precinct is still Ignacio Marquina, *El Templo Mayor de México* (Mexico: INAH, 1960). Also see Alfredo López Austin, "El Templo Mayor de México-Tenochtitlan según los informantes indígenas," *Estudios de Cultura Náhuatl* 5 (1965): 75–102.

79. Sahagún, *Florentine Codex*, 2:182.

80. Ibid., 2:179–194.

81. Ibid., 8:3.

82. Sahagún, *Florentine Codex*, 12:1. The following quotes about omens are from Miguel León-Portilla, *The Broken Spears* (Boston: Beacon Press, 1972), pp. 4–5.

83. An alternative approach using structuralist principles appears in Michel Graulich, *Montezuma* (Paris: Fayard, 1994).84. *The Broken Spears: The Aztec Account of the Conquest of Mexico,* edited and with an introduction by Miguel Leon Portilla (Boston: Beacon Press, 1990), p. 5.

85. León-Portilla, *Broken Spears*, p. 116.

86. Fuentes, *Where the Air Is Clear*, pp. 4–5.

2. Templo Mayor

The first epigraph of this chapter is taken from Mircea Eliade, *The Sacred and the Profane: The Nature of Religion* (New York: Harcourt, Brace & World, Inc., 1959), p. 43.

The second epigraph is from Walter Burkert, *Homo Necans: The Anthropology of Ancient Greek Sacrificial Ritual and Myth* (Berkeley: University of California Press, 1983), p. 1.

1. Bernal Díaz del Castillo, *The Discovery and Conquest of Mexico*, ed. Genaro García and trans. Alfred P. Maudslay (New York: Farrar, Strauss, and Giroux, 1956), p. 191.

2. Ibid., p. 436.

3. See Benjamin Keen's expansive *The Aztec Image in Western Thought* (New Brunswick: Rutgers University Press, 1971) for an entertaining and thorough outline of the ways that modern scholars and artists have responded to the Aztec enigma. For a more general and very compelling interpretation of European responses and debates about the New World, see Anthony Grafton, *New Worlds, Ancient Texts* (Cambridge, Mass.: Belknap Press of Harvard University Press, 1992). A remarkable book by Walter Mignolo, *The Darker Side of the Renaissance: Literacy, Territoriality, and Colonization* (Ann Arbor: University of Michigan Press, 1995), illustrates how European identity, literacy, and power derived in part from the discovery and invention of the New World.

4. This huge circular stone is more accurately referred to as the Stone of the Suns because, while it has a series of calendrical signs on it, it primarily depicts the story of the four ages, or "suns," through which the universe had passed, organized around an image of the fifth, or Aztec, sun. See H. B. Nicholson, "The Problem of the Identification of the Central Images of the 'Aztec Calendar Stone,'" in Alana Cordy-Collins and Douglas Sharon, eds., *Current Topics in Aztec Studies: Essays in Honor of H. B. Nicholson* (San Diego: San Diego Museum of Man, 1993). This concern with cosmic cycles was focused through a pervasive calendar system best described in Alfonso Caso's authoritative introduction to the Mesoamerican calendar in "Calendrical Systems of Central Mexico," in G. F. Eckholm and Ignacio Bernal, eds., *Handbook of Middle American Indians* (Austin: University of Texas Press,

1971) 10:333–348, hereafter referred to as *Handbook*. A more extensive version of the work appears in Caso's *Los calendarios prehispanicos* (Mexico, D. F.: Universidad Nacional Autonoma de Mexico, 1967).

5. Diego Durán, *Book of the Gods and Rites and the Ancient Calendar*, trans. F. Horcasitas and D. Heyden (Norman: University of Oklahoma Press, 1977), has a startling number of human sacrifices listed in relation to the calendar festivals in Tenochtitlan. And Book 2 of the *Florentine Codex* provides detailed descriptions of sacrifice associated with the ritual calendar.

6. H. B. Nicholson's introduction to Mesoamerican sculpture, "Major Sculpture in Pre-Hispanic Central Mexico," in *Handbook*, 10:92–135, discusses the character and creativity of Aztec sculpture in the round. Also see Esther Pasztory, *Aztec Art* (New York: Henry N. Abrams, 1983); Eduardo Matos Moctezuma, *Obras maestras del Templo Mayor* (Mexico: Fomento Cultural Banamex, 1988); and Felipe Solís, *Gloria y fama Mexicas* (Mexico: S.A. de C.V., 1991).

7. See Miguel León-Portilla's "Pre-Hispanic Literature," in *Handbook*, 10:452–458, for a short introduction to Aztec poetic forms. Also see his *La filosofía náhuatl estudiada en sus fuentes*, 2nd edition (Mexico City: UNAM-Instituto de Investigaciones Historicas-Seminario de Cultura Nahuatl, 1959), and "Cuicatl y tlahtolli: Las formas de expresión en náhuatl," *Estudios de Cultura Náhuatl*, 6:13–108. The authoritative texts can be found in Angel Maria Garibay K., *Poesía náhuatl*, 3 vols. (Mexico City: UNAM, 1964–1968).

8. Jonathan Z. Smith explains the importance of knowing a people's vision of place this way: "The question of the character of the place upon which one stands is *the* fundamental symbolic and social question. Once an individual or culture has expressed its vision of its place, a whole language of symbols and social structure will follow," in his "The Influence of Symbols Upon Social Change: A Place on Which to Stand," *Worship* (October, 1970): 469. For an elaboration of Smith's ingenious approach to sacred space/place studies, see his *To Take Place: Toward Theory in Ritual* (Chicago: University of Chicago Press, 1987).

9. Charles Gibson, "Structure of the Aztec Empire," in *Handbook,* 10:376–396. Also see Nigel Davies, *The Aztecs: A History* (London: Macmillan, 1973).

10. Durán's *Book of the Gods* refers to many of the rituals performed at the Templo Mayor.

11. See the December 1980 issue of *National Geographic Magazine*, "The Aztecs," for an introduction to the discoveries at the Templo Mayor excavation. Eduardo Matos Moctezuma, *The Great Temple of the Aztecs: Treasures of Tenochtitlan* (London: Thames & Hudson, 1988); Johanna Broda, Davíd Carrasco, and Eduardo Matos Moctezuma, *The Great Temple of Tenochtitlan: Center and Periphery in the Aztec World* (Berkeley: University of California Press, 1987); and Leonardo López Luján, *The Offerings of the Templo Mayor of Tenochtitlan*, trans. Bernard Ortiz de Montellano and Thelma Ortiz de Montellano (Niwot: University Press of Colorado, 1994), are all indispensable for understanding the significance of the Templo Mayor.

12. The phases of excavation at the Templo Mayor are: First Period of Excavation: 1978–1982; Second Period of Excavation: 1987; Third Period of Excavation: 1989; Fourth Period: 1991–1992; Fifth Period: 1994–1995. For useful summaries of the continuing excavations, see the relevant essays in Elizabeth H. Boone, ed., *The Aztec Templo Mayor* (Washington, D.C.: Dumbarton Oaks, 1987), and López Luján, *The Offerings of the Templo Mayor of Tenochtitlan*.

13. The nature of pre-Hispanic primary sources presents a distinct set of problems for the scholar interested in working with Mesoamerican materials. For a sampling of these problems and helpful approaches to them, see Donald Robertson, *Mexican Manuscript Painting of the Early Colonial Period: The Metropolitan Schools* (New Haven: Yale University Press, 1959), and Charles Gibson, "A Survey of Middle American Prose Manuscripts in the Native Historical Tradition," in *Handbook*, 15:311–321. Alternative approaches appear in Elizabeth H. Boone and Walter D. Mignolo, eds., *Writing Without Words: Alternative Literacies in Mesoamerica & the Andes* (Durham and London: Duke University Press, 1994), especially Boone's "Aztec Pictorial Histories: Records Without Words," pp. 50–77, Peter van der Loo's "Voicing the Painted Image: A Suggestion for Reading the Reverse of the Codex Cospi," pp. 77–87, and Dana Leibsohn's "Primers for Memory: Cartographic Histories and Nahua Identity," pp. 161–188.

14. See Miguel León-Portilla, "The Ethnohistorical Record of the Huey Teocalli of Tenochtitlan," in *The Aztec Templo Mayor*, pp. 71–96, and Boone's "Templo Mayor Research, 1521–1978," pp. 5–70, in the same book. The excavation provides, among other things, a golden moment for the historian of religions seeking to understand the interrelationship between urban form and symbolic order in central Mesoamerica. We now have the growing opportunity of combining, cross-checking, and interweaving the written and pictorial evidence about the Aztec shrine with the mute evidence from the dig, which both confirms and negates the written evidence and reveals surprising facts about the Templo Mayor's history, structure, and its relationship with distant and peripheral communities in the Aztec empire. There is more written, pictorial, and archaeological evidence about the Templo Mayor than about any other single building in Mesoamerica. Never before have we had the opportunity to understand with such coordination the significance of a major Mesoamerican religious shrine in terms of its history, architecture, symbolic meaning, and the dynamics that existed between the capital city it crowned and the empire it integrated.

15. See especially Eduardo Matos Moctezuma, *The Great Temple of the Aztecs*, p. 91.

16. Jonathan Z. Smith raised a similar point about the category of the Center when he asked, ". . . I would query whether one can pay such attention to the 'Center' without giving equal attention to the periphery," in his essay "The Wobbling Pivot," in *Map Is Not Territory: Studies in the History of Religions* (Leiden: E. J. Brill, 1978), which is his early critique of Eliade's morphologies.

17. Other scholars who have explored this theory in relation to particular manifestations include Clifford Geertz, *Negara: The Theatre State in Nineteenth Century Bali*

(Princeton: Princeton University Press, 1980), p. 13, and Paul Wheatley, *The Pivot of the Four Quarters, A Preliminary Enquiry into the Origins and Nature of the Ancient Chinese City* (Chicago: Aldine, 1973), p. 225. Wheatley's work as developed in this swollen seed is particularly germane to this hermeneutical work. He has combined the methods of urban studies with insights from the history of religions and tested them against a multitude of sources from seven areas of primary urban generation to show how ceremonial centers were the "primary instruments for the creation of political, social, economic, and sacred space." Stanley Tambiah, "The Galactic Polity in Southeast Asia," in *Culture, Thought and Social Action: An Anthropological Approach* (Cambridge: Harvard University Press, 1985), pp. 252–287, and Clifford Geertz present important variations on Wheatley's approach. One of Tambiah's points bears mentioning here. He criticizes Wheatley and others, "But what I question is seeing the rationale for this model in a cosmological mode of thought as an ontological priority, which is so interpreted as to constitute a sociological anteriority as well, such that for the imputed 'traditional' or 'archaic' mentality a notion of the 'sacred' is alleged to engulf the 'secular' and to serve as the ground of reality" (p. 257). While making an important point about the role of the social world, Tambiah misses what was the key contribution of Wheatley's model, namely, the magisterial description of what the rulers of the kingdoms sought to represent and have their followers believe! The power of the periodic stability of the galactic polity derives directly from the indigenous claim to an ontological basis, and any achievement of indigenous "totalization" was based on the model that Wheatley deciphered.

18. Leonardo López Luján discusses Mexica strategies for eliminating these cosmic threats in *La recuperación Mexica del pasado teotihuacano* (México: INAH, 1989).

19. Michael E. Smith has effectively explored the role of social stratification in the center/periphery dynamics of the Aztec empire in at least two important articles, "The Role of Social Stratification in the Aztec Empire: A View from the Provinces," *American Anthropologist* 88 (1986):70–90, and "The Expansion of the Aztec Empire: A Case Study in the Correlation of Diachronic Archaeological and Ethnohistorical Data," *American Antiquity* 52 (1987): 37–54. Smith claims that the center/periphery propaganda of the Mexica elites, expressed through their quadripartite symbolism projected onto the historical and social struggles and differences of their empire, masked the crucial social reality of noble/commoner distinctions. This is an important reflection on Mexica propaganda, but I wonder if the Mexica were as intent on this kind of mystification as Smith claims. The record collected by Sahagún on the people, merchants, kings, and lords, as well as the *huehuetlatolli* (ancient words) of Book 6 of *The Florentine Codex,* make it evident that the class distinctions were well known, publicly proclaimed, celebrated, and ritually affirmed. Mexica propaganda was as much concerned with illustrating the divine basis of this division as it was in fitting it into the cosmovision. It is more likely that scholarly approaches, with their own propagandistic itineraries, are responsible for the lack of attention to

social stratification. One area of scholarship that may still impede such work is the resistance to a fuller awareness of what urbanization is and does to social relationships.

20. Written evidence concerning the Templo Mayor is contained in Díaz del Castillo, *The Discovery and Conquest of Mexico*; Diego Durán, *Historia de las Indias de Nueva España y Islas de tierra firme* (Mexico, 1951); Alvarado Tezozomoc, *Crónica Mexicana* (Mexico, 1944); Bernardino de Sahagún, *Historia general de las cosas de Nueva España* (2 vols., introduction, paleography, glossary, and notes by Alfredo López Austin and J. Garcia Quintana [Madrid: Alianza Editorial, 1988]). The best anthology of primary sources about the Templo Mayor is Barbro Dahlgren, Emma Pérez Rocha, Lourdes Suárez Díez, and Perla Valle de Revueltas, *Corazón de Copíl: El Templo Mayor y el Recinto Sagrado de México-Tenochtitlan según fuentes del siglo xvi, México* (México: INAH, 1982). Also see the well-illustrated *Arqueología Mexicana: recientes en el Templo Mayo* 6:3, for more recent discoveries about the ritual life at Templo Mayor.

21. Leonardo López Luján suggests that some of these women were priestesses who were decapitated and deposited in the sacred precinct (personal communication).

22. Benjamin Keen, *The Aztec Image in Western Thought* (New Brunswick: Rutgers University Press, 1971).

23. Peter Brown, *Society and the Holy in Late Antiquity* (Berkeley, Los Angeles, and London: University of California Press, 1982), p. 8.

24. Other colonial representations of the Templo Mayor appear in the Codices *Aubin, Magliabechiano, Matritense,* and *Telleriano-Remensis.*

25. *Códice Durán,* proyecto and textos por Electra y Tonatiuh Gutiérrez (Mexico: Arrendadora Internacional, 1991), Apendice: lamina 16, fig. 23.

26. Díaz del Castillo, *The Discovery and Conquest of Mexico,* p. 218.

27. See H. B. Nicholson's detailed interpretation of the Coyolxauhqui stone in "The New Tenochtitlan Templo Mayor Coyolxauhqui-Chantico Monument," in the Festschrift honoring Professor Gerdt Kutscher, Ibero-Amerikanisches Institut, Berlin, Germany (1985) 10, part 2, pp. 77–98.

28. Miguel León-Portilla's *Native Mesoamerican Spirituality* (New York: Paulist Press, 1980) contains a number of *teocuicatl* (divine songs) and *huehuetlatolli* (ancient words), making the volume a useful collection of indigenous fragments available in English. The following quotes regarding Huitzilopochtli are taken from pp. 220–225.

29. The most impressive discussion of Tula's overall significance in Mesoamerica appears in Lindsay Jones, *Twin City Tales: A Hermeneutical Reassessment of Tula and Chichén Itzá* (Niwot: University Press of Colorado, 1995). For an interpretation of Tula's religious significance, see Davíd Carrasco's *Quetzalcoatl and the Irony of Empire* (Chicago: University of Chicago Press, 1992), especially pp. 72–92, 104–128, and the bibliography.

30. Beatriz de la Fuente, "Escultura en el tiempo: Retorno al pasado tolteca," *Artes de México*, 7:36–53, writes about the Mexica search for the Toltec past through art.

31. Alfredo López Austin's *Hombre-dios: Religión y política en el mundo náhuatl* (Mexico: Universidad Nacional Autónoma de México, 1973) is a complex and innovative interpretation of Mesoamerican religion.

32. See Mircea Eliade's discussion of "magical heat" and "berserker" experiences in the history of religions for useful connections to not only the myth of Huitzilopochtli but also the warrior mentality that animated segments of Aztec religion, in *Rites and Symbols of Initiation* (New York: Harper and Row, 1958), pp. 81–107.

33. Documents that relate Coatepec and the Templo Mayor include Alvarado Tezozomoc, *Crónica Mexicana* (Mexico: Leyenda, 1944), p. 300; Bernardino de Sahagún, *Códice Florentino* (México: AGN, 1979) Book 2, folio 108r; *Códice Azcatitlan*, Introducción, Michel Graulich, Comentario, Robert H. Barlow (Paris: Bibliotheque Nacional de France/Société des Americanistes, 1995), plate 6.

34. Eduardo Matos Moctezuma, "Los hallazgos de la arqueología," in *El Templo Mayor* (Mexico: Bancomer, 1981), pp. 102–283; Yólotl González de Lesur, "El dios Huitzilopochtli en la peregrinacion Mexica de Aztlan a Tula," *Anales del INAH* (México) 19:175–190; Miguel León-Portilla, *México-Tenochtitlan: su espacio y tiempo sagrado* (México: INAH), pp. 50–65; Eduardo Matos Moctezuma, *Life and Death at the Templo Mayor* (Niwot: University Press of Colorado, 1995).

35. This pattern of integrating foreign sacred elements as a sign of dominance is repeated in the construction and use of the Coacalco, the temple in which the sacred images of the gods of conquered communities were collected.

36. Durán, *Book of the Gods and Rites*, p. 458.

37. Edward Shils, "Center and Periphery," in *Center and Periphery: Essays in Macrosociology* (Chicago and London: University of Chicago Press, 1975), p. 9. In the use of categories like center and periphery, which are literary categories that reflect Aztec conceptions of space and social order, I am building upon the work of Shils; Jonathan Z. Smith, "The Wobbling Pivot"; Richard Hecht, "Center and Periphery: Some Aspects of the Social World of Ptolemaic and Early Roman Alexandria" (mimeographed, Santa Barbara, 1979); and Alfonso Ortiz, *The Tewa World*, (Chicago: University of Chicago Press, 1979). Shils makes a relevant comment in his elegant essay when he writes, "The more territorially dispersed the institutional system, the less the likelihood of an intense affirmation of the central value system. Indeed, it might be said that the degree of affirmation inevitably shades off from the center of the exercise of authority and of the promulgation of values" (p. 11). See Andrea Stone's innovative essay on the ways that social centers "capture" peripheral landscapes by replicating them in ritual architecture within ceremonial enclaves. "From Ritual in the Landscape to Capture in the Urban Center," *Journal of Ritual Studies* 6(7) (Winter 1992): 109–132. In fact, the Aztec imperial arrangement was not only territorially dispersed over very difficult terrain, but the boundaries fluctuated radically in Tenochtitlan's short, less than one hundred years, domination. The

escalation of human sacrifice is related to this territorial, temporal fluctuation and dispersal.

38. Stanley Tambiah, "The Galactic Polity."

39. Diego Durán, *The History of the Indies of New Spain* (Norman: University of Oklahoma, 1994), pp. 335–336.

40. See the articles by Francis Berdan in *The Codex Mendoza*, ed. Frances E. Berdan and Patricia Rieff Anawalt (Berkeley: University of California Press, 1992).

41. López Luján, *The Offerings of the Templo Mayor of Tenochtitlan*, p. 130.

42. Leonardo López Luján writes, "Forty-two percent of the chordates belong to two classes of aquatic vertebrates: fish and elasmobranchs. Almost all the identified specimens came from the estuaries and reefs of the Gulf of Mexico; the grouper is the only one from the Pacific Ocean. Paradoxically, the freshwater species that lived in the lakes of the Basin of Mexico hardly appear in the archaeological record. Starting with the presence of specific characteristics in the examples studied, we can infer selective fishing. We know these were not food offerings because the number of edible species is only 30 percent. To the contrary, poisonous fauna predominated, which is enormously important for symbolic analysis. Fish like the porcupine fish, fugu fish, puffer fish, trunkfish, and the barracuda are toxic when eaten. The scorpion fish and the ray inject poison into the victim. Additionally, most species had strange peculiarities; sharp teeth (shark, sawfish, and barracuda), strange bodies (needlefish and half-beak), bright colors (angelfish and parrot fish). . . . The predominance in the excavated context of dental, premaxillar, preopercular, and neurocranial remains and the absence of vertebrae or hipural plates is meaningful. This means that the Mexica did not deposit the bodies of the fish but only their heads and scales. A triggerfish found in offering 23 is the only complete specimen. All this is evidence that the Mexica observed strict rules in selecting animal material and prepared it in various ways before it was deposited," pp. 132–133.

43. The best description of this religio-political organization appears in Alfredo López Austin's *The Human Body and Ideology: Concepts Among the Ancient Nahuas* (Salt Lake City: University of Utah Press, 1988), pp. 77–87. Also see Pedro Carrasco, "Social Organization of Ancient Mexico," in *Handbook*, 10:347–375.

44. López Luján, *The Offerings of the Templo Mayor of Tenochtitlan.*

45. Ibid., p. 144.

46. Ibid., p. 135.

47. Johanna Broda, "Templo Mayor as Ritual Space," in Broda, Carrasco, Matos, *The Great Temple of Tenochtitlan*, pp. 97–100.

48. Stanley Tambiah, "A Reformulation of Geertz's Conception of the Theatre State," in *Culture, Thought and Social Action*, p. 321.

49. Durán, *The History of the Indies of New Spain*, pp. 349–354.

50. See López Luján, *The Offerings of the Templo Mayor*, pp. 316–319.

51. Eduardo Matos Moctezuma, "Una máscara olmeca en el Templo Mayor de Tenochtitlan," *Anales de Antropología* (1979): 11–19. Also see Leonardo López Luján, *"La recuperación Mexica del pasado Teotihuacano* (Mexico: INAH/Asociación de Amigos del Templo Mayor/GV Editores, 1989); and Eduardo Matos Moctezuma and Leonardo López Luján, "Teotihuacan and Its Mexica Legacy," in K. Berrin and Esther Pasztory, *Teotihuacan: Art from the City of the Gods* (San Francisco: Thames and Hudson/The Fine Arts Museum, 1993), pp. 155–165.

52. Esther Pasztory, *Aztec Stone Sculpture* (The Center for Inter-American Relations, January 1976).

53. Ibid.

54. Ibid.

55. Durán, *Book of the Gods and Rites*, p. 160.

56. Esther Pasztory, "The Aztec Tlaloc: God of Antiquity," in *Smoke and Mist: Mesoamerican Studies in Memory of Thelma D. Sullivan,* vol. 402, ed. J. K. Josserand and Karin Dakin (Oxford: BAR, 1988): 289–327. A more sophisticated interpretation of the Aztec application of Teotihuacan's prestige into the Templo Mayor appears in Pasztory's *Teotihuacan: An Experiment in Living* (Norman: University of Oklahoma Press, 1997), pp. 74–77.

57. López Luján, *Offerings of the Templo Mayor*, p. 91.

58. Johanna Broda, López Austin, and Matos Moctezuma share some of these opinions as described in López Luján, *Offerings of the Templo Mayor*, pp. 93–96.

59. Ibid., p. 92.

60. Durán, *The History of the Indies of New Spain*, p. 329.

61. Broda, "Aztec Ideology," pp. 24–35.

62. In some cases, it appears that sacrifices had double purposes. The heart was sacrificed to renew the sun, and the head was taken to revitalize the earth. In one scholar's view, the Aztecs were not the people of the sun, but the people of the sun and the earth. See especially Michel Graulich, "Double Immolations in Ancient Mexica Sacrificial Ritual, *History of Religions,* 27, 4:393–404.

63. Broda, "Aztec Ideology," pp. 24–38.

64. Ibid., pp. 30–31.

65. Ibid.

66. López Luján, *Offerings of the Templo Mayor*, p. 281.

67. Durán, *The History of the Indies of New Spain*, p. 331.

68. Sahagún, *Florentine Codex*, 3:1.

69. Ibid.

70. Ibid., 7:6.

71. Ibid.

72. Ibid., p. 7.

73. Ibid., p. 8. My work with myths of creation is deeply indebted to Charles H. Long, especially his *Alpha: Myths of Creation* (Chico, Calif.: Scholars Press, 1963).

74. According to Michel Graulich and Leonardo López Luján, the principal festival used to inaugurate the Templo Mayor (for each of its enlargements) was always Tlacaxipehualiztli. This was the festival related to war and the birth of the sun. Graulich argues that the gladiatorial sacrifice is a recreation of the myth of the Fifth Sun in Teotihuacan and also of the first war, the massacre of the four hundred Mimixcoa ordered by Tonatiuh. See Michel Graulich, "Tlacaxipehualiztli ou la fête aztèque de la moisson et de la guerre," *Revista espanola de antropología americana,* 12:15–254. Also see López Luján, *Offerings of the Templo Mayor,* pp. 286–296.

75. Durán, *The History of the Indies of New Spain,* pp. 333–339.

76. Broda, "Ideology of the Aztec State and Human Sacrifice" (manuscript delivered at 1979 Conference in Boulder, Colorado), pp. 24–35, to be published in Roger Joseph, Frances F. Berdan, and Hugo G. Nutini, eds., *Societies in Transition: Essays in Honor of Pedro Carrasco* (in press).

77. Broda, "Ideology of the Aztec State," pp. 24–38. See also Davíd Carrasco, "Human Sacrifice: Aztec Rites," *The Encyclopedia of Religion* (New York: Macmillan, 1987), 6:518–523.

78. Philip P. Arnold, *Eating Landscape: Aztec and European Occupation of Tlalocan* (Niwot: University Press of Colorado, 1999).

79. This general discussion of ritual human sacrifice is derived from H. B. Nicholson's "Religion in Pre-Hispanic Central Mexico," in *Handbook* (1971), Book 10, and the *Florentine Codex,* Book 2, *The Ceremonies;* see especially the appendix. The best summary of everyday sacrifice is found in Cecelia Klein, "The Ideology of Autosacrifice at the Templo Mayor," *The Aztec Templo Mayor,* ed. Elizabeth Hill Boone (Dumbarton Oaks: Trustees for Harvard University, Washington, D.C., 1987).

80. Peggy Reeves Sanday, *Divine Hunger: Cannibalism as a Cultural System* (New York: Cambridge University Press, 1986).

81. Friedrich Katz, *Ancient American Civilizations* (Chicago: Praeger Press, 1972), see especially chapter 10.

82. Roy Rappaport, *Ecology, Meaning and Religion* (Richmond, Calif.: North Atlantic Books, 1979), p. 148.

3. The New Fire Ceremony and the Binding of the Years

The combination of skillful and fearful symmetry in the New Fire Ceremony, referred to in the chapter title, has a compelling resonance with William Blake's passage from "The Tyger": "Tyger! Tyger! burning bright / in the forests of the night, / What immortal hand or eye / Dare frame thy fearful symmetry?"

1. James Thurber, *My Life and Hard Times*, quoted in *The Art of Interpretive Speech*, ed. Charles H. Woolbert and Severina E. Nelson (New York: Appleton-Century-Crofts, 1956), pp. 493–495. I am grateful to my teacher, Esther Smith, for introducing me to the significance of this episode.

2. My own concern with interdisciplinary work and the engagement in a more extensive analysis of Mesoamerican religions stems from the creative hermeneutics of a number of historians of religions, including Gerardus van der Leeuw, Mircea Eliade, Charles Long, J. Z. Smith, Wendy Doniger, and Lawrence Sullivan. Each in their own way has explored the limits and values of interdisciplinary work in order to enlarge and deepen our understanding of the pervasive role of religious experience and expressions in human society. While this is always a complex task that often promises more than it produces, one of the best starting points was described by Mircea Eliade in his essay on the quest for a new humanism, which involves an intellectual orientation designed to transcend cultural and disciplinary provincialism. He wrote that it is "useful to repeat that *homo religiosus* represents the 'total man'; hence, the science of religions must become a total discipline in the sense that it must use, integrate, and articulate the results obtained by the various methods of approaching a religious phenomenon. It is not enough to grasp the meaning of a religious phenomenon in a certain culture and, consequently, to decipher its 'message' (for every religious phenomenon constitutes a 'cipher'); it is also necessary to study and understand its 'history,' that is, to unravel its changes and modifications and, ultimately, to elucidate its contribution to the entire culture. In the past few years a number of scholars have felt the need to transcend the alternative *religious phenomenology* or *history of religions* and to reach a broader perspective in which these two intellectual operations can be applied together. It is toward the integral conception of the science of religions that the efforts of scholars seem to be orienting themselves today. To be sure, these two approaches correspond in some degree to different philosophical temperaments. And it would be naive to suppose that the tension between those who try to understand the *essence* and the *structures* and those whose only concern is the *history* of religious phenomena will one day be completely done away with. But such a tension is creative. It is by virtue of it that the science of religions will escape dogmatism and stagnation," in *The Quest* (Chicago: University of Chicago Press, 1969), p. 8. Among many important statements about attempts to explore this creative hermeneutics, see especially Wendy Doniger, *Other People's Myths* (New York: Macmillan Publishing Company, 1988); Charles Long, *Significations: Signs, Symbols and Images in the Interpretation of Religion* (Philadelphia: Fortress Press, 1986); and Lawrence Sullivan, *Icanchu's Drum: An Orientation to Meaning in South American Religions* (New York: Macmillan Publishers, 1989).

3. See Anthony Aveni's introductory comments in *World Archaeoastronomy* (Cambridge: Cambridge University Press, 1989), pp. xi–12.

4. Ibid., pp. 3–4.

5. I am following Clifford Geertz's approach to "analogy" in his essay "Blurred Genres: The Reconfiguration of Social Thought," reprinted in *Local Knowledge: Further Essays in Interpretive Anthropology* (New York: Basic Books, 1983).

6. This question was recently discussed in Lawrence Sullivan's article "Astral Myths Rise Again: Interpreting Religious Astronomy," *Criterion* 22(1) (1981): 12–17. Summarizing two previous periods in Western scholarship when the tie between astronomy and religion was in vogue, Sullivan noted a single tendency that hindered the construction of a sound theoretical framework for understanding the relationship between religious symbolism and astronomy. This was the tendency to "impose upon the data an assumption of mutual incompatibility between religious and scientific purposes which appear to be built into the data."

The problems caused by this assumption were evident in the 1798 publication of Charles François Dupuis's twelve-volume *The Origin of All Religious Worship: Universal Religion*. Dupuis argued that all religious ideas and practices originated in fantastic distortions of one process of nature, the regular movement of the stars. Sullivan writes, "Examining evidence of religious belief and practice in Chinese, Siamese, Greek, Molluccan, Persian, Philippino, Norse, Madagascan, Formosan, and Japanese traditions he attributed the origin and order of all myth . . . to nothing more than the unnecessary veil of allegory drawn across the visible events of . . . the equinox, solstices, seven planets, and 12 signs of the Zodiac." Dupuis's point was that religion obstructed the acquisition of true knowledge about the stars. True knowledge of the heavens would be achieved through reasonable and precise astronomic data. It is interesting to note, as an aside about cultural fashions and astronomy, that Dupuis's book was dedicated to the French Revolutionary Assembly of 1795 and that in the intervening twenty-five years, according to Sullivan, "this last significant mythography of the Enlightenment had sold out of every edition of its three-, eight-, and single-volume formats and had been the center of a raging controversy. Joseph Priestley, the one time Unitarian minister and scientist, refuted it at length and, in exile from England, discussed it vehemently with his new found American friends, John Adams and Thomas Jefferson."

A second interest in astromythology appeared in the early twentieth century among the Pan-Babylonianists, whose researches in Babylonian, Assyrian, Sumerian, and Semitic civilizations argued that nearly all myths "were literal statements about the movement of heavenly bodies, especially the multiform synodical phases of the moon." Again the position argued that religion had a narrow origin in human history and that it was, in part, a distortion of observable nature.

7. Anthony Aveni, ed., *World Archaeoastronomy: Selected Papers from the 2nd Oxford International Conference on Archaeoastronomy Held at Merida, Yucatan, Mexico* (Cambridge: Cambridge University Press, 1989), p. xii. It appears that one of the characteristics of contemporary archaeoastronomy is the interest in discovering intersections, crossroads, and conjunctions between the multiple aspects of ecology, the patterns of astronomy, and the complex aspects of the religious imagination. This development in archaeoastronomy finds a conversation partner in the position

expressed by Ninian Smart in his essay on the future of the history of religions. Smart persuasively argues that scholars in religious studies need intellectual interchanges with scholars from other disciplines. These interchanges would result not only in the usual process of "importing" ideas into religious studies but also in the much-needed process of "exporting" ideas from the history of religions into other disciplines. Also, Smart urges historians of religions to carry out more theoretical work that relates what we call religion to other areas of human experience.

8. Paul Wheatley, *The Pivot of the Four Quarters: A Preliminary Enquiry into the Origins and Character of the Ancient Chinese City* (Chicago: Aldine Publishing Company, 1971), p. 414.

9. Kent V. Flannery, ed., *The Early Mesoamerican Village* (New York: Academic Press, 1976), p. 331.

10. Ibid.

11. A significant advance in archaeology and religion has been achieved in the publications of the Templo Mayor project in Mexico City. See especially the excellent synthetic work by Leonardo López Luján, *The Offerings of the Templo Mayor of Tenochtitlan* (Niwot: University Press of Colorado, 1994), especially chapter 8 and the various works by Eduardo Matos Moctezuma.

12. Alfredo López Austin, *The Myths of the Opossum: Pathways of Mesoamerican Mythology*, trans. B. R. Ortiz de Montellano and T. Ortiz de Montellano (Albuquerque: University of New Mexico Press, 1993). See also his highly useful *Tamoanchan, Tlalocan: Places of Mist* (Niwot: University Press of Colorado, 1994), especially chapters 1 and 3, for an illuminating discussion of the Mesoamerican religious tradition.

13. Inga Clendinnen, *Ambivalent Conquests: Maya and Spaniard in Yucatan, 1517–1570* (Cambridge: Cambridge University Press, 1987), pp. 131–132.

14. Ibid., p. 132. Clendinnen is overstating the case here. The Maya voices may have been a murmur to some of the Spaniards, but they were also too loud for many of the priests. And of course among themselves, they cried, shouted, prayed, conversed, and narrated eloquently.

15. Alfredo López Austin, "The Research Method of Fray Bernardino de Sahagún: The Questionnaires," *Sixteenth Century Mexico,* ed., Munro Edmonson (Albuquerque: University of New Mexico Press, 1974), p. 136.

16. See Aveni's "Introduction: Whither Archaeoastronomy?" in *World Archaeoastronomy,* for a summary of the problem and use of the category of "alignment." Also see how the category of alignment, contrary to what some scholars expected, has continued to be one of the guiding concepts and metaphors for what archaeoastronomers seek, in Johanna Broda, "The Sacred Landscape of Aztec Calendar Festivals: Myth, Nature and Society," in *Aztec Ceremonial Landscapes,* ed. Davíd Carrasco, (Niwot: University Press of Colorado, 1999), paperback, pp. 74–121, and numerous articles in her edited volume.

17. An impressive work on the symmetry of Aztec art appears in Richard Town-

send, *State and Cosmos in the Art of Tenochtitlan* (Washington, D.C.: Dumbarton Oaks, 1979). Also see his "Coronation at Tenochtitlan," in *The Imagination of Matter: Religion and Ecology in Mesoamerican Traditions,* ed. Davíd Carrasco (B. A. R. International Series 515, 1989).

18. Rudolph van Zantwijk, *The Aztec Arrangement: The Social History of Pre-Spanish Mexico* (Norman: University of Oklahoma Press, 1977).

19. Bernardino de Sahagún, *Florentine Codex: The General History of the Things of New Spain,* ed. and trans. J. O. Anderson and Charles E. Dibble, 12 vols. (Santa Fe, N.M.: School of American Research and University of Utah, 1955–1982), 7:27.

20. Ibid.

21. Ibid., pp. 26–28.

22. Ibid., p. 28.

23. Ibid., p. 28.

24. Ibid., p. 29.

25. Motolinía (Toribio de Benavente), *Motolinía's History of the Indians of New Spain,* trans. Francis Borgia Steck (Washington, D.C.:s Academy of American Franciscan History, Documentary Series, 1951), vol. 1.

26. Sahagún, 7:29–30.

27. Ibid., p. 25.

28. Ibid., p. 31.

29. Henry Nicholson, "Some Remarks on the Provenience of the *Codex Borbonicus,*" *Adeva Mitteilungen* 40: 14–18 (Graz: Akademische Druck-u.Verlagsanstalt, 1974), argues for a non-Mexica location of the temple and the manuscript. A more extensive version of this argument appears in "The Provenience of the *Codex Borbonicus*: An Hypothesis," in *Smoke and Mist,* edited by J. Kathryn Josserand and Karen Dakin, coordinated by H. B. Nicholson, Doris Heyden, Karen Dakin, and Nicholas A. Hopkins (Oxford, England: BAR [British Archaeological Reports], International Series 402(i), part i, pp. 77–97.

30. Christopher Couch, *The Festival Cycle of the Aztec Codex Borbonicus* (Oxford: British Archaeological Reports, 1985), p. 84.

31. A meridian is a great circle that passes through the zenith and the north and south celestial poles. So, this passage does not mean that the Pleiades passed through the zenith, or the point directly over the head of the observer, but rather it passed through the arched line of the great circle at the highest possible point on that night's passage. See Anthony Aveni, *Skywatchers of Ancient Mexico* (Austin: University of Texas Press, 1980), p. 98.

32. Sahagún, *Florentine Codex,* 4 & 5:143. This passage comes from a short but rich account of the Toximmolpilia ceremony and adds some important details about the general populace's response to the lighting of the New Fire that appears in Book 7.

33. Ibid., p. 144.

34. See Johanna Broda's exhaustive account in "Tlacaxipeualiztli: A Reconstruction of an Aztec Calendar Festival from 16th Century Sources," *Revista española de antropología americana* 5 (1970): 197–274.

35. Sahagún, 7:31.

36. This quote is actually Clifford Geertz's gloss on Shils's work in "Centers, Kings and Charisma: Symbolics or Power," in *Local Knowledge*, p. 122.

37. The narrative in Diego Durán's *The History of the Indies of New Spain* indicates that the New Fire goes from the mountain directly to the towns and cities throughout the empire, but the more detailed, though inadequate, account in Sahagún makes it very likely that the circuit is from the mountain to the Templo Mayor to all temples, schools, homes, and bodies in the city and then to the empire. What is also impressive about Durán's account are the historical references to a particular New Fire Ceremony and the war and conquest against Teuctepec, "So it was on that day the two thousand captives who had been brought from the destruction and conquest of Teuctepec (which I have described) were sacrificed there. This sacrifice began at midnight and lasted most of the next day" (p. 446). The priests were bathed in blood, and vessels of blood were taken to the temples and smeared on lintels, altars, and statues of the gods. It is not clear if these warriors died of sacrifice by fire.

38. Quoted in López Austin, p. 274.

39. Newborn children were placed near the hearth fire in order to provide them with *tonalli,* one of the animistic entities, or souls, upon which human life depended for growth and survival.

40. I am attracted to López Austin's approach to symbolism, where he writes, "The symbols depicted on the codices, on the walls, on implements, and on stone monuments make up codes whose referents go far beyond the sphere of esthetic emotion. These symbols include the taxonomic and structural bases of the cosmos and were produced by peoples who oriented their actions in the belief in a universal harmony and organization. Iconographic research cannot always guide us toward the historical event, but it can tell us much about what ought to be: an archetype, a justification or elaboration, a model, or a pattern within which behavior took place" in "The Masked God of Fire," in *The Great Aztec Temple,* ed., Elizabeth Boone (Washington, D.C.: Dumbarton Oaks, 1987), p. 259.

41. Ibid., p. 275.

42. Ibid., p. 279.

43. Ibid., p. 276. López Austin writes that to step on a hearthstone was to offend the god and await his punishment.

44. See especially Jonathan Z. Smith, "The Influence of Symbols upon Social Change: A Place upon Which to Stand," in *Map Is Not Territory.*

45. Sahagún, 2:61.

46. Ibid., pp. 109–110.

47. Ibid.

48. Ibid.

49. Ibid.

50. Ibid., p. 68.

51. Ibid., p. 69.

52. Johanna Broda, "The Sacred Landscape of Aztec Calendar Festivals: Myth, Nature, and Society," in *Aztec Ceremonial Landscapes*, ed. Davíd Carrasco, with a preface by William Fash (Niwot: University Press of Colorado, 1999), p. 75.

53. Broda writes that through the careful investigation of mountain cult relations with astronomy and ecology, "we discover one of the many ways in which the Aztecs became the heirs of the civilizations that had preceded them in the old cultural land of the Basin of Mexico. It makes us realize that there operated in pre-Hispanic times a historical consciousness and tradition with respect to 'holy places' that became manifest in the existence of certain important sanctuaries. These were closely linked to astronomical observations and thus, 'visual lines' of particularly significant alignments are found to connect them. We are beginning to discover a structured whole of calendar alignments and geometrical proportions, that seem to have originated in Preclassic times, although, naturally, it continued to evolve during the nearly two millennia that succeeded Cuicuilco as the first major center in the Basin of Mexico. Increasingly, more data accumulate indicating that the Mexica purposefully inserted themselves into this ancient landscape of the Valley and established the island of Tenochtitlan, with Templo Mayor as its center, as the principal pivot of this realm" (Ibid., pp. 111–112).

54. I was assisted by Phil Arnold, who did the initial study of the articles published in the *History of Religions*.

55. Miguel León-Portilla, in his overview article "A Reflection of the Ancient Mesoamerican Ethos," in *World Archaeoastronomy*, ed., Anthony Aveni, pp. 219–227, cautions archaeoastronomers against the projection of modern astronomical knowledge onto the sky watching practices of ancient peoples. He writes, "If skywatching—the observing and measuring of the running of the stars—was an essential part of Mesoamerican culture, modern 'discoveries' of any of its ancient achievements will have always to do with celestial phenomena intrinsically related to the world view, religion and practices of Mesoamericans. 'Discoveries' of archaeoastronomers dealing with celestial bodies or cosmic cycles, about whose meaning in the culture itself nothing is known, have to be held suspicious and put in parenthesis" (p. 225).

56. Two notable exceptions are Alex Wayman, "Climactic Times in Indian Mythology and Religion," *History of Religions* 4:2 (Winter 1965): 295 318; and Schuyler Cammann, "The Magic Square of Three in Old Chinese Philosophy and Religion," *History of Religions* 1:1 (Summer 1961): 37–80. I am grateful to my former research assistant, Phil Arnold, for his assistance in this research.

57. See Anthony Aveni's discussion of "special assemblages," such as the Group E-VII sub/structure in Uaxactun, in *Conversations with Aveni: Archaeoastronomy and the History of Religions in Mesoamerica*, working paper 1, ed., Davíd Carrasco, Phil Arnold, Lawrence Desmond, and Rebecca Herr (Boulder: Mesoamerican Archive and Research Project, University of Colorado).

58. The research program of the Mesoamerican Archive has attempted to widen the notion of periphery by associations with (1) frontiers, that is, the social and symbolic limits to political order and within cosmovision; these frontiers occasionally functioned as buffer areas for exchange and conflict, (2) battlefields, specifically chosen spaces of combat and ritual where explosive political relationships were transformed and negotiated and often mediated by astronomical observations, (3) plants and soils from outlying regions utilized in market exchange and religious/medical practices; these materials reflect the diverse ecological niches of Mesoamerican landscapes. What is central to the use of this expanding model of center and periphery are the various dynamics that created reciprocal and recurrent patterns of relationships. The three most outstanding dynamics are the energy and action of the marketplace, the symbolism and action of warfare, and the ritual performances that mapped out the ceremonial world. As the archaeoastronomers have shown, each of these dynamics was mediated in part through astronomical movements, events, and appearances.

59. Sahagún, 2:216.

60. Ulrich Köhler, "Comets and Falling Stars in the Perception of Mesoamerican Indians," in *World Archaeoastronomy*, ed., Anthony Aveni (Cambridge: Cambridge University Press, 1989). Kohler's concise article surveys native Mesoamerican attitudes toward comets and falling stars from pre-Hispanic times to the present day.

61. Sahagún, 7:6-7.

62. Fray Toribio de Benavente, or Motolinía, *Historia de los Indios de la Nueva España* (Mexico: Editorial Porrua, 1973).

63. Quoted in Anthony F. Aveni, Edward Calnek, Horst Hartung, "On the Orientation of the Templo Mayor of Tenochtitlan," *American Antiquity* 53 (1988): 287-309.

64. Earlier calculations were made by Franz Tichy, "Order and Relationship of Space and Time in Mesoamerica: Myth or Reality," in *Mesoamerican Sites and World Views*, ed. E.P. Benson, pp. 217-245 (Washington, D.C.: Dumbarton Oaks, 1981), and Arturo Ponce de Leon, *Fechamiento arqueoastronómico en el Altiplano de México* (Mexico: Departamento del Distrito Federal, 1982).

65. Aveni, Calnek, Hartung, "On the Orientation of the Templo Mayor," p. 306.

66. Broda, "Tlacaxipeualiztli: A Reconstruction of an Aztec Calendar Festival from the 16th Century Sources," in *Revista Española de Antropología Americana*, vol. 5 (Madrid), pp. 197-274.

67. Sahagún, 2:55.

68. I have borrowed this phrase from Geertz's discussion of charisma in *Local Knowledge*.

4. The Sacrifice of Tezcatlipoca

The first epigraph is taken from Jonathan Z. Smith, *Map Is Not Territory: Studies in the History of Religions* (Leiden: E. J. Brill, 1978), p. 134.

The second epigraph is from Bernardino de Sahagún, *Florentine Codex: A History of the Things of New Spain*, ed. and trans. Arthur J. O. Anderson and C. E. Dibble (Santa Fe: School of American Research and the University of Utah, 1950–1982), 6:22.

1. Jonathan Z. Smith, *To Take Place: Toward Theory in Ritual* (Chicago: University of Chicago Press, 1987), p. xii.

2. As Maarten Jansen and others have shown, certain dates in Mesoamerican calendars are intimately related to, or locked into, specific places and communities. See Jansen's "Dates, Deities and Dynasties, Non-Durational Time in Mixtec Historeography," in *Continuity and Identity in Native America*, ed., M. Jansen, P. van der Loo, and R. Manning (Leiden: E. J. Brill, 1988).

3. Sahagún, 2:67.

4. Ibid., p. 68.

5. Ibid.

6. Ibid., p. 71.

7. Alfredo López Austin, *The Human Body and Ideology: Concepts of the Ancient Nahuas*, 2 vols. (Salt Lake City: University of Utah Press, 1988), 1:8.

8. Lawrence Sullivan, "Sound and Sense: Toward a Hermeneutics of Performance," *History of Religions* 26 (1986): 8.

9. Rhys Isaac, *The Transformation of Virginia, 1740–1790* (Chapel Hill: University of North Carolina Press, 1982), p. 10.

10. It may be that this pattern of metamorphosis is present in many, if not all, Aztec ceremonies. Likewise, as Leonardo López Luján has suggested in a personal communication, all the Aztec gods were wonders of transformation.

11. Sahagún, 2:54.

12. Ibid., p. 132.

13. Thelma Sullivan, "The Rhetorical Orations or Huehuetlatolli, collected by Sahagún," in *Sixteenth-Century Mexico: The Work of Sahagún*, ed. Monro S. Edmonson (Albuquerque: University of New Mexico Press, 1974), p. 86.

14. Diego Durán, *Book of the Gods and Rites and the Ancient Calendar*, trans. and ed. F. Horcasitas and D. Heyden (Norman: University of Oklahoma Press, 1977), p. 99.

15. A number of gods used these mirrors as instruments of divination into the profound processes of the cosmos. In Book 1 of *The Florentine Codex*, we find references to mirrors associated with Cahlchiuhtlicue, Huitzilopochtli, and Xiuhtecuhtli.

16. Sahagún, 6:25.

17. The *tonalli* and the *teyolia* are the animistic entities given by the gods to humans at conception and during maturation; see Alfredo López Austin, *Human Body and Ideology,* and Bernardo Ortiz de Montellano, *Aztec Medicine, Heath, and Nutrition* (New Brunswick: Rutgers University Press, 1990), for helpful discussions of these two "souls." An illuminating study of the soul is Jill Leslie McKeever Furst, *The Natural History of the Soul in Ancient Mexico* (New Haven: Yale University Press, 1995).

18. Durán, *Book of the Gods,* p. 107.

19. Otto von Simson, *The Gothic Cathedral* (Chicago: University of Chicago Press, 1956), p. 161.

20. Ibid., p. 163.

21. López Austin, *Human Body and Ideology,* 1:377.

22. See Alfredo López Austin's *The Myths of the Opossum: Pathways of Mesoamerican Mythology* (Albuquerque: University of New Mexico Press, 1993), especially chapters 10–12 on the "Nature of the Gods," pp. 104–155.

23. Ibid., pp. 136–138.

24. Durán, *Book of the Gods,* p. 111.

25. Ibid., p. 110.

26. Ibid., p. 100.

27. Ibid.

28. Ibid., p. 101.

29. Richard Schechner, *Between Theater and Anthropology* (Philadelphia: University of Pennsylvania Press, 1985).

30. Sahagún, 2:71.

31. Ibid., p. 10.

32. Durán, *Book of the Gods,* p. 107.

33. Sahagún, 2:10.

34. Ibid., p. 71.

35. Ibid., p. 7.

36. Ibid.

37. Ibid., 6:8.

38. Ibid., p. 9.

39. Ibid., p. 23.

5. Give Me Some Skin

The epigraph opening the chapter is taken from Paul Wheatley, in *Melaka: The Transformation of a Malay Capital, c. 1400–1980,* ed., Kernial Singh Sandhu and Paul Wheatley (Oxford: Oxford University Press, 1983), p. 18.

1. This description comes from three major sixteenth-century sources on Aztec ritual compiled by two Franciscan friars, Bernardino de Sahagún and Toribio de Benavente (Motolinía), and a Dominican, Diego Durán. Sahagún, *Florentine Codex: General History of the Things of New Spain, Book II: The Ceremonies*, trans. Arthur J. O. Anderson and Charles E. Dibble (Santa Fe, N. M.: The School of American Research and the University of Utah, 1981); Motolinía, *Historia de los Indios de la Nueva España*, estudio crítico, apéndices, notas e índice de Edmundo O'Gorman (México: Editorial Porrúa, 1959); and Durán, *The Book of the Gods and the Rites and the Ancient Calendar*, trans. Fernando Horcasitas and Doris Heyden (Norman: University of Oklahoma Press, 1971).

2. In working on this festival, I am following the exceptional research of Johanna Broda, whose crucial articles on imperial expansion, human sacrifice, and the cults of various deities at the Templo Mayor raise the standard of knowledge about Aztec religion. See especially her "La expansión imperial mexica y los sacrificios del Templo Mayor," in *Mesoamérica y el Centro de México*, Jesús Monjarás-Ruiz, Rosa Brambila, Emma Pérez-Rocha, recopiladores (México: Instituto Nacional de Antropología e Historia, 1985). Earlier, Broda mapped out the ritual architecture of Tlacaxipeualiztli in her seminal "Tlacaxipeualiztli: A Reconstruction of an Aztec Calendar Festival from the 16th-Century Sources," *Revista española de antropología americana* 5 (1970): 197–279.

3. See Alfredo López Austin's focused discussion of human sacrifice in *The Human Body and Ideology: Concepts of the Ancient Nahuas*, trans. Thelma and Bernardo Ortiz de Montellano (Salt Lake City: University of Utah Press, 1988), pp. 375–380. He writes that the *teteo imixiptlahuan* were "men possessed by the gods, and, as such, died in a rite of renewal. . . . It was not men who died, but gods—gods within a corporeal covering that made possible their ritual death on earth" (p. 376).

4. Sahagún, 2:48.

5. Ibid., p. 50. Another version of this ceremony appears in *Book VIII: Kings and Lords* of the *Florentine Codex*. The skirmishes in the streets are described in some detail, including, "And then the chieftains started forth and fell upon the tototecti: they pinched their navels. Very swiftly they pinched them, and then they took after them and went skirmishing with them there in the place where they were, a place called Totectzontecontitlan" (p. 85).

6. Johanna Broda's insights into the relationship of these ceremonies to the formation of the Aztec empire emphasize the relationship of inauguration and sacrificial stones. In "La expansión imperial mexica," she writes, "Cierto tiempo después Motecuhzoma mandó tallar una nueva piedra de sacrificio con la imagen del sol (*cuauhxicalli*) inaugurándola con el sacrificio de los cautivos de la guerra contra el señorío mixteco de Coaixtlahuaca. Para la fiesta convidó a los señores de Tetzcoco, Tlacopan, Chalco, Xhochimilco, Culhuacan, Cuitlahuac, y del Marquesado. El día siguiente, los caballeros águila (*cuaucuauhtin*) celebraron la fiesta del quinto sol, *nahua ollin*, sacrificando una víctima sobre la piedra nueva. A partir de entonces, los señores convidados empezaron a imitar las costumbres rituales de los mexica, introduciéndolas en sus propios pueblos" ("Sometime later Moctezuma ordered carved a new sacri-

ficial stone with the image of the Sun [cuauhxicalli] and inaugurated it with the sacrifice of war captives from the Mixtec region of Coaixtlahuaca. He invited to the festival the rulers of Tetzcoco, Tlacopan, Chalco, Xochimilco, Culhuacan, Cuitlahuac, and of the Marquessate. On the following day the eagle warriors celebrated the festival of the Fifth Sun by sacrificing a victim on the new stone. As a result the invited rulers began to imitate the ritual customs of the Mexica, introducing them in their own communities.") (pp. 448–449).

7. Sahagún, 2:51.

8. Ibid., p. 53.

9. Ibid.

10. Ibid., p. 54.

11. Sahagún's Book 8 gives interesting details to this penetration of domestic spaces by the impersonators, "thereupon the tototecti visited house after house. Nowhere did they omit a house or one's home. Indeed everywhere they entered: and the common folk, seasoned to this, awaited them in order to offer them the things with which they expected them—bunches of ears of maize, tortillas made of uncooked maize, and tamales of maize, amaranth seed, and honey mixed together. For the whole day they went from house to house, (thus treated with) esteem" (p. 85).

12. Sahagún, 2:55.

13. Ibid., p. 57.

14. Throughout this essay, I am indebted to the synthetic work of Doris Heyden on Xipe Totec and a number of Aztec deities. Roaming over the scattered evidence about this ancient Mesoamerican deity, Heyden has presented a critical overview of Xipe's significance, origin, and meaning. She writes of Xipe's widespread influence, "Xipe totec . . . was a deity of prehispanic Mexico whose image—or that of his surrogate—appears in clay figurines from Teotihuacan, the Gulf Coast region, Western Mexico as well as in pictorial codices of central Mexico. He also appears in early colonial written sources which describe his frightening figure, that of a man dressed in another person's skin" (from "Xipe the Flayed God: A Reevaluation of His Character and Place of Origin," unpublished manuscript, p. 1). Heyden has also done illuminating work on the flora of the Aztecs and their ritual significance. See especially her "Las diosas del agua y de la vegetación," Anales de Antropología 2 (1983): 129–145.

15. Ross Hassig, Aztec Warfare: Imperial Expansion and Political Control (Norman: University of Oklahoma Press, 1989), pp. 18–21. Hassig's well-researched monograph describes the rational basis of Mexica warfare and the efficient spatial arrangements achieved through the preparations, mobilizations, marches, combat, and campaigns of various kings, which made up what he calls the "military life cycle." Using Edward N. Luttwak's analysis of political relations and the distinction between force and power, Hassig insists that while force is direct physical action, power (in which force is a component) is primarily psychological, the perception of

the possessor's ability to achieve its ends. The Aztec control of its empire was based on perceived power, i.e., perceived by those enemy and allied polities. In Hassig's self-assured prose, "To the Aztecs, war was not simply the fulfillment of some religious imperative or the defense of what they perceived as vital interests. War *was* the empire" (p. 20). While I am persuaded by Professor Hassig's insistence on the ways in which Aztec warfare organized the political relations of the empire, I doubt that Aztec psychology or perceptions were ever free of the religious dimensions and emotions that defined the nature, timing, and actions of war.

16. This linkage between the spaces of practical life and the spaces of ceremonial action in the history of religions has recently been explored by Jonathan Z. Smith in his "The Bare Facts of Ritual," in *Imagining Religion: From Babylon to Jonestown* (Chicago: University of Chicago Press, 1982), where he defines ritual as a "controlled environment" rather than a gesture of sympathetic magic. Working from material as diverse as Siberian bear ceremonialism, Kafka's *Great Wall of China*, and Borges's *Death and the Compass*, Smith argues that ritual represents "the creation of a controlled environment where the variables (i.e., the accidents) of ordinary life may be displaced precisely because they are felt to be so overwhelmingly present and powerful. Ritual is a means of performing the way things ought to be in conscious tension to the way things are in such a way that this ritualized perfection is recollected in the ordinary, uncontrolled course of things" (p. 63). Interestingly for students of Aztec religions, Smith's chief example of ritualized perfection in a controlled environment comes from bear festivals of circumpolar peoples who hunt and capture bears, keep them in the village for several years fattening them up, and then rope and parade them through the village, tie them down, shoot them through the heart, strangle them, cut up their bodies, and eat them, believing that the bear's soul returns to the Master of the Animals who provides bears for the sustenance of the community in the future. In Smith's view, the ritual treatment, etiquette, roles, and prayers of the bear ritual demonstrate that the "bear festival represents a perfect hunt."

17. See the fruits of collaborative scholarly work in Anthony Aveni's "Mapping the Ritual Landscape: Debt-Payment to Tlaloc during the Month of Atlcahualo," in *Aztec Ceremonial Landscapes*. Aveni, Johanna Broda, Davíd Carrasco, Robert Bye, Philip Arnold, and Elizabeth Boone participated in a series of meetings and field trips to map out the prodigious movements of Atl Cuaulo.

18. Paul Wheatley, *The Pivot of the Four Quarters* (Chicago: Aldine, 1971).

19. Henri Hubert and Marcel Mauss, *Sacrifice: Its Nature and Function*, trans. W. D. Halls (Chicago: University of Chicago Press, 1964), p. 27.

20. These places are at once the location of maximum visibility and communication and a place of fusion between gods and humans. But Tlacaxipeualiztli reveals another mode of place—not the pivot of the four quarters or a static conception of a magic circle, but the sacred, which pivots and moves through the four quarters giving and taking power at each opportunity. I am building upon Arnold van Gennep's seminal study of rites of passage, which took the notion of a magic circle and gave it

a dynamic sense of movement. Noting the variability of the presence of the sacred, he wrote, "Thus, the magic circles pivot, shifting as a person moves from one place in society to another. The categories and concepts which embody them operate in such a way that whoever passes through the various positions of a life one day sees the sacred where before he has seen the profane, or vice versa." Van Gennep, *The Rites of Passage*, trans. Monika B. Vizedom and Gabrielle L. Caffee (Chicago: University of Chicago Press, 1960), p. 12.

21. Durán, *Book of the Gods and the Rites,* p. 175.

22. The dynamic ceremonial landscape of this ritual draws some of its shape from the movements in the *teocuicatl,* or divine song of Huitzilopochtli's birth and the dismemberment of Coyolxauhqui. I am impressed that the warriors who traveled from great distances to Serpent Mountain, where they were vanquished by Huitzilopochtli on the slopes, is the path taken by enemy warriors in a number of Mexican ceremonies. See Carrasco, "Myth, Cosmic Terror, and the Templo Mayor," in Johanna Broda, Davíd Carrasco, and Eduardo Matos Moctezuma, *The Great Temple of Tenochtitlan: Center and Periphery in Aztec Religion* (Berkeley: University of California Press, 1987), pp. 124–162.

23. See "Introduction," in *Great Temple of Tenochtitlan,* pp. 1–14.

24. Sahagún, 2:48.

25. See the entire text translated in Eduardo Matos Moctezuma, "Templo Mayor: History and Interpretation," in *Great Temple of Tenochtitlan,* pp. 51–55.

26. Sahagún, 2:51.

27. Ibid., p. 53.

28. López Austin, *The Human Body and Ideology,* p. 383.

29. Stanley Jeyaraja Tambiah, *The Buddhist Saints of the Forest and the Cult of Amulets: A Study in Charisma, Hagiography, Sectarianism, and Millennial Buddhism* (Cambridge: Cambridge University Press, 1984), p. 5.

30. Stanley Jeyaraja Tambiah, "A Performative Approach to Ritual," Radcliffe Brown Lecture in Social Anthropology, *Proceedings of the British Academy* 65 (1979).

31. Durán, p. 176.

32. Ibid.

33. See Lawrence Sullivan's synthetic "Sound and Sense: Toward a Hermeneutics of Performance," *History of Religions* 11 (1986): 1–33.

34. Durán, p. 184.

35. Quoted in Hassig, *Aztec Warfare,* p. 124.

36. This sustained concentration on death to the point of seeing and wearing a decomposing human body finds a similar practice in Tibetan Buddhism in a ritual complex called "Meditation on the Ten Foul Things." One purpose of this and other meditation techniques was the incorporation of magical powers of the dead

into one's "self." For instance, meditation was sometimes accompanied by beating drums made of human skulls stretched with human skins to place the practitioner in direct encounter with the sound and substance of death. As D. L. Snellgrove tells us in his study of the Hevajra Tantra, there are Tantric songs describing the Siddhu's quest for perfection, telling of the imagination of eating of human flesh as a means of "consuming the notion of the self. . . . Here one eats the flesh in order to transform one's own body so that it can be endowed with the powers of an aerial being" [*The Hevajra Tantra*, 9], i.e., the acquisition of magical power. This practice of incorporating magical powers of the dead into the self extended to the "Meditation on the Ten Foul Things," which involved visiting cemeteries and meditating on (1) The Swollen Corpse, (2) The Discolored Corpse, (3) The Festering Corpse, (4) The Fissured Corpse, (5) The Mangled Corpse, (6) The Dismembered Corpse, (7) The Limb-37Scattered Corpse, (8) The Bloody Corpse, (9) The Worm Foul Corpse, and (10) The Skeleton. The words of the practitioner are "I earnestly ask to acquire in the inmost shrine of my being, of the ten foul things regarded as objects of meditation . . . piercing the stream of the span of life, and entering the threshold of the mind, the element of the ten foul things appear" [*Manual of a Mystic: The Yogavachara's Manual*, ed. Mrs. Rhys Davids (London, 1916), pp. 80–85].

37. Johanna Broda "Relaciones políticas ritualizadas: el ritual como expresión de una ideología," in *Economía Política e Ideología en el México Prehispánico*, ed. Pedro Carrasco and Johanna Broda (México: CISINAH/Editorial Nueva Imagen, 1978).

6. Cosmic Jaws

1. See Anthony Grafton, *New Worlds, Ancient Texts: The Power of Tradition and the Shock of Discovery* (Cambridge: Belknap Press of Harvard University Press, 1992), for an extended discussion of how the West perceived the "Rest" during the age of discovery.

2. Grafton, who has a fine capacity for presenting complex materials in the form of helpful overviews, writes about the earliest Western tradition for making monsters out of "others." "This tradition had begun in the fifth century B.C.E. when Greeks lived near, and often within, the large and cosmopolitan empire of the Persians and reported to their countrymen of Persian, Egyptian, and even Indian customs and institutions. It developed further after the conquests of Alexander the Great, as writers followed his armies all the way to the court of Chandragupta in India. The Greeks who wrote these reports did like to describe monsters and marvels: Herodotus told his readers about the gold digging ants of India, and Ctesias, not much later, wrote about dog-headed men and pygmies . . . Herodotus, describing Egypt, sometimes used the simplest of principles for organizing the description of a foreign society; he defined it by opposition to everything Greek. . . . Sometimes, however, he took exactly the opposite tack, arguing that Egyptian civilization was not only far older than Greek, but also the source of Greek ideas and practices" (pp. 37–40). For reference to the cannibal who ate two hundred human beings, see p. 83 in Grafton.

3. Ibid., p. 72.

4. Ibid., p. 73.

5. This scene has a paradigmatic quality reserved for interpreting the first encounters between Europeans and native Americans. The setting is the beach, the liminal edge between the awesome Atlantic traversed by Europeans and the New World. It appeared in Johann Froschauer's *Dise Figur anzaigt uns das Folck und Insel die gefunden ist durch den christenlichen Kunig zu Prodigal oder von Seinen Underthonen.* As Greg Dening shows in his remarkable *Islands and Beaches: Discourse on a Silent Land: Marquesas 1774–1880* (Chicago: Dorsey Press, 1980), beaches were the contact zones where the first meetings, exchanges, perceptions and misperceptions, and murders took place. In the Americas, these exchanges often set in endless motion the discourse of America about race, religion, and the nature of the humans encountered.

6. Henry Lewis Morgan, "Moctezuma's Dinner," *North American Review* 122 (April 1876): 265–308.

7. Bernal Díaz del Castillo, *The Discovery and Conquest of New Spain* (New York: Farrer, Straus and Giroux, 1976), p. 209.

8. Ibid., p. 213.

9. See Marvin Harris, "The Cannibal Kingdom," in *Cannibals and Kings: The Origins of Culture* (New York: Random House, 1977), pp. 147–168. This book is a superior example of a scholar moving from the almost sublime to the ridiculous. Early in his work he states that his "aim is to show the relationship between material and spiritual well being and the cost benefits of various systems for increasing production and controlling population growth" (p. xii). As the narrative continues, however, it is clearer that he doesn't care at all about understanding relationships of "well-being," but is very much concerned about the cost benefits of military action and is drawn to scenes of blood spurting from wounds, loud shrieks, and the "uncontrollable desire to drink human blood." What seems clear is that Harris had an uncontrollable desire to create a scandal that, soon after publication, turned directly in his direction.

10. See especially the work of Bernard Ortiz de Montellano, "Aztec Cannibalism: An Ecological Necessity?" *Science* 200 (1978): 4342, for the best critique based on empirical research of the Harris/Harner thesis.

11. See Stanley J. Tambiah, *Culture, Thought and Action* (Cambridge: Harvard University Press, 1985), for this more detailed statement, "My own preoccupations have led me to elaborate the implications of rituals as amalgams or totalities constituted by both word and deed, of speech interlaced with the manipulation of objects, of a simultaneous and sequential use of multiple media of communication (auditory, tactile, visual, and olfactory) and of presentational modes (song, dance, music, recitations and so on)" (p. 85). I especially like the dramatic repertoire of Tambiah's approach and his awareness of ritual as a channel for not just the repetitions of myth, but the living *experience* of myth.

12. See Jacob Neusner, *The Way of the Torah: An Introduction to Judaism,* 2nd edition (Encino, Calif.: Dickenson, 1974), for a concise discussion of how mythic structures influence everyday life.

13. See Miguel León-Portilla, *Aztec Thought and Culture: A Study of the Ancient Nahuatl Mind* (Norman: University of Oklahoma Press, 1971), for an excellent introduction into the mercurial worldview held by the Aztecs and its impact on their artistic expressions.

14. Diego Durán, *Book of the Gods and Rites and the Ancient Calendar,* trans. Fernando Horcasitas and Doris Heyden (Norman: University of Oklahoma Press, 1971), p. 191.

15. See Peggy Reeves Sanday, *Divine Hunger: Cannibalism as a Cultural System* (New York: Cambridge University Press, 1986), for a comparative discussion of cannibalism as a mythic system. She interprets the meaning of this metaphor of the human heart as a kind of edible fruit.

16. Tambiah, *Culture, Thought and Action,* p. 87.

17. Quoted in Johanna Broda, "Templo Mayor as Ritual Space," in *The Great Temple of Tenochtitlan: Center and Periphery in the Aztec World,* ed. Johanna Broda, Davíd Carrasco, and Eduardo Matos Moctezuma (Berkeley: University of California Press, 1987), p. 107.

18. Linda Schele and Mary Ellen Miller, *The Blood of Kings: Dynasty and Ritual in Maya Art* (New York and Ft. Worth: Braziller and the Kimbell Art Museum, 1986), p. 268.

19. Philip Arnold, "Eating Landscape: Human Sacrifice and Sustenance in Aztec Mexico," *To Change Place: Aztec Ceremonial Landscapes,* ed. Davíd Carrasco (Niwot: University Press of Colorado, 1991), pp. 219–232.

20. Schele and Miller, *The Blood of Kings,* p. 268.

21. Ibid., p. 269.

22. In *Teogonía e Historia de los Mexicanos,* Angel Ma. Garibay, ed. (Histoyre du Mechique, 1965), pp. 91–116. Editorial Porrúa, S. A., México. For a discussion of the kinds of crocodiles that actually lived in Mesoamerica, see Donald Lathrap's "Jaws: The Control of Power in the Early Nuclear American Ceremonial Center," in *Early Ceremonial Architecture in the Andes: A Conference at Dumbarton Oaks, 8th to 10th October 1982,* ed., Christopher B. Donnan (Washington, D.C.: Dumbarton Oaks, 1985), pp. 246–249.

23. This combination of dismemberment and creation is an emphatic characteristic of Mesoamerican mythology. The creation of the world is constantly joined to the destruction of the world in the mythic narratives. These myths of creation are also myths of destruction, a form of *coincidentia oppositorium,* a juxtaposition of breaking and making.

24. Doris Heyden, "The Skin and Hair of Tlaltecuhtli," in *The Imagination of Mat-*

ter: Religion and Ecology in Mesoamerican Tradition, ed. Davíd Carrasco (Oxford: B. A. R. International Series, 1977), 515:211–224.

25. Ibid., p. 320.

26. Nelly Gutiérrez Solana, "Relieve del Templo Mayor con Tláloc Tlaltecuhtli y Tláloc" *Anales del Instituto de Investigaciones Estéticas* 61 (1990), pp. 15–32.

27. Cecelia Klein, "Snares and Entrails: Mesoamerican Symbols of Sin and Punishment," *RES* 19/20 (1990), p. 92.

28. The most vivid, succinct summary of the meaning of cave symbolism in Mesoamerica is Doris Heyden's "Caves, Gods, and Myths: World View & Planning in Teotihuacan," in *Mesoamerican Sites and World Views,* ed. Elizabeth P. Benson (Washington, D.C.: Dumbarton Oaks Research Library & Collections, Trustees for Harvard University, 1981), pp. 1–41. She demonstrates the association of caves with part of the human body, in addition to caves being repositories for dead bodies, external to the mouth of the womb in Heyden's analysis. In another of Klein's works, "Post-Classic Mexican Death Images as a Sign of Cyclic Completion," in *Death and After Life in Pre-Columbian America,* ed. Elizabeth P. Benson (Washington, D.C.: Dumbarton Oaks, 1973), pp. 69–88, she shows how the death imagery of Mesoamerican ceremonial centers is part of a "unified and coherent cosmic system" rather than a demonstration of the collapse into chaos and nonrational thinking of Mesoamerican peoples. She goes on to discuss the most prominent images of death, which are the images of the god Tlaltecuhtli, the female earth monster discussed earlier in this chapter. Many of Tlaltecuhtli's images appear *en face,* with their face and body directly confronting the viewer. These images are either in dorsal (with back facing the viewer and the head upturned, often with a gaping mouth) or squatting position related to women in childbirth. In some cases, the image has a protruding tongue in the form of a sacrificial knife, suggesting the hunger for blood available through human sacrifice. In her view, this is all a part of the cyclic and regenerative ideology of the Mesoamerican cultures. Also see Doris Heyden's "The Skin and Hair of Tlaltecuhtli," in *The Imagination of Matter: Religion and Ecology in Mesoamerican Traditions,* ed., Davíd Carrasco (B. A. R. International Series 515, Oxford, 1989), pp. 211–224, for a broader interpretation of this goddess's meaning in Aztec religion.

29. Mircea Eliade, *Patterns in Comparative Religion* (New York: Meridian, 1957); Charles H. Long, *Alpha: Myths of Creation* (New York: George Braziller, 1963); Kees Bolle, "Myth: An Overview," in *The Encyclopedia of Religion,* vol. 10, ed. Mircea Eliade (New York: Macmillan, 1987), pp. 261–273.

30. Alfredo López Austin, *The Human Body and Ideology: Concepts Among the Ancient Nahuas* (Salt Lake City: University of Utah Press, 1988), p. 336.

31. Ibid., p. 335.

32. Ibid., p. 336.

33. See *The Book of the Life of the Ancient Mexicans/Codex Magliabechiano,* ed. Zelia Nuttall and Elizabeth H. Boone (Berkeley: University of California Press, 1983).

34. Bernardino de Sahagún, *Florentine Codex: General History of the Things of New Spain,* 13 vols., ed. and trans. Arthur J. O. Anderson and Charles E. Dibble (Santa Fe, N.M.: School of American Research and University of Utah, 1950–1982), 6:21.

35. Quoted in López Austin, *The Human Body and Ideology,* p. 314. He is translating a passage from Sahagún, *Florentine Codex,* 6:115.

36. Ibid., p. 334. López Austin is quoting from the *Primeros Memoriales,* one of the primary texts collected by Sahagún.

37. Davíd Carrasco, *Quetzalcoatl and the Irony of Empire: Myths and Prophecies in the Aztec Tradition* (Chicago: University of Chicago Press, 1981), pp. 148–204; and "Myth, Cosmic Terror, and the Templo Mayor," in *The Great Temple of Tenochtitlan,* ed. Broda, Carrasco, and Matos Moctezuma, pp. 124–162.

38. Quoted in Elizabeth Baquedano, "Aztec Earth Deities," *Polytheistic Systems,* ed. Glenys Davies (Edinburgh: Edinburgh University Press, 1989), p. 192.

39. Arnold, "Eating Landscape," pp. 225–226.

40. Sahagún, 1:23.

41. Ibid.

42. Ibid.

43. Ibid., p. 24.

44. Ibid.

45. Ibid.

46. Ibid.

47. Ortiz de Montellano, *Aztec Medicine,* p. 152.

48. Ibid., p. 25.

49. Ibid.

50. Sahagún, 1:25.

51. Ibid.

52. Ibid.

53. Ibid., p. 26.

54. Alfredo López Austin, personal communication.

55. Sahagún, 1:26.

56. Ibid.

57. Cecelia Klein, "The Ideology of Autosacrifice at the Templo Mayor," in *The Aztec Templo Mayor,* ed. Elizabeth Boone (Washington D. C.: Dumbarton Oaks, 1987), pp. 293–395.

58. Sahagún, 1:27.

59. Klein, "The Ideology of Autosacrifice," p. 355.

60. Sahagún, 6:202. The speech to the baby girl as reported in Sahagún does not

include an extensive statement about original evil. Rather it says, ". . . she cleaned of thievery. Everywhere on its body, its groin, it was said, she cleaned it of vice" (p. 206).

7. The Sacrifice of Women

The first epigraph in chapter 7 is taken from Alfredo López Austin, *Tlalocan, Tamoanchan: Places of Mist* (Niwot: University Press of Colorado, 1997), p. 186. The second epigraph is from Bernardino de Sahagún, *Florentine Codex*, 2:122.

1. There are six ceremonies dedicated to the killing of women, including Huey Tocoztli (The Great Vigil, also known as the time of the Taking of the God of Maize), Tecuilhuitontli (The Small Festival of the Lords), Huey Tecuilhuitl (The Great Festival of the Lords, also called The Eating of Fresh Maize Tortillas), Ochpanitzli (Sweeping, also called The Hanging of the Gourds), Tepeilhuitl (The Festival of the Mountains), and Tititl (Stretching). The translations of the names of these ceremonies are from the highly valuable *Primeros Memoriales*, Fray Bernardino de Sahagún, with *Paleography of Nahuatl Text and English Translations* by Thelma Sullivan, completed and revised, with additions, by H. B. Nicholson, Arthur J. O. Anderson, Charles E. Dibble, Eloise Quiñones Keber, and Wayne Ruwet (Norman: University of Oklahoma Press, in cooperation with the Patrimonio Nacional and the Real Academia de la Historia, Madrid, 1997), pp. 56–66.

2. I am by no means the first to draw attention to this combination of regenerating fertility and warfare in these rituals. Eduard Seler, representing the work of specialists, and Mircea Eliade, representing the work of comparativists, drew attention to this combination. Also, Johanna Broda in her seminal "Tlacaxipehualiztli: A Reconstruction of an Aztec Calendar Festival from 16th Century Sources," *Revista Español de Antropología Americana*, 5:197–273, provides a valuable overview of these patterns. And Betty Ann Brown, "Ochpaniztli in Historical Perspective," in *Ritual Human Sacrifice in Mesoamerica*, ed. Elizabeth H. Boone (Washington, D.C.: Dumbarton Oaks Research Library and Collection, 1984), pp. 195–211, provides a useful interpretation of the historic basis of Ochpaniztli. In particular, Eliade wrote, "A whole series of ceremonies followed upon these: the warriors marched by (for, like many eastern gods and goddesses of fertility, Toci was also the goddess of war and of death), dances were performed and, finally, the king, followed by all his people, threw everything that came to hand at the head of the person representing Toci and then withdrew." Mircea Eliade, *Patterns in Comparative Religion* (New York: Meridian, 1958), p. 344. The most eloquent invocation of women's powers in Aztec society comes from Inga Clendinnen's *Aztecs: An Interpretation* (Cambridge: Cambridge University Press, 1991), especially chapters 6–8 where she writes about "the female being revealed" (pp. 153–212).

3. See López Austin's *Tamoanchan* for a concise outline of the ways in which death played a creative role in cosmic creation.

4. The notion of the "magic circle" that pivots comes from Arnold van Gennep, *Rites of Passage* (Chicago: University of Chicago Press, 1960). See my "Give Me Some Skin: The Charisma of the Aztec Warrior" in *History of Religions*, for an earlier application of this concept to Aztec ritual.

5. One of the most useful essays on the symbols of sacrifice is by Patricia Rieff Anawalt, "Memory Clothing: Costumes Associated with Aztec Human Sacrifice," in *Ritual Human Sacrifice in Mesoamerica* (Washington, D.C.: Dumbarton Oaks Research Library and Collection, 1984), pp. 165–194.

6. Sahagún, 2:104.

7. Paul Wheatley, *The Pivot of the Four Quarters: A Preliminary Enquiry into the Origins and Character of the Ancient Chinese City* (Chicago: Aldine Publishing Company, 1971), p. 436.

8. Johanna Broda has published many articles illustrating the nature and power of the cosmovision, including "El culto mexica de los cerros y del agua," *Multidisciplina* 3, 7:45–56 (Escuela Nacional de Estudios Professionales Acatlan, UNAM); "Geography, Climate and the Observation of Nature in pre-Hispanic Mesoamerica," in *The Imagination of Matter: Religion and Ecology in Mesoamerican Traditions,* ed. David Carrasco (Oxford: B. A.R International Series). Also see Alfredo López Austin's *Tamoanchan,* especially pp. 9–13. López Austin describes cosmovision as "a concept of the world sufficiently organized and coherent . . . present in all of the acts of social life, chiefly in those that include the different kinds of production, family life, care of the body, community relationships, and relations with authorities." Also see David Carrasco, *Religions of Mesoamerica: Ceremonial Centers and Cosmovision* (San Francisco: HarperCollins, 1991).

9. Paul Wheatley, *Pivot of the Four Quarters,* see especially "The Ancient Chinese City as a Cosmo-Magical Symbol," pp. 400–453.

10. See Nancy Jay's *Throughout Your Generations Forever: Sacrifice, Religion and Paternity* (Chicago: University of Chicago Press, 1991), especially p. 147; and Peggy Reeves Sandy, *Divine Hunger: Cannibalism as a Cultural System* [Cambridge: Cambridge University Press, 1986]). Perhaps, as Wendy Doniger remarked after I described the flaying ritual of Ochpaniztli to her, "There is an extraordinary meanness in these rituals." Jay's work may offer a useful perspective for understanding these sacrifices. She argues that gender dichotomy is fundamental to sacrifice, which works to reconstruct descent structures to favor males. Men sacrifice in order to do birth better, that is, to overcome the profound problem for males of having been born of women. Male control of sacrificial rituals recreates social relations, biologically established in childbirth, so that social reproduction of all types will be in the hands of men. She writes, "Opposition between sacrifice and childbirth, or between sacrifice and childbearing women, that is, mothers or potential mothers, is present in countless different sacrificial traditions. This opposition is manifested in a number of different ways; for example, the gender roles of sacrificial practice. It is a common feature of unrelated traditions that only adult males—fathers, real and met-

aphorical—may perform sacrifice. Where women are reported as performing sacrifice it is never as mothers, but almost always in some specifically non-childbearing role, as virgins (or dressed as if they were virgins), as consecrated unmarried women, or as post-menopausal women" (p. xxiii).

11. Davíd Carrasco, "The Sacrifice of Tezcatlipoca: To Change Place," in *Aztec Ceremonial Landscapes: To Change Place,* ed. Davíd Carrasco (Niwot: University Press of Colorado, 1998), pp. 31–58.

12. Alfredo López Austin, *Tamoanchan, Tlalocan,* pp. 123–199. On the complex matter of the unity and diversity of gods, he argues that there is (1) a hidden, primordial essence expressed in nature and history through and balanced by countless oppositional pairs (death/life, cold/hot, female/male, water/ fire, rainy season/dry season) of divine beings who are capable of uniting and separating with other essences, creating a widely shared coessence; and (2) these gods can be in more than one place at the same time and can share their power with other beings. Essence undergoes orderly but continual and complex metamorphosis.

13. Alfredo López Austin, *Hombre-Dios, Religíon y Política en el Mundo Náhuatl* (Mexico: Universidad Nacional Autonoma de Mexico, 1973).

14. Alfredo López Austin, *Tamoanchan, Tlalocan,* p. 153.

15. Sahagún, 1:44.

16. Ibid.

17. Ibid., 2:8.

18. Ibid., p. 64.

19. Sahagún states that in nobles' homes, the liquid of life and revitalization, blood, was sprinkled on fir branches and balls of grass, the latter with maguey thorns placed in the middle. In the evening, all the neighborhood temples were swept clean and women prepared the "shining . . . scintillating" *atole* drink. In Diego Durán's description of rites to Chicomecoatl, a blood offering rite at a later stage of the ritual, we read that after the female *ixiptla* is carried into a chamber where a wooden effigy of the same goddess is waiting, she stands on ears of corn and vegetables. "While she stood there, the lords and nobles came in; forming a line and one by one, they approached her. They squatted on their knees and removed the dry blood they had preserved on their temples and ears during the seven days. They scratched this off with their hands and flung it in front of the girls consecrated as a goddess. . . . the women came in to perform the same ceremony" (*Book of the Gods and Rites and the Ancient Calendar* [Norman: University of Oklahoma Press, 1971], p. 225).

20. It appears that these alms or offerings included different types of *atole* such as *cuauhnexatolli, nextamalatolli,* and *xocoatolli.*

21. Sahagún, 2:63.

22. Ibid., p. 64.

23. Ibid.

24. López Austin, *Tamoanchan*, pp. 190–191.

25. Sahagún. "Her paper crown was covered completely with red ochre; her embroidered shift also was red; her skirt was a red covering." Apparently she carried a symbol of the ruler's designed shield, embellished in red.

26. Ibid., pp. 64–65.

27. Ibid., p. 94.

28. Ibid., p. 92.

29. Ibid., p. 93.

30. López Austin, personal communication, 1999.

31. Sahagún, 2:94.

32. Ibid.

33. Ibid.

34. Ibid., p. 102.

35. The eighth month was a time when the plants were growing but supplies of food stuffs were scarce, and the rulers and nobles appeared on the ritual stage to provide gifts of foods, principally different kinds of tamales, for the community. The rulers claimed they were showing benevolence to the common folk, who were also referred to as the "greedy poor." Cheaters, those who took more than offered, were beaten and the food was taken from them. People jostled in crowds and had to be pushed apart. There was public weeping among the poor, who expressed their sense of misery, and they broke out in public near riots.

36. Ibid., p. 102.

37. Ibid.

38. Ibid.

39. Doris Heyden, "Entering the Sand," unpublished manuscript.

40. Sahagún, 2:104.

41. Ibid., p. 105.

42. The harshest of punishments, including the actual killing of people, were meted out by the ruler, "when Moctezuma's slayers, his executioners, struck the backs of each (of the criminals heads)," which created terror. These punishments reflect again the cycle of payments and debt payments that animate this religious system. The gods gave, in mythic time, alcoholic drinks to humans to bring them happiness. Humans were required to consume this happiness in moderation because drunkenness meant one was possessed by the god of the *pulque*—he who drinks *pulque* imbibes the god into the body, of which the god then takes possession. To take too much of the god into one's body is a dangerous offense to the gods.

43. Ibid., pp. 119–120.

44. Ibid., p. 119.

45. Ibid.

46. Ibid., p. 120.

47. Ibid.

48. Centeotl sometimes referred to the fertility goddess Chicomecoatl, "or Seven Snake," but more frequently referred to the male aspect of the maize god. See *Primeros Memoriales* by Fray Bernardino de Sahagún, trans. Thelma D. Sullivan, completed and revised with additions by H. B. Nicholson, Arthur J. O. Anderson, Charles E. Dibble, Eloise Quiñones Keber and Wayne Ruwet (Norman: University of Oklahoma Press, 1997), p. 58.

49. Sahagún, 2:120.

50. Ibid.

51. Eduard Seler, *Gesammelte Abhandlungen zur amerikanischen Sprach-und Altertumskunde* (Berlin: 1902–1923), 1, 433.

52. Sahagún, 2:123.

53. Ibid., p. 126.

54. Clendinnen makes the claim "The identification of the woman's womb with the great womb of the earth was the foundation of the Mexica system of thought. It was that understanding which sustained the meanings played out through the medium of the human body in each 'human sacrifice,' by a dismemberment and analysis at once physical and conceptual" (*Aztecs,* p. 208). There were more ingredients in the "foundation" of Aztec cosmo-magical thought, but Clendinnen's illumination of female roles has opened the way for many new considerations.

8. When Warriors Became Walls, When the Mountain of Water Crumbled

The epigraph at the beginning of this chapter is taken from Bernardino de Sahagún, *The Florentine Codex,* 12:116.

1. See Jonathan Z. Smith, "The Influence of Symbols upon Social Change: A Place upon Which to Stand," in his *Map Is Not Territory: Studies in the History of Religions* (Leiden: E. J. Brill, 1978), pp. 129–147.

2. For these episodes I have switched to Miguel León-Portilla's excellent translation in *The Broken Spears: The Aztec Account of the Conquest of Mexico* (Boston: Beacon Press, 1990), p. 112.

3. Ibid., p. 113.

4. Ibid. The translation in Dibble and Anderson reads, "And when our foes saw him, *it was if a mountain crumbled.* All the Spaniards indeed were terrified; he terrorized them."

5. Sahagún, 12:118.

6. "Critical games of arrival" is a phrase used by Jose Piedra in "A Game of Critical Arrival," *Diacritics* 19 (1989): 34–61.

7. Miguel León-Portilla, *The Broken Spears: The Aztec Account of the Conquest of Mexico* (Boston: Beacon Press, 1990), p. 149.

8. Mary Louise Pratt, *Imperial Eyes: Travel Writing and Transculturation* (New York: Routledge, 1992).

9. Sahagún, p. 5.

10. Consider the abundance of riches of these gifts. Just the list of the first costume includes, beside the turquoise mask, "a decoration for the breast made of quetzal feathers, a collar woven in the petatillo style with a gold disk in the center, and a shield decorated with gold and mother of pearl and bordered with quetzal feathers with a pendant of the same feathers. There was a mirror like those which the ritual dancers wore on their buttocks. The reverse of the mirror was a turquoise mosaic: it was encrusted and adorned with turquoises. And there was a spear-thrower inlaid with turquoise, a bracelet of chalchiuites, hung with little gold bells and a pair of sandals as black as obsidian" (León-Portilla, *The Broken Spears*, p. 23). It is significant that we also have Cortés's list of some of these gifts and while some items in the list are the same, the mask of Quetzalcoatl does not appear in the Spaniards' account.

11. Ibid., p. 22.

12. Ibid., p. 21.

13. Ibid., p. 23.

14. Ibid., p. 33.

15. Ibid., p. 34.

16. Ibid.

17. Ibid.

18. Ibid., p. 45.

19. Ibid., p. 99.

20. Ibid., p. 100.

21. Ibid., p. 114.

22. Ibid., p. 122.

23. Ibid.

24. Ibid., p. 126.

25. Ibid.

26. Ibid.

ACKNOWLEDGMENTS

Many scholars and friends helped me write, rewrite, and imagine the shape and content of this book. Leonardo López Luján, archaeologist at the Templo Mayor in Mexico City, read the entire manuscript and offered critical questions while affirming the fundamental direction of the project. Eduardo Matos Moctezuma, "mi hermano mayor," welcomed me time and time again to the excavations and museum of the Great Aztec Temple. Phil Arnold, Anthony Aveni, Charles Long, Steven Lestition, William Taylor, and Paul Wheatley read substantial parts of what I wrote, listened to my queries, and sustained me in efforts to develop a broader understanding of ritual violence and ceremonial landscapes in the Aztec city. Patti Anawalt, Frances Berdan, Elizabeth Boone, Tom Bremer, Miguel Centeno, John Gager, Ronald Grimes, Doris Heyden, Eloise Quiñones Keber, Ken Mills, H. B. Nicholson, Scott Sessions, Michael Wood, and Jody Zepp read individual chapters and offered helpful criticism and encouragement.

Alfredo Lopez Austin worked with me on the Nahuatl translations, and his deep knowledge of the Mesoamerican religious tradition opened up new possibilities in my thinking. The entire project was sustained by the resources of the Raphael and Fletcher Lee Moses Mesoamerican Archive and Research Project at Princeton University. Scott Sessions in particular assisted with the selection of the illustrations and the editing. Other colleagues at Princeton, especially Lorraine Fuhrmann, Jeffrey Stout, and Gail Eshleman, came to my aid in professional ways.

Very early versions of some of these chapters were given as lectures at the University of Chicago, University of California at Santa Barbara, San Diego State University, Universidad Nacional Autonoma de Mexico, Harvard University, and Western Maryland College.

The special efforts of Micah Kleit and Deb Chasman at Beacon Press and of copyeditor Patti Waldygo helped the book find its final form. A special thanks for Calvern Narcisi for his encouragement. Above all I wish to thank my wife, Lugene Ann Whitley, for her editorial skill and graceful guidance. The creative sacrifice was hers.

INDEX